# Pro OpenGL ES for Android

D0801093

Mike Smithwick
Mayank Verma

Apress®

**Pro OpenGL ES for Android**

Copyright © 2012 by Mike Smithwick and Mayank Verma

This work is subject to copyright. All rights are reserved by the Publisher, whether the whole or part of the material is concerned, specifically the rights of translation, reprinting, reuse of illustrations, recitation, broadcasting, reproduction on microfilms or in any other physical way, and transmission or information storage and retrieval, electronic adaptation, computer software, or by similar or dissimilar methodology now known or hereafter developed. Exempted from this legal reservation are brief excerpts in connection with reviews or scholarly analysis or material supplied specifically for the purpose of being entered and executed on a computer system, for exclusive use by the purchaser of the work. Duplication of this publication or parts thereof is permitted only under the provisions of the Copyright Law of the Publisher's location, in its current version, and permission for use must always be obtained from Springer. Permissions for use may be obtained through RightsLink at the Copyright Clearance Center. Violations are liable to prosecution under the respective Copyright Law.

ISBN-13 (pbk): 978-1-4302-4002-0
ISBN-13 (electronic): 978-1-4302-4003-7

Trademarked names, logos, and images may appear in this book. Rather than use a trademark symbol with every occurrence of a trademarked name, logo, or image we use the names, logos, and images only in an editorial fashion and to the benefit of the trademark owner, with no intention of infringement of the trademark.

The images of the Android Robot (01 / Android Robot) are reproduced from work created and shared by Google and used according to terms described in the Creative Commons 3.0 Attribution License. Android and all Android and Google-based marks are trademarks or registered trademarks of Google, Inc., in the U.S. and other countries. Apress Media, L.L.C. is not affiliated with Google, Inc., and this book was written without endorsement from Google, Inc.

The use in this publication of trade names, trademarks, service marks, and similar terms, even if they are not identified as such, is not to be taken as an expression of opinion as to whether or not they are subject to proprietary rights.

While the advice and information in this book are believed to be true and accurate at the date of publication, neither the authors nor the editors nor the publisher can accept any legal responsibility for any errors or omissions that may be made. The publisher makes no warranty, express or implied, with respect to the material contained herein.

President and Publisher: Paul Manning
Lead Editor: Richard Carey
Technical Reviewer: Leila Muhtasib
Editorial Board: Steve Anglin, Mark Beckner, Ewan Buckingham, Gary Cornell, Morgan Ertel, Jonathan Gennick, Jonathan Hassell, Robert Hutchinson, Michelle Lowman, James Markham, Matthew Moodie, Jeff Olson, Jeffrey Pepper, Douglas Pundick, Ben Renow-Clarke, Dominic Shakeshaft, Gwenan Spearing, Matt Wade, Tom Welsh
Coordinating Editor: Corbin Collins
Copy Editor: Kim Wimpsett, Linda Seifert
Compositor: Mac,PS
Indexer: SPi Global
Artist: SPi Global
Cover Designer: Anna Ishchenko

Distributed to the book trade worldwide by Springer Science+Business Media New York, 233 Spring Street, 6th Floor, New York, NY 10013. Phone 1-800-SPRINGER, fax (201) 348-4505, e-mail orders-ny@springer-sbm.com, or visit www.springeronline.com.

For information on translations, please e-mail rights@apress.com, or visit www.apress.com.

Apress and friends of ED books may be purchased in bulk for academic, corporate, or promotional use. eBook versions and licenses are also available for most titles. For more information, reference our Special Bulk Sales–eBook Licensing web page at www.apress.com/bulk-sales.

Any source code or other supplementary materials referenced by the author in this text is available to readers at www.apress.com. For detailed information about how to locate your book's source code, go to www.apress.com/source-code/.

*To a couple of the greatest parents in the world, who always supported me, never flinching at my wacky requests such as sending me back to see an Apollo launch or buying a telescope.*

**–Mike Smithwick**

# Contents at a Glance

# Contents

# About the Authors

**Mike Smithwick**'s slow descent into programming computers began when he first got a little 3-bit plastic DigiComp 1 computer in 1963 (http://en.wikipedia.org/wiki/Digi-Comp_I). Not too long before that, he got interested in planetariums. Eventually he graduated to programming NASA flight simulator graphics through the 1980s. But what he really wanted to do was become a syndicated cartoonist (really!). Failing to get any syndication deals, he wrote and sold the popular Distant Suns planetarium program for the Commodore Amiga, old-school Mac, and Microsoft Windows while selling himself as a contract programmer on the side, working for Apple, 3DO, Sense-8, and Epyx. Eventually he landed a "real" job at Live365, working on client software Windows and Windows Mobile 6, TiVo, Symbian (ahhh ... Symbian ...), and iPhone. After 13 short years he decided to go back to the dark side of contracting, writing, and working on Distant Suns for mobile devices after it became modest success in the App Store. Sometimes late at night, he thinks he can hear his Woz-autographed Apple II sobbing for attention from the garage. He may be contacted via www.distantsuns.com, lazyastronomer on AIM, and @distantsuns or @lazyastronomer on Twitter.

**Mayank Verma** completed his master's degree in computer science from Arizona State University in 2008. During the program, he published several research papers in the area of security. Since then, he has been working as a software developer specializing in software application design and development. Mayank is passionate about mobile application development and became interested in Android programming when the platform was first launched by Google. When he's is not working on Android projects, he spends his spare time reading technical blogs, researching, analyzing, and testing mobile applications, and hacking gadgets. He can be contacted at verma.mayank@gmail.com.

# About the Technical Reviewer

 **Leila Muhtasib** has been passionate about programming since she wrote her first program on MS-DOS. Since then, she's graduated with a Computer Science degree from the University of Maryland, College Park. Fascinated by mobile technology and its increasing ubiquity, she has been programming mobile apps since the first Android SDK was released. She is now a Senior Software Engineer and Tech Lead of a mobile development team at Cisco Systems.

# Acknowledgments

Thanks to Corbin Collins and Richard Carey, our long-suffering editors, for putting up with first-time authors, who clearly need to read *Writing Android Books for Beginners*. And to Leila Muhtasib, our tech editor, who was every bit as good as we thought she would be.

# Introduction

In 1985 I brought home a new shiny Commodore Amiga 1000, about one week after they were released. Coming with a whopping 512K of memory, programmable colormaps, a Motorola 68K CPU, and a modern multitasking operating system, it had "awesome" writ all over it. Metaphorically speaking, of course. I thought it might make a good platform for an astronomy program, as I could now control the colors of those star-things instead of having to settle for a lame fixed color palette forced upon me from the likes of Hercules or the C64. So I coded up a 24-line basic routine to draw a random star field, turned out the lights, and thought, "Wow! I bet I could write a cool astronomy program for that thing!" Twenty-six years later I am still working on it and hope to get it right one of these days. Back then my dream device was something I could slip into my pocket, pull out when needed, and aim it at the sky to tell me what stars or constellations I was looking at.

It's called a smartphone.

I thought of it first.

As good as these things are for playing music, making calls, or slinging birdies at piggies, it really shines when you get to the 3D stuff. After all, 3D is all around us—unless you are a pirate and have taken to wearing an eye patch, in which case you'll have very limited depth perception. Arrrggghhh.

Plus 3D apps are fun to show off to people. They'll "get it." In fact, they'll get it much more than, say, that mulch buyer's guide app all the kids are talking about. (Unless they show off their mulch in 3D, but that would be a waste of a perfectly good dimension.)

So, 3D apps are fun to see, fun to interact with, and fun to program. Which brings me to this book. I am by no means a guru in this field. The real gurus are the ones who can knock out a couple of NVIDIA drivers before breakfast, 4-dimensional hypercube simulators by lunch, and port Halo to a TokyoFlash watch before the evening's *Firefly* marathon on SyFy. I can't do that. But I am a decent writer, have enough of a working knowledge of the subject to make me harmless, and know how to spell "3D." So here we are.

First and foremost this book is for experienced Android programmers who want to at least learn a little of the language of 3D. At least enough to where at the next game programmer's cocktail party you too can laugh at the quaternion jokes with the best of them.

This book covers the basics in both theory of 3D and implementations using the industry standard OpenGL ES toolkit for small devices. While Android can support both flavors—version 1.x for the easy way, and version 2.x for those who like to get where the nitty-is-gritty—I mainly cover the former, except in the final chapter which serves as an intro to the latter and the use of programmable shaders.

Chapter 1 serves as an intro to OpenGL ES alongside the long and tortuous path of the history of computer graphics. Chapter 2 is the math behind basic 3D rendering, whereas Chapters 3 through 8 lead you gently through the various issues all graphics programmers eventually come across, such as how to cast shadows, render multiple OpenGL screens, add lens flare, and so on. Eventually this works its way into a simple (S-I-M-P-L-E!) solar-system model consisting of the sun, earth, and some stars—a traditional 3D exercise. Chapter 9 looks at best practices and development tools, and Chapter 10 serves as a brief overview of OpenGL ES 2 and the use of shaders.

So, have fun, send me some M&Ms, and while you're at it feel free to check out my own app currently just in the Apple App Store: Distant Suns 3. Yup, that's the same application that started out on a Commodore Amiga 1000 in 1985 as a 24-line basic program that drew a couple hundred random stars on the screen.

It's bigger now.

—**Mike Smithwick**

# Chapter 1

# Computer Graphics: From Then to Now

*To predict the future and appreciate the present, you must understand the past.*

—Probably said by someone sometime

Computer graphics have always been the darling of the software world. Laypeople can appreciate computer graphics more easily than, say, increasing the speed of a sort algorithm by 3 percent or adding automatic tint control to a spreadsheet program. You are likely to hear more people say "Coooool!" at your nicely rendered image of Saturn on your iPad than at a Visual Basic script in Microsoft Word (unless, of course, a Visual Basic script in Microsoft Word can render Saturn; then that really would be cool). The cool factor goes up even more when said renderings are on a device you can carry around in your back pocket. Let's face it—the folks in Silicon Valley are making the life of art directors on science-fiction films very difficult. After all, imagine how hard it must be to design a prop that looks more futuristic than a Samsung Galaxy Tab or an iPad. (Even before Apple's iPhone was available for sale, the prop department at ABC's *Lost* borrowed some of Apple's screen iconography for use in a two-way radio carried by a mysterious helicopter pilot.)

If you are reading this book, chances are you have an Android-based device or are considering getting one in the near future. If you have one, put it in your hand now and consider what a miracle it is of 21st-century engineering. Millions of work hours, billions of dollars of research, centuries of overtime, plenty of all-nighters, and an abundance of Jolt-drinking, T-shirt–wearing, comic-book-loving engineers coding into the silence of the night have gone into making that little glass and plastic miracle-box so you can play Angry Birds when *Mythbusters* is in reruns.

# Your First OpenGL ES Program

Some software how-to books will carefully build up the case for their specific topic ("the boring stuff") only to get to the coding and examples ("the fun stuff") by around page 655. Others will jump immediately into some exercises to address your curiosity and save the boring stuff for a little later. This book will attempt to be of the latter category.

> **NOTE:** OpenGL ES is a 3D graphics standard based on the OpenGL library that emerged from the labs of Silicon Graphics in 1992. It is widely used across the industry in everything from pocketable machines running games up to supercomputers running fluid dynamics simulations for NASA (and playing really, really fast games). The ES variety stands for *Embedded Systems*, meaning small, portable, low-power devices.

When installed, the Android SDK comes with many very good and concise examples ranging from Near Field Communications (NFC) to UI to OpenGL ES projects. Our earliest examples will leverage those that you will find in the wide-ranging ApiDemos code base. Unlike its Apple-lovin' cousin Xcode, which has a nice selection of project wizards that includes an OpenGL project, the Android dev system unfortunately has very few. As a result, we have to start at a little bit of a disadvantage as compared to the folks in Cupertino. So, you'll need to create a generic Android project, which I am sure you already know how to do. When done, add a new class named Square.java, consisting of the code in Listing 1–1. A detailed analysis follows the listing.

**Listing 1–1.** *A 2D Square Using OpenGL ES*

```
package book.BouncySquare;

import java.nio.ByteBuffer;
import java.nio.ByteOrder;
import java.nio.FloatBuffer;
import java.nio.IntBuffer;

import javax.microedition.khronos.opengles.GL10;           //1
import javax.microedition.khronos.opengles.GL11;

/**
 * A vertex shaded square.
 */
class Square
{
    public Square()
    {
        float vertices[] =                                  //2
```

```
    {
        -1.0f, -1.0f,
        1.0f, -1.0f,
        -1.0f,  1.0f,
        1.0f,  1.0f
    };

    byte maxColor=(byte)255;

    byte colors[] =                                         //3
    {
        maxColor,maxColor,        0,maxColor,
        0,        maxColor,maxColor,maxColor,
        0,        0,        0,maxColor,
        maxColor,        0,maxColor,maxColor
    };

    byte indices[] =                                        //4
    {
        0, 3, 1,
        0, 2, 3
    };

    ByteBuffer vbb = ByteBuffer.allocateDirect(vertices.length * 4);     //5
    vbb.order(ByteOrder.nativeOrder());
    mFVertexBuffer = vbb.asFloatBuffer();
    mFVertexBuffer.put(vertices);
    mFVertexBuffer.position(0);

    mColorBuffer = ByteBuffer.allocateDirect(colors.length);
    mColorBuffer.put(colors);
    mColorBuffer.position(0);

    mIndexBuffer = ByteBuffer.allocateDirect(indices.length);
    mIndexBuffer.put(indices);
    mIndexBuffer.position(0);

}

public void draw(GL10 gl)                                   //6
{
    gl.glFrontFace(GL11.GL_CW);                             //7
    gl.glVertexPointer(2, GL11.GL_FLOAT, 0, mFVertexBuffer);   //8
    gl.glColorPointer(4, GL11.GL_UNSIGNED_BYTE, 0, mColorBuffer);  //9
    gl.glDrawElements(GL11.GL_TRIANGLES, 6,                 //10
    GL11.GL_UNSIGNED_BYTE, mIndexBuffer);
    gl.glFrontFace(GL11.GL_CCW);                            //11
}
```

```
    private FloatBuffer mFVertexBuffer;
    private ByteBuffer   mColorBuffer;
    private ByteBuffer   mIndexBuffer;
}
```

Before I go on to the next phase, I'll break down the code from Listing 1–1 that constructs a polychromatic square:

- Java hosts several different OpenGL interfaces. The parent class is merely called GL, while OpenGL ES 1.0 uses GL10, and version 1.1 is imported as GL11, shown in line 1. You can also gain access to some extensions if your graphics hardware supports them via the GL10Ext package, supplied by the GL11ExtensionPack. The later versions are merely subclasses of the earlier ones; however, there are still some calls that are defined as taking only GL10 objects, but those work if you cast the objects properly.

- In line 2 we define our square. You will rarely if ever do it this way because many objects could have thousands of vertices. In those cases, you'd likely import them from any number of 3D file formats such as Imagination Technologies' POD files, 3D Studio's .3ds files, and so on. Here, since we're describing a 2D square, it is necessary to specify only x and y coordinates. And as you can see, the square is two units on a side.

- Colors are defined similarly, but in this case, in lines 3ff, there are four components for each color: red, green, blue, and alpha (transparency). These map directly to the four vertices shown earlier, so the first color goes with the first vertex, and so on. You can use floats or a fixed or byte representation of the colors, with the latter saving a lot of memory if you are importing a very large model. Since we're using bytes, the color values go from 0 to 255, That means the first color sets red to 255, green to 255, and blue to 0. That will make a lovely, while otherwise blinding, shade of yellow. If you use floats or fixed point, they ultimately are converted to byte values internally. Unlike its big desktop brother, which can render four-sided objects, OpenGL ES is limited to triangles only. In lines 4ff the connectivity array is created. This matches up the vertices to specific triangles. The first triplet says that vertices 0, 3, and 1 make up triangle 0, while the second triangle is comprised of vertices 0, 2, and 3.

- Once the colors, vertices, and connectivity array have been created, we may have to fiddle with the values in a way to convert their internal Java formats to those that OpenGL can understand, as shown in lines 5ff. This mainly ensures that the ordering of the bytes is right; otherwise, depending on the hardware, they might be in reverse order.

- The `draw` method, in line 6, is called by `SquareRenderer.drawFrame()`, covered shortly.

- Line 7 tells OpenGL how the vertices are ordering their faces. Vertex ordering can be critical when it comes to getting the best performance out of your software. It helps to have the ordering uniform across your model, which can indicate whether the triangles are facing toward or away from your viewpoint. The latter ones are called *backfacing triangles* the back side of your objects, so they can be ignored, cutting rendering time substantially. So, by specifying that the front face of the triangles are GL_CW, or clockwise, all counterclockwise triangles are culled. Notice that in line 11 they are reset to GL_CCW, which is the default.

- In lines 8, 9, and 10, pointers to the data buffers are handed over to the renderer. The call to `glVertexPointer()` specifies the number of elements per vertex (in this case two), that the data is floating point, and that the "stride" is 0 bytes. The data can be eight different formats, including floats, fixed, ints, short ints, and bytes. The latter three are available in both signed and unsigned flavors. Stride is a handy way to let you interleave OpenGL data with your own as long as the data structures are constant. Stride is merely the number of bytes of user info packed between the GL data so the system can skip over it to the next bit it will understand.

- In line 9, the color buffer is sent across with a size of four elements, with the RGBA quadruplets using unsigned bytes (I know, Java doesn't have unsigned anything, but GL doesn't have to know), and it too has a stride=0.

- And finally, the actual `draw` command is given, which requires the connectivity array. The first parameter says what the format the geometry is in, in other words, triangles, triangle lists, points, or lines.

- Line 11 has us being a good neighbor and resetting the front face ordering back to GL_CCW in case the previous objects used the default value.

Now our square needs a driver and way to display its colorful self on the screen. Create another file called `SquareRenderer.java`, and populate it with the code in Listing 1–2.

**Listing 1–2.** *The Driver for Our First OpenGL Project*

```
package book.BouncySquare;

import javax.microedition.khronos.egl.EGL10;                    //1
import javax.microedition.khronos.egl.EGLConfig;
import javax.microedition.khronos.opengles.GL10;

import android.opengl.GLSurfaceView;                            //2
import java.lang.Math;
```

```java
class SquareRenderer implements GLSurfaceView.Renderer
{
    public SquareRenderer(boolean useTranslucentBackground)
    {
        mTranslucentBackground = useTranslucentBackground;
        mSquare = new Square();                                          //3
    }

    public void onDrawFrame(GL10 gl)                                     //4
    {

        gl.glClear(GL10.GL_COLOR_BUFFER_BIT | GL10.GL_DEPTH_BUFFER_BIT);  //5

        gl.glMatrixMode(GL10.GL_MODELVIEW);                             //6
        gl.glLoadIdentity();                                           //7
        gl.glTranslatef(0.0f,(float)Math.sin(mTransY), -3.0f);          //8

        gl.glEnableClientState(GL10.GL_VERTEX_ARRAY);                   //9
        gl.glEnableClientState(GL10.GL_COLOR_ARRAY);

        mSquare.draw(gl);                                              //10

        mTransY += .075f;
    }

    public void onSurfaceChanged(GL10 gl, int width, int height)       //11
    {
        gl.glViewport(0, 0, width, height);                            //12

        float ratio = (float) width / height;
        gl.glMatrixMode(GL10.GL_PROJECTION);                          //13
        gl.glLoadIdentity();
        gl.glFrustumf(-ratio, ratio, -1, 1, 1, 10);                   //14
    }

    public void onSurfaceCreated(GL10 gl, EGLConfig config)           //15
    {
        gl.glDisable(GL10.GL_DITHER);                                  //16

        gl.glHint(GL10.GL_PERSPECTIVE_CORRECTION_HINT,                //17
                GL10.GL_FASTEST);

        if (mTranslucentBackground)                                    //18
        {
            gl.glClearColor(0,0,0,0);
        }
        else
        {
```

```
            gl.glClearColor(1,1,1,1);
        }
        gl.glEnable(GL10.GL_CULL_FACE);                              //19
        gl.glShadeModel(GL10.GL_SMOOTH);                            //20
        gl.glEnable(GL10.GL_DEPTH_TEST);                            //21
    }
    private boolean mTranslucentBackground;
    private Square mSquare;
    private float mTransY;
    private float mAngle;
}
```

A lot of things are going on here:

- The EGL libraries in line 1 bind the OpenGL drawing surface to the system but are buried within GLSurfaceview in this case, as shown in line 2. EGL is primarily used for allocating and managing the drawing surfaces and is part of an OpenGL ES extension, so it is platform independent.

- In line 3, the square object is allocated and cached.

- onDrawFrame() in line 4 is the root refresh method; this constructs the image each time through, many times a second. And the first call is typically to clear the entire screen, as shown in line 5. Considering that a frame can be constructed out of several components, you are given the option to select which of those should be cleared every frame. The color buffer holds all of the RGBA color data, while the depth buffer is used to ensure that the closer items properly obscure the further items.

- Lines 6 and 7 start mucking around with the actual 3D parameters; these details will be covered later. All that is being done here is setting the values to ensure that the example geometry is immediately visible.

- Next, line 8 translates the box up and down. To get a nice, smooth motion, the actual translation value is based on a sine wave. The value mTransY is simply used to generate a final up and down value that ranges from -1 to +1. Each time through drawFrame(), the translation is increased by .075. Since we're taking the sine of this, it isn't necessary to loop the value back on itself, because sine will do that for us. Try increasing the value of mTransY to .3 and see what happens.

- Lines 9f tells OpenGL to expect both vertex and color data.

- Finally, after all of this setup code, we can call the actual drawing routine of the mSquare that you've seen before, as shown in line 10.

▦ onSurfaceChanged(), here in line 11, is called whenever the screen changes size or is created at startup. Here it is also being used to set up the viewing *frustum*, which is the volume of space that defines what you can actually see. If any of your scene elements lay outside of the frustum, they are considered invisible so are clipped, or culled out, to prevent that further operations are done on them.

▦ glViewport merely permits you to specify the actual dimensions and placement of your OpenGL window. This will typically be the size of your main screen, with a location 0.

▦ In line 13, we set the matrix mode. What this does is to set the current working matrix that will be acted upon when you make any general-purpose matrix management calls. In this case, we switch to the GL_PROJECTION matrix, which is the one that *projects* the 3D scene to your 2D screen. glLoadIdentity() resets the matrix to its initial values to erase any previous settings.

▦ Now you can set the actual frustum using the aspect ratio and the six clipping planes: near/far, left/right, and top/bottom.

▦ In this final method of Listing 1–2, some initialization is done upon surface creation line 15. Line 16 ensures that any dithering is turned off, because it defaults to on. Dithering in OpenGL makes screens with limited color palettes look somewhat nicer but at the expense of performance of course.

▦ glHint() in line 17 is used to nudge OpenGL ES to do what it thinks best by accepting certain trade-offs: usually speed vs. quality. Other hintable settings include fog and various smoothing options.

▦ Another one of the many states we can set is the color that the background assumes when cleared. In this case, which is black, if the background is translucent, or white, (all colors max out to 1), if not translucent. Go ahead and change these later to see what happens.

▦ At last, the end of this listing sets some other handy modes. Line 19 says to cull out faces (triangles) that are aimed away from us. Line 20 tells it to use smooth shading so the colors blend across the surface. The only other value is GL_FLAT, which, when activated, will display the face in the color of the last vertex drawn. And line 21 enables depth testing, also known as *z-buffering*, covered later.

Finally, the activity file will need to be modified to look like Listing 1–3.

**Listing 1–3.** *The Activity File*

```
package book.BouncySquare;
```

```
import android.app.Activity;
import android.opengl.GLSurfaceView;
import android.os.Bundle;
import android.view.WindowManager;
import book.BouncySquare.*;

public class BouncySquareActivity extends Activity
{
    /** Called when the activity is first created. */
    @Override
    public void onCreate(Bundle savedInstanceState)
    {
    super.onCreate(savedInstanceState);
        getWindow().setFlags(WindowManager.LayoutParams.FLAG_FULLSCREEN,
            WindowManager.LayoutParams.FLAG_FULLSCREEN);
            GLSurfaceView view = new GLSurfaceView(this);
            view.setRenderer(new SquareRenderer(true));
            setContentView(view);
    }
}
```

Our activity file is little modified from the default. Here the GLSurfaceView is actually allocated and bound to our custom renderer, SquareRenderer.

Now compile and run. You should see something that looks a little like Figure 1–1.

**Figure 1–1.** *A bouncy square. If this is what you see, give yourself a high-five.*

Now as engineers, we all like to twiddle and tweak our creations, just to see what happens. So, let's change the shape of the bouncing-square-of-joy by replacing the first number in the vertices array with -2.0, instead of -1.0. And replace maxcolor, the first value in the color array with a 0. That will make the lower-left vertex stick out quite a ways and should turn it to green. Compile and stand back in awe. You should have something like Figure 1–2.

**Figure 1–2.** *After the tweakage*

Don't worry about the simplicity of this first exercise; you'll build stuff fancier than a bouncing rainbow-hued cube of Jell-O at some point. The main project will be to construct a simple solar-system simulator based on some of the code used in Distant Suns 3. But for now, it's time to get to the boring stuff: where computer graphics came from and where they are likely to go.

> **NOTE:** The Android emulator is notoriously buggy and notoriously slow. It is strongly recommended that you do all of your OpenGL work on real hardware, especially as the exercises get a little more complex. You will save yourself a lot of grief.

# A Spotty History of Computer Graphics

To say that 3D is all the rage today is at best an understatement. Although forms of "3D" imagery go back to more than a century ago, it seems that it has finally come of age. First let's look at what 3D is and what it is not.

## 3D in Hollywood

In 1982 Disney released *Tron*, the first movie to widely use computer graphics depicting life inside a video game. Although the movie was a critical and financial flop, it would eventually join the ranks of cult favorites right up there with *The Rocky Horror Picture Show*. Hollywood had taken the bite out of the apple, and there was no turning back.

Stretching back to the 1800s, what we call "3D" today was more commonly referred to as *stereo vision*. Popular Victorian-era *stereopticons* would be found in many parlors of the day. Consider this technology an early Viewmaster. The user would hold the stereopticon up to their face with a stereo photograph slipped into the far end and see a view of some distant land, but in stereo rather than a flat 2D picture. Each eye would see only one half of the card, which carried two nearly identical photos taken only a couple of inches apart.

Stereovision is what gives us the notion of a depth component to our field of view. Our two eyes deliver two slightly different images to the brain that then interprets them in a way that we understand as depth perception. A single image will not have that effect. Eventually this moved to movies, with a brief and unsuccessful dalliance as far back as 1903 (the short *L'arrivée du Train* is said to have had viewers running from the theater to avoid the train that was clearly heading their way*)* and a resurgence in the early 1950s, with *Bwana Devil* being perhaps the best known.

The original form of 3D movies generally used the "anaglyph" technique that required the viewers to wear cheap plastic glasses with a red filter over one eye and a blue one over the other. Polarizing systems were incorporated in the early 1950s and permitted color movies to be seen in stereo, and they are still very much the same as today. Afraid that television would kill off the movie industry, Hollywood needed some gimmick that was impossible on television in order to keep selling tickets, but because both the cameras and the projectors required were much too impractical and costly, the form fell out of favor, and the movie industry struggled along just fine.

With the advent of digital projection systems in the 1990s and fully rendered films such as *Toy Story*, stereo movies and eventually television finally became both practical and affordable enough to move it beyond the gimmick stage. In particular, full-length 3D animated features (*Toy Story* being the first) made it a no-brainer to convert to stereo. All one needed to do was simply rerender the entire film but from a slightly different viewpoint. This is where stereo and 3D computer graphics merge.

# The Dawn of Computer Graphics

One of the fascinating things about the history of computer graphics, and computers in general, is that the technology is still so new that many of the giants still stride among us. It would be tough to track down whoever invented the buggy whip, but I know who to call if you wanted to hear firsthand how the Apollo Lunar Module computers were programmed in the 1960s.

Computer graphics (frequently referred to as CG) come in three overall flavors: 2D for user interface, 3D in real time for flight or other forms of simulation as well as games, and 3D rendering where quality trumps speed for non-real-time use.

## MIT

In 1961, an MIT engineering student named Ivan Sutherland created a system called Sketchpad for his PhD thesis using a vectorscope, a crude light pen, and a custom-made Lincoln TX-2 computer (a spin-off from the TX-2 group would become DEC). Sketchpad's revolutionary graphical user interface demonstrated many of the core principles of modern UI design, not to mention a big helping of object-oriented architecture tossed in for good measure.

> **NOTE:** For a video of Sketchpad in operation, go to YouTube and search for *Sketchpad* or *Ivan Sutherland.*

A fellow student of Sutherland's, Steve Russell, would invent perhaps one of the biggest time sinks ever made, the computer game. Russell created the legendary game of Spacewar in 1962, which ran on the PDP-1, as shown in Figure 1–3.

**Figure 1–3.** *The 1962 game of Spacewar resurrected at the Computer History Museum in Mountain View, California, on a vintage PDP-1. Photo by Joi Itoh, licensed under the Creative Commons Attribution 2.0 Generic license (*http://creativecommons.org/licenses/by/2.0/deed.en*).*

By 1965, IBM would release what is considered the first widely used commercial graphics terminal, the 2250. Paired with either the low-cost IBM-1130 computer or the IBM S/340, the terminal was meant largely for use in the scientific community.

Perhaps one of the earliest known examples of computer graphics on television was the use of a 2250 on the CBS news coverage of the joint Gemini 6 and Gemini 7 mannded space missions in December 1965 (IBM built the Gemini's onboard computer system). The terminal was used to demonstrate several phases of the mission on live television from liftoff to rendezvous. At a cost of about $100,000 in 1965, it was worth the equivalent of a nice home. See Figure 1–4.

**Figure 1–4.** *IBM-2250 terminal from 1965. Courtesy NASA.*

## University of Utah

Recruited by the University of Utah in 1968 to work in its computer science program, Sutherland naturally concentrated on graphics. Over the course of the next few years, many computer graphics visionaries in training would pass through the university's labs.

Ed Catmull, for example, loved classic animation but was frustrated by his inability to draw—a requirement for artists back in those days as it would appear. Sensing that computers might be a pathway to making movies, Catmull produced the first-ever computer animation, which was of his hand opening and closing. This clip would find its way into the 1976 film *Future World*.

During that time he would pioneer two major computer graphics innovations: texture mapping and bicubic surfaces. The former could be used to add complexity to simple forms by using images of texture instead of having to create texture and roughness using discrete points and surfaces, as shown in Figure 1–5. The latter is used to generate algorithmically curved surfaces that are much more efficient than the traditional polygon meshes.

**Figure 1–5.** *Saturn with and without texture*

Catmull would eventually find his way to Lucasfilm and, later, Pixar and eventually serve as president of Disney Animation Studios where he could finally make the movies he wanted to see. Not a bad gig.

Many others of the top names in the industry would likewise pass through the gates of University of Utah and the influence of Sutherland:

- John Warnock, who would be instrumental in developing a device-independent means of displaying and printing graphics called PostScript and the Portable Document Format (PDF) and would be cofounder of Adobe.

- Jim Clark, founder of Silicon Graphics that would supply Hollywood with some of the best graphics workstations of the day and create the 3D framework now known as OpenGL. After SGI he cofounded Netscape Communications, which would lead us into the land of the World Wide Web.

▓ Jim Blinn, inventor of both bump mapping, which is an efficient way of adding true 3D texture to objects, and environment mapping, which is used to create really shiny things. Perhaps he would be best known creating the revolutionary animations for NASA's Voyager project, depicting flybys of the outer planets, as shown in Figure 1–6 (compare that with Figure 1–7 using modern devices). Of Blinn, Sutherland would say, "There are about a dozen great computer graphics people, and Jim Blinn is six of them." Blinn would later lead the effort to create Microsoft's competitor to OpenGL, namely, Direct3D.

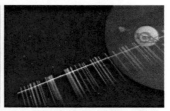

*Figure 1–6. Jim Blinn's depiction of Voyager II's encounter with Saturn in August of 1981. Notice the streaks formed of icy particles while crossing the ring plane. Courtesy NASA.*

*Figure 1–7. Compare with Figure 1–6, using some of the best graphics computers and software at the time, with a similar view of Saturn from Distant Suns 3 running on a $500 iPad.*

## Coming of Age in Hollywood

Computer graphics would really start to come into their own in the 1980s thanks both to Hollywood and to machines that were increasingly powerful while at the same time costing less. For example, the beloved Commodore Amiga that was introduced in 1985 cost less than $2,000, and it brought to the consumer market an advanced multitasking operating system and color graphics that had been previously the domain of workstations costing upwards of $100,000. See Figure 1–8.

**Figure 1–8.** *Amiga 1000, circa 1985. Photo by Kaivv, licensed under the Creative Commons Attribution 2.0 Generic license (http://creativecommons.org/licenses/by/2.0/deed.en).*

Compare this to the original black-and-white Mac that was released a scant 18 months earlier for about the same cost. Coming with a very primitive OS, flat file system, and 1–bit display, it was fertile territory for the "religious wars" that broke out between the various camps as to whose machine was better (wars that would also include the Atari ST).

> **NOTE:** One of the special graphics modes on the original Amiga could compress 4,096 colors into a system that would normally max out at 32. Called Hold and Modify (HAM mode), it was originally included on one of the main chips for experimental reasons by designer Jay Miner. Although he wanted to remove the admitted kludge that produced images with a lot of color distortion, the results would have left a big empty spot on the chip. Considering that unused chip landscape was something no self-respecting engineer could tolerate, he left it in, and to Miner's great surprise, people started using it.

A company in Kansas called NewTek pioneered the use of Amigas for rendering high-quality 3D graphics when coupled with its special hardware named the Video Toaster. Combined with a sophisticated 3D rendering software package called Lightwave 3D, NewTek opened up the realm of cheap, network-quality graphics to anyone who had a few thousand dollars to spend. This development opened the doors for elaborate science-fiction shows such as *Babylon 5* or *Seaquest* to be financially feasible considering their extensive special effects needs.

During the 1980s, many more techniques and innovations would work their way into common use in the CG community:

- Loren Carpenter developed a technique to generate highly detailed landscapes algorithmically using something called *fractals*. Carpenter was hired by Lucasfilm to create a rendering package for a new company named Pixar. The result was REYES, which stood for Render Everything You Ever Saw.

- Turner Whitted developed a technique called *ray tracing* that could produce highly realistic scenes (at a significant CPU cost), particularly when they included objects with various reflective and refractive properties. Glass items were common subjects in various early ray-tracing efforts, as shown in Figure 1–9.

- Frank Crow developed the first practical method of *anti-aliasing* in computer graphics. Aliasing is the phenomenon that generates jagged edges (jaggies) because of the relatively poor resolution of the display. Crow's method would smooth out everything from lines to text, making it look more natural and pleasing. Note that one of Lucasfilm's early games was called Rescue on Fractalus. The bad guys were named *jaggies*.

- *Star Trek II: The Wrath of Khan* brought with it the first entirely computer-generated sequence used to illustrate how a device called the Genesis Machine could generate life on a lifeless planet. That one simulation was called "the effect that wouldn't die" because of its groundbreaking techniques in flame and particle animation and fractal landscapes.

**Figure 1–9.** *Sophisticated images such as this are within the range of hobbyists with programs such as the open source POV-Ray. Photo by Gilles Tran, 2006.*

The 1990s brought the T1000 "liquid metal" terminator in *Terminator 2: Judgment Day*, the first completely computer-generated full-length feature film of *Toy Story*, believable animated dinosaurs in *Jurassic Park*, and James Cameron's *Titanic*, all of which helped solidified CG as a common tool in the Hollywood director's arsenal.

By the decade's end, it would be hard to find any films that didn't have computer graphics as part of the production in either actual effects or in postproduction to help clean up various scenes. New techniques are still being developed and applied in ever more spectacular fashion, as in Disney's delightful *Up!* or James Cameron's beautiful *Avatar*.

Now, once again, take out your i-device and realize what a little technological marvel it is. Feel free to say "wow" in hushed, respectful tones.

# Toolkits

All of the 3D wizardry referenced earlier would never have been possible without software. Many CG software programs are highly specialized, and others are more general purpose, such as OpenGL ES, the focus of this book. So, what follows are a few of the many toolkits available.

## OpenGL

Open Graphics Library (OpenGL) came out of the pioneering efforts of Silicon Graphics (SGI), the maker of high-end graphics workstations and mainframes. Its own proprietary graphics framework, IRIS-GL, had grown into a de facto standard across the industry. To keep customers as competition increased, SGI opted to turn IRIS-GL into an open framework so as to strengthen their reputation as the industry leader. IRIS-GL was stripped of non-graphics-related functions and hardware-dependent features, renamed OpenGL, and released in early 1992. As of this writing, version 4.1 is the most current.

As small handheld devices became more common, OpenGL for Embedded Systems (OpenGL ES) was developed, which was a stripped-down version of the desktop version. It removed a lot of the more redundant API calls and simplified other elements to make it run efficiently on the lower-power CPUs in the market. As a result, it has been widely adopted across many platforms such as Android, iOS, HP's WebOS, Nintendo 3DS, and BlackBerry (OS 5.0 and newer).

There are two main flavors of OpenGL ES, 1.*x* and 2.*x*. Many devices support both. Version 1.*x* is the higher-level variant, based on the original OpenGL specification. Version 2.*x* (yes, I know it's confusing) is targeted toward more specialized rendering chores that can be handled by programmable graphics hardware.

# Direct3D

Direct3D (D3D) is Microsoft's answer to OpenGL and is heavily oriented toward game developers. In 1995, Microsoft bought a small company called RenderMorphics that specialized in creating a 3D framework named RealityLab for writing games. RealityLab was turned into Direct3D and first released in the summer of 1996. Even though it was proprietary to Windows-based systems, it has a huge user base across all of Microsoft's platforms: Windows, Windows 7 Mobile, and even Xbox. There are constant ongoing debates between the OpenGL and Direct3D camps as to which is more powerful, flexible, and easier to use. Other factors include how quickly hardware manufacturers can update their drivers to support new features, ease of understanding (Direct3D uses Microsoft's COM interface that can be very confusing for newcomers), stability, and industry support.

# The Other Guys

While OpenGL and Direct3D remain at the top of the heap when it comes to both adoption and features, the graphics landscape is littered with numerous other frameworks, many which are supported on today's devices.

In the computer graphics world, graphics libraries come in two very broad flavors: low-level rendering mechanisms represented by OpenGL and Direct3D and high-level systems typically found in game engines that concentrate on resource management with special extras that extend to common game-play elements (sound, networking, scoring, and so on). The latter are usually built on top of one of the former for the 3D portion. And if done well, the higher-level systems might even be abstracted enough to make it possible to work with both GL and D3D.

## QuickDraw 3D

An example of a higher-level general-purpose library is QuickDraw 3D (QD3D). A 3D sibling to Apple's 2D QuickDraw, QD3D had an elegant means of generating and linking objects in an easy-to-understand hierarchical fashion (*a scene-graph*). It likewise had its own file format for loading 3D models and a standard viewer and was platform independent. The higher-level part of QD3D would calculate the scene and determine how each object and, in turn, each piece of each object would be shown on a 2D drawing surface. Underneath QD3D there was a very thin layer called RAVE that would handle device-specific rendering of these bits.

Users could go with the standard version of RAVE, which would render the scene as expected. But more ambitious users could write their own that would display the scene in a more artistic fashion. For example, one company generated the RAVE output so as to look like their objects were hand-painted on the side of a cave. It was very cool when you could take this modern version of a cave drawing and spin it around. The plug-in architecture also made QD3D highly portable to other machines. When potential users balked at using QD3D since it had no hardware solution on PCs, a version of RAVE was produced that would use the hardware acceleration available for Direct3D by actually using its competitor as its rasterizer. Sadly, QD3D was almost immediately killed on the second coming of Steve Jobs, who determined that OpenGL should be the 3D standard for Macs in the future. This was an odd statement because QD3D was not a competitor to the other but an add-on that made the lives of programmers much easier. After Jobs refused requests to make QD3D open source, the Quesa project was formed to re-create as much as possible the original library, which is still being supported at the time of this writing. And to nobody's surprise, Quesa uses OpenGL as its rendering engine.

A disclaimer here: I wrote the RAVE/Direct3D layer of QD3D only to have the project canceled a few days after going "gold master" (ready to ship). Bah.

## OGRE

Another scene-graph system is Object-oriented Rendering Engine (OGRE). First released in 2005, OGRE can use both OpenGL and Direct3D as the low-level rasterizing solution, while offering users a stable and free toolkit used in many commercial products. The size of the user community is impressive. A quick peek at the forums shows more than 6,500 topics in the General Discussion section alone at the time of this writing.

## OpenSceneGraph

Recently released for iOS devices, OpenSceneGraph does roughly what QuickDraw 3D did, by providing a means of creating your objects on a higher level, linking them together, and performing scene management duties and extra effects above the OpenGL layer. Other features include importing multiple file formats, text support, particle effects (used for sparks, flames, or clouds), and the ability to display video content in your 3D applications. Knowledge of OpenGL is highly recommended, because many of the OSG functions are merely thin wrappers to their OpenGL counterparts.

## Unity3D

Unlike OGRE, QD3D, or OpenSceneGraph, Unity3D is a cross-platform full-fledged game engine that runs on both Android and iOS. The difference lies in the scope of the product. Whereas the first two concentrated on creating a more abstract wrapper around OpenGL, game engines go several steps further, supplying most if not all of the other supporting functionality that games would typically need such as sound, scripting, networked extensions, physics, user interface, and score-keeping modules. In addition, a good engine will likely have tools to help generate the assets and be platform independent.

Unity3D has all of these so would be overkill for many smaller projects. Also, being a commercial product, the source is not available, and it is not free to use but costs only a modest amount (compared to other products in the past that could charge $100,000 or more).

## And Still Others

Let's not ignore A6, Adventure Game Studio, C4, Crystal Space, VTK, Coin3D, SDL, QT, Delta3D, Glint3D, Esenthel, FlatRedBall, Horde3D, Irrlicht, Leadwerks3D, Lightfeather, Raydium, Panda3D (from Disney Studios and CMU), Torque, and many others. Although they're powerful, one drawback of using game engines is that more often than not your world is executed in their environment. So, if you need a specific subtle behavior that is unavailable, you may be out of luck.

# OpenGL Architecture

Now since we've analyzed to death a simple OpenGL program, let's take a brief look at what goes on under the hood at the graphics pipeline.

The term *pipeline* is commonly used to illustrate how a tightly bound sequence of events relate to each other, as illustrated in Figure 1–10. In the case of OpenGL ES, the process accepts a bunch of numbers in one end and outputs something really cool-looking at the other end, be it an image of the planet Saturn or the results of an MRI.

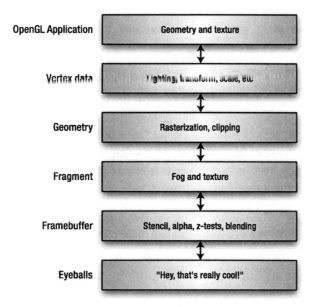

**Figure 1–10.** *Basic overview of the OpenGL ES 1.x pipeline*

- The first step is to take the data that describes some geometry along with information on how to handle lighting, colors, materials, and textures and send it into the pipeline.

- Next the data is moved and rotated, after which lighting on each object is calculated and stored. The scene—say, a solar-system model—must then be moved, rotated, and scaled based on the viewpoint you have set up. The viewpoint takes the form of a frustrum, a rectangular cone of sorts, which limits the scene to, ideally, a manageable level.

- Next the scene is clipped, meaning that only stuff that is likely to be visible is actually processed. All of the other stuff is culled out as early as possible and discarded. Much of the history of real-time graphics development has to do with object culling techniques, some of which are very complex.

  Let's get back to the example of a solar system. If you are looking at the earth and the moon is behind your viewpoint, there is no need whatsoever to process the moon data. The clipping level does just this, both on an object level on one end and on a vertex level on the other. Of course, if you can pre-cull objects on your own before submitting to the pipeline, so much the better. Perhaps the easiest is to simply tell whether an object is behind you making it completely skippable. Culling can also take place if the object is just too far away to see or is completely obscured by other objects.

- The remaining objects are now *projected* against the "viewport," a virtual display of sorts.

- At this point is where *rasterization* takes place. Rasterization breaks apart the image into *fragments* that are in effect single pixels.

- Now the fragments can have texture and fog effects applied to them. Additional culling can likewise take place if the fog might obscure the more distant fragments, for example.

- The final phase is where the surviving fragments are written to the frame buffer, but only if they satisfy some last-minute operations. Here is where the fragment's alpha values are applied for translucency, along with depth tests to ensure that the closest fragments are drawn in front of further ones and stencil tests used to render to nonrectangular viewports.

And when this is done, you might actually see something that looks like that teapot shown in Figure 1–11b.

**NOTE:** The more you delve into computer graphics, the more you'll see a little teapot popping up here and there in examples in books all the way to television and movies (*The Simpsons*, *Toy Story*). The legend of the teapot, sometimes called the Utah Teapot (everything can be traced back to Utah), began with a PhD student named Martin Newell in 1975. He needed a challenging shape but one that was otherwise a common object for his doctoral work. His wife suggested their white teapot, at which point Newell laboriously digitized it by hand. When he released the data into the public domain, it quickly achieved the status of being the "Hello World!" of graphics programming. Even one of the early OpenGL ES examples from Apple's developer web site had a teapot demo. The original teapot now resides at the Computer History Museum in Mountain View, California, just a few blocks from Google. See the left side of Figure 1-11.

**Figure 1–11a, b.** *The actual teapot used by Newell, currently on display at the Computer History Museum in Mountain View, California, on the left. Photo by Steve Baker. An example OpenGL application from Apple's developer site on the right.*

# Summary

In this chapter, we covered a little bit of computer graphics history, a simple example program, and, most importantly, the Utah Teapot. Next up is a deep and no doubt overly detailed look into the mathematics behind 3D imagery.

# Chapter 2

# All That Math Jazz

No book on 3D programming would be complete without at least one chapter on the mathematics behind 3D transformations. If you care nothing about this, move on—there's nothing to see here. After all, doesn't OpenGL take care of this stuff automatically? Certainly. But it is helpful to be familiar with what's going on inside, if nothing more but to understand the lingo of 3D-speak.

Let's define some terminology first:

- *Translation*: Moving an object from its initial position (see Figure 2–1, left)
- *Rotation*: Rotating an object around a central point of origin (see Figure 2–1, right)
- *Scaling*: Changing the size of an object
- *Transformation*: All of the above

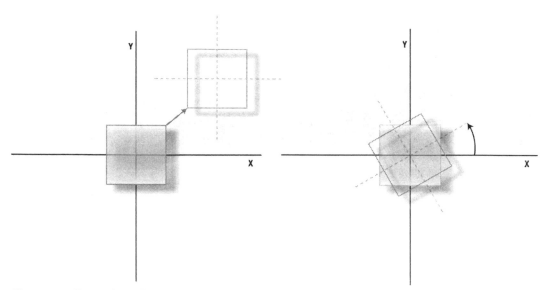

**Figure 2–1.** *Translation (left) and rotation (right)*

# 2D Transformations

Without knowing it, you probably have used 2D transformations already in the form of simple translations. If you create a UIImageView object and want to move it based on where the user is touching the screen, you might grab its frame and update the x and y values of the origin.

## Translations

You have two ways to visualize this process. The first is that the object itself is moving relative to a common origin. This is called a *geometric transformation*. The second means to move the world origin while the object stays stationary. This is called a *coordinate transformation*. In OpenGL ES, both descriptions are commonly used together.

A translational operation can be expressed this way:

$$x' = x + T_x \qquad y' = y + T_y$$

The original coordinates are *x* and *y*, while the translations, *T*, will move the points to a new location. Simple enough. As you can tell, translations are naturally going to be very fast.

NOTE: Lowercase letters, such as *xyz*, are the coordinates, while uppercase letters, such as *XYZ*, reference the axis.

## Rotations

Now let's take a look at rotations. In this case, we'll rotate around the world origin at first to keep things simple (see Figure 2–2).

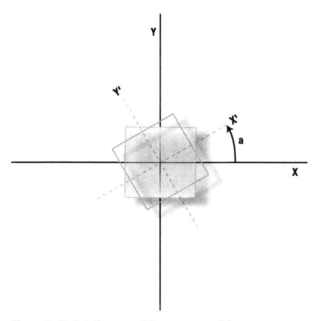

**Figure 2–2.** *Rotating around the common origin*

Naturally things get more complicated while we have to dust off the high-school trig. So, the task at hand is to find out where the corners of the square would be after an arbitrary rotation, *a*. Eyes are glazing over across the land.

NOTE: By convention counterclockwise rotations are considered positive, while clockwise are negative.

So, consider *x* and *y* as the coordinates of one of our square's vertices, and the square is normalized. Unrotated, any vertex would naturally map directly into our coordinate system of *x* and *y*. Fair enough. Now we want to rotate the square by an angle *a*. Although its corners are still at the "same" location in the square's own local coordinate system, they are different in ours, and if we're wanting to actually draw the object, we need to know the new coordinates of *x'* and *y'*.

Now we can jump directly to the trusty rotation equations, because ultimately that's what the code will express:

$$x' = x\cos(a) - y\sin(a) \qquad y' = x\sin(a) + y\cos(a)$$

Doing a really quick sanity check, you can see that if *a* is 0 degrees (no rotation), *x'* and *y'* reduce to the original *x* and *y* coordinates. If the rotation is 90 degrees, then *sin(a)=1, cos(a)=0*, so *x'=-y*, and *y'=x*. It's exactly as expected.

Mathematicians are always fond of expressing things in the most compact form possible. So, 2D rotations can be "simplified" using matrix notation:

$$R_a = \begin{bmatrix} \cos(a) & -\sin(a) \\ \sin(a) & \cos(a) \end{bmatrix}$$

> **NOTE:** One of the most overused words in *Star Trek* is *matrix*. Pattern-matrix here, buffer-matrix there, "Number One, I have a headache-matrix and need to take a nap-matrix." (And don't get me started on the use of *protocol* in *24*.) Every self-respecting *Star Trek* drinking game (as if any drinking game would be self-respecting) should use *matrix* in its selection of words. Unless one of your friends has a drinking problem, in which case substitute matrix for *rabid badger.* I am almost sure there was never a mention of badgers, rabid or otherwise, in the *Star Trek* pantheon.

$R_a$ is shorthand for our 2D rotation matrix. Although matrices might look busy, they are actually pretty straightforward and easy to code because they follow precise patterns. In this case, *x* and *y* can be represented as a teeny matrix:

$$\begin{bmatrix} x' \\ y' \end{bmatrix} = \begin{bmatrix} \cos(a) & -\sin(a) \\ \sin(a) & \cos(a) \end{bmatrix} \begin{bmatrix} x \\ y \end{bmatrix}$$

Translations can also be encoded in a matrix form. Since translations are merely moving the point around, the translated values of *x* and *y* come from adding the amount of movement to the point. What if you wanted to do a rotation and a translation on the same object? The translation matrix requires just a tiny bit of nonobvious thought. Which is the right one, the first or second shown here?

$$T = \begin{bmatrix} 1 & 1 \\ T_x & T_y \end{bmatrix} \text{ or } T = \begin{vmatrix} 1 & 0 & 0 \\ 0 & 1 & 0 \\ T_x & T_y & 1 \end{vmatrix}$$

The answer is *obviously* the second one, or maybe it's not so obvious. The first one ends up as the following, which doesn't make much sense:

$$x' = x + yT_x \text{ and } y' = x + yT_y$$

So, in order to create a matrix for translation, we need a third component for our 2D point, commonly written as *(x,y,1)*, as is the case in the second expression. Ignoring where the 1 comes from for a moment, notice that this can be easily reduced to this:

$$x' = x + T_x \quad \text{and} \quad y' = y + T_y$$

The value of *1* is not to be confused with a third dimension of *z*; rather, it is a means used to express an equation of a line (in 2D space for this example) that is a slightly different from the slope/intercept we learned in grade school. A set of coordinates in this form is called *homogeneous coordinates*, and in this case it helps to create a 3x3 matrix that can now be combined or concatenated to other 3x3 matrices. Why would we want to do this? What if we wanted to do a rotation and translation together? Two separate matrices could be used for each point, and that would work just fine. But instead, we can precalculate a single matrix out of several using matrix multiplication (also known as *concatenation*) that in turn represents the cumulative effect of the individual transformations. Not only can this save some space, but it can substantially increase performance.

In Java2D, you will at some point stumble across java.awt.geom.AffineTransform. You can think of this as transformations that can be decomposed into one or more of the following: rotation, translation, shear, and scale. All of the possible 2D affine transformations can be expressed as $x' = ax + cy + e$ and $y = bx + dy + f$. That makes for a very nice matrix, a lovely one at that:

$$T = \begin{bmatrix} a & b & 0 \\ c & d & 0 \\ e & f & 1 \end{bmatrix} \text{ so } \begin{bmatrix} x' & y' & 1 \end{bmatrix} = \begin{vmatrix} a & b & 0 \\ c & d & 0 \\ e & f & 1 \end{vmatrix} \begin{bmatrix} x & y & 1 \end{bmatrix}$$

The following is a simple code segment that shows how to use AffineTransform both for translation and for scaling. As you can see, it is pretty straightforward.

```
public void paint(Graphics g)
{
    AffineTransform transform = new AffineTransform();
    transform.translate(5,5);
```

```
    transform.scale(2,2);
    Graphics2D g2d = (Graphics2D)g;
    g2d.setTransform(transform);
}
```

## Scaling

Of the other two transforms, let's just take a look at the scaling, or simple resizing, of an object:

$$x' = xS_x \text{ and } y = yS_y$$

In matrix form, this becomes as follows:

$$S = \begin{vmatrix} S_x & 0 & 0 \\ 0 & S_y & 0 \\ 0 & 0 & 1 \end{vmatrix}$$

With scaling, as with the other two transformations, the order is *very* important when applied to your geometry. Say, for instance, you wanted to rotate and move your object. The results will clearly be different depending on whether you do the translation first or last. The more common sequence is to rotate the object first and then translate, as shown at the left in Figure 2–3. But if you invert the order, you'll get something like the image at the right in Figure 2–3. In both these instances, the rotation is happening around the point of origin. If you wanted to rotate the object around its own origin, then the first example is for you. If you meant for it to be rotated with everything else, the second works. (A typical situation might have you translate the object to the world origin, rotate it, and translate it back.)

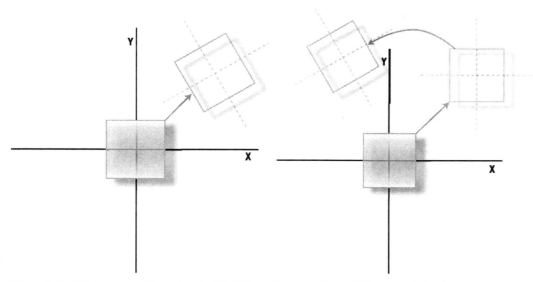

**Figure 2–3.** *Rotation around the point of origin followed by a translation (left) vs. translation followed by rotation (right)*

So, what does this have to do with the 3D stuff? Simple! Most if not all of the principles can be applied to 3D transformations and are more clearly illustrated with one less dimension.

# 3D Transformations

When moving everything you've learned to 3D space (also referred to as *3-space*), you'll see that, as in 2D, 3D transformations can likewise be expressed as a matrix and as such can be concatenated with other matrices. The extra dimension of *Z* is now the depth of the scene going in and out of the screen. OpenGL ES has +*Z* coming out
and −*Z* going in. Other systems may have that reversed or even have *Z* being the vertical, with *Y* now assuming depth. I'll stay with the OpenGL convention, as shown in Figure 2–4.

> **NOTE:** Moving back and forth from one frame of reference to another is the quickest road to insanity next to trying to figure out why Fox canceled *Firefly*. The classic 1973 book *Principles of Interactive Computer Graphics* has *Z* going up and +*Y* going into the screen. In his book, Bruce Artwick, the creator of Microsoft's Flight Simulator, shows *X* and *Y* in the viewing plane but +*Z* going *into* the screen. And yet another book has (get this!) *Z* going up, *Y* going *right*, and *X* coming toward the viewer. There oughtta be a law....

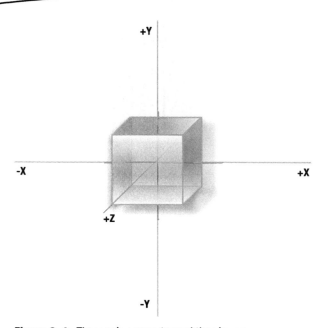

+Y

-X                    +X

+Z

-Y

**Figure 2–4.** *The z-axis comes toward the viewer.*

First we'll look at 3D transformation. Just as the 2D variety was merely adding the desired deltas to the original location, the same thing goes for 3D. And the matrix that describes that would look like the following:

$$T = \begin{bmatrix} 1 & 0 & 0 & 0 \\ 0 & 1 & 0 & 0 \\ 0 & 0 & 1 & 0 \\ T_x & T_y & T_z & 1 \end{bmatrix} \text{ so } \begin{bmatrix} x' \\ y' \\ z' \\ 1 \end{bmatrix} = \begin{bmatrix} 1 & 0 & 0 & 0 \\ 0 & 1 & 0 & 0 \\ 0 & 0 & 1 & 0 \\ T_x & T_y & T_z & 1 \end{bmatrix} \begin{bmatrix} x \\ y \\ z \\ 1 \end{bmatrix}$$

And of course that would yield the following:

$$x' = x + T_x, \ y' = y + T_y \text{ and } z' = z + T_z$$

Notice the extra 1 that's been added; it's the same as for the 2D stuff, so our point location is now in *homogeneous* form.

So, let's take a look at rotation. One can safely assume that if we were to rotate around the z-axis (Figure 2–5), the equations would map directly to the 2D versions. Using the matrix to express this, here is what we get (notice the new notation, where *R(z,a)* is used to make it clear which axis is being addressed). Notice that z remains a constant because it is multiplied by 1:

$$R(z,a) = \begin{bmatrix} \cos(a) & -\sin(a) & 0 & 0 \\ \sin(a) & \cos(a) & 0 & 0 \\ 0 & 0 & 1 & 0 \\ 0 & 0 & 0 & 1 \end{bmatrix}$$

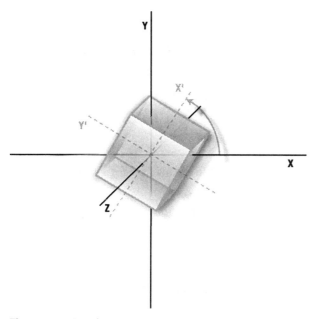

**Figure 2–5.** *Rotation around the z-axis*

This looks almost exactly like its 2D counterpart but with $z = z$. But now we can also rotate around $x$ or $y$ as well. For $x$ we get the following:

$$R(x,a) = \begin{bmatrix} 1 & 0 & 0 & 0 \\ 0 & \cos(a) & -\sin(a) & 0 \\ 0 & \sin(a) & \cos(a) & 0 \\ 0 & 0 & 0 & 1 \end{bmatrix}$$

And, of course, for $y$ we get the following:

$$R(y,a) = \begin{bmatrix} \cos(a) & 0 & \sin(a) & 0 \\ 0 & 1 & 0 & 0 \\ -\sin(a) & 0 & \cos(a) & 0 \\ 0 & 0 & 0 & 1 \end{bmatrix}$$

But what about multiple transformations on top of each other? Now we're talking ugly. Fortunately, you won't have to worry too much about this because you can let OpenGL do the heavy lifting. That's what it's for.

Assume we want to rotate around the $y$-axis first, followed by $x$ and then $z$. The resulting matrix might resemble the following (using $a$ as the rotation around $x$, $b$ for $y$, and $c$ for $z$):

$$R = \begin{bmatrix} \cos(b)\cos(c) - \sin(b)\sin(a)\sin(c) & -\cos(b)\sin(c) + \sin(b)\sin(a)\cos(c) & \sin(b)\cos(a) & 0 \\ \sin(c)\cos(a) & \cos(c)\cos(a) & -\sin(a) & 0 \\ -\sin(b)\cos(c) + \cos(b)\sin(a)\sin(c) & \sin(c)\sin(b) + \cos(b)\sin(a)\cos(c) & \cos(a)\cos(b) & 0 \\ 0 & 0 & 0 & 1 \end{bmatrix}$$

Simple, eh? No wonder why the mantra for 3D engine authors is *optimize, optimize, optimize*. In fact, some of my inner loop in the original Amiga version of Distant Suns needed to be in 68K assembly. And note that this doesn't even include scaling or translation.

Now let's get to the reason for this book: all of this can be done by the following three lines:

```
glRotatef(b,0.0,1.0,0.0);
glRotatef(a,1.0,0.0,0.0);
glRotatef(c,0.0,0.0,1.0);
```

> **NOTE:** There are many functions in OpenGL ES 1.1 that are not available in 2.0. The latter is oriented toward lower-level operations, sacrificing some of the ease-of-use utility routines for flexibility and control. The transformation functions have vanished, leaving it up to developers to calculate their own matrices. Fortunately, there are a number of different libraries to mimic these operations and ease the transition tasks.

When dealing with OpenGL, this particular matrix is called the modelview because it is applied to anything that you draw, which are either models or lights. There are two other types that we'll deal with a little later: the *Projection* and *Texture* matrices.

It bears repeating that the actual order of the rotations is absolutely critical when trying to get this stuff to work. For example, a frequent task is to model an aircraft or spacecraft with a full six degrees of freedom: three translational components and three rotational components. The rotational parts are usually referred to as *roll*, *pitch*, and *yaw* (RPY). Roll would be rotations around the *z*-axis, pitch is around the *x*-axis (in other words, aiming the nose up or down), and yaw, of course, is rotation around the *y*-axis, moving the nose left and right. Figure 2–6 shows this at work in the Apollo spacecraft from the moon landings in the 1960s. The proper sequence would be yaw, pitch, and roll, or rotation around *y, x,* and finally *z.* (This requires 12 multiplications and 6 additions, while premultiplying the three rotation matrices could reduce that to 9 multiplications and 6 additions.) The transformations would be incremental, comprising the changes in the RPY angles since the last update, not the total ones from the beginning. In the good ol' days, round-off errors could compound distorting the matrix, leading to very cool but otherwise unanticipated results (but still cool nonetheless).

## ENGINE LOCATION

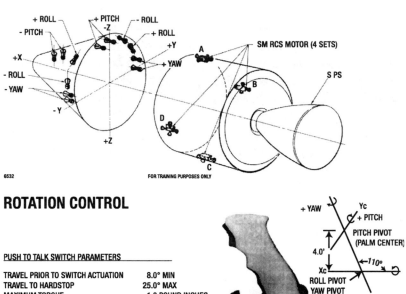

## ROTATION CONTROL

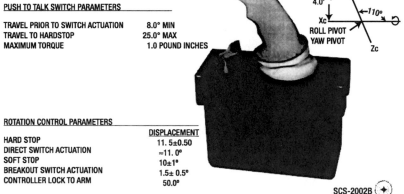

<u>PUSH TO TALK SWITCH PARAMETERS</u>

| | |
|---|---|
| TRAVEL PRIOR TO SWITCH ACTUATION | 8.0° MIN |
| TRAVEL TO HARDSTOP | 25.0° MAX |
| MAXIMUM TORQUE | 1.0 POUND INCHES |

<u>ROTATION CONTROL PARAMETERS</u>

| | <u>DISPLACEMENT</u> |
|---|---|
| HARD STOP | 11. 5±0.50 |
| DIRECT SWITCH ACTUATION | ≈11. 0° |
| SOFT STOP | 10±1° |
| BREAKOUT SWITCH ACTUATION | 1.5± 0.5° |
| CONTROLLER LOCK TO ARM | 50.0° |

## FLIGHT DIRECTOR ATTITUDE INDICATOR

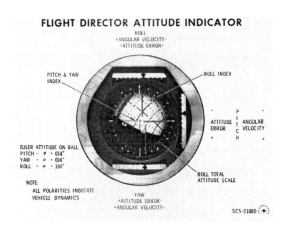

**Figure 2–6**. *Illustration of the Apollo's frame of reference, its joystick, and artificial horizon*

# Picture This: Projecting the Object onto the Screen

Whew, even after all of that we're not quite done yet. Once you have performed all the rotations, scaling, and translations of your objects, you still need to get them *projected* onto your screen. Converting a 3D scene onto a 2D surface has troubled mankind since he sketched the first mammoth on a cave wall. But it is actually quite easy to grasp, as opposed to transformations.

There are two main kinds of projections at work here: *perspective* and *parallel*. Perspective projection is the way we see the 3D world on our 2D retina. Perspective views consist of vanishing points and foreshortening. Vanishing points are where all parallel lines converge in the distance, providing the perception of depth (think of railroad tracks heading toward the horizon). The result is that the closer something is, the bigger it appears, and vice versa, as shown in Figure 2–7. The parallel variety, also called *orthographic projection*, simply removes the effects of distance by effectively setting the $z$ component of each vertex to 0 (the location of our viewing plane), as shown in Figure 2–8.

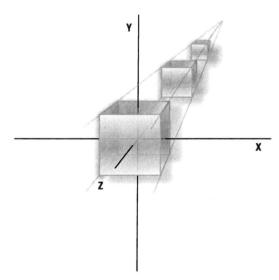

**Figure 2–7**. *Perspective projection*

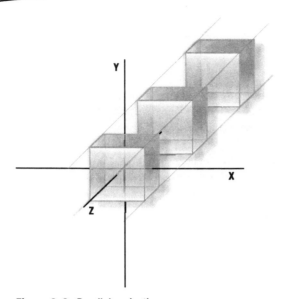

**Figure 2–8**. *Parallel projection*

In perspective projection, the distance component, *z*, is used to scale what will ultimately be the screen *x* and screen *y* values. So, the larger the *z*, or the distance away from the viewer, the smaller the pieces are visually. What one needs is the dimension of the *viewport* (OpenGL's version of your window or display screen) and its center point, which is typically the origin of the XY plane.

This final phase involves setting up the viewing *frustum*. The frustum establishes six clipping planes (top, bottom, left, right, near, and far) needed to precisely determine what should be visible to the user and how it is projected onto their *viewport*, which is OpenGL's version of your window or screen. This acts something like a lens into your OpenGL virtual world. By changing the values, you can zoom in or out and clip stuff really far away or not at all, as shown in Figures 2–9 and 2–10. The *perspective* matrix is defined by these values.

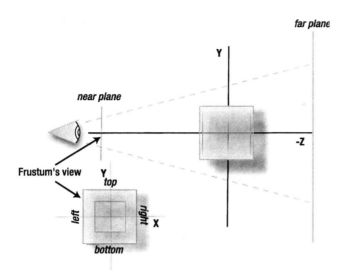

**Figure 2–9.** *Narrow bounds for the frustum give you a high-power lens.*

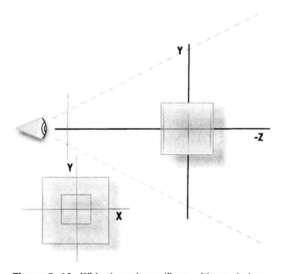

**Figure 2–10**. *Wider bounds are like a wide-angle lens.*

With these boundaries established, the one final transformation is that to the *viewport*, OpenGL's version of your screen. This is the point where OpenGL is fed the screen's dimensions, those of your display area, and the origin, which is likely the lower-left corner of the screen. On small devices such as a phone or tablet, you will likely fill up the entire screen and so will use the screen's full width. But should you want to place the image into a subwindow of the main display, you could simply pass smaller values to the viewport. The law of similar triangles plays out here.

In Figure 2–11 we want to find what the projected $x'$ is, given the $x$ of an arbitrary vertex on the model. Consider two triangles, one formed by the corners CBA and the other smaller one by COA' (the *O* is for *origin*). The distance from C (where the eye is, to O is *d*). The distance from C to B is *d+z*. So, just taking the ratio of those, as follows:

$$\frac{x'}{d_{eye}} = \frac{x}{z + d_{eye}} \text{ and } \frac{y'}{d_{eye}} = \frac{y}{z + d_{eye}}$$

yields the following:

$$x' = \frac{x d_{eye}}{z + d_{eye}} \text{ and } y' = \frac{y d_{eye}}{z + d_{eye}}$$

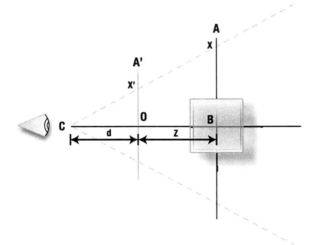

**Figure 2–11.** *Mapping a vertex to the viewport using the Law of Similar Triangles*

Figure 2–12 shows the final translations. Those can be added to *x'* and *y'*:

$$x' = \frac{x d_{eye}}{z + d_{eye}} + T_x \text{ and } y' = \frac{y d_{eye}}{z + d_{eye}} + T_y$$

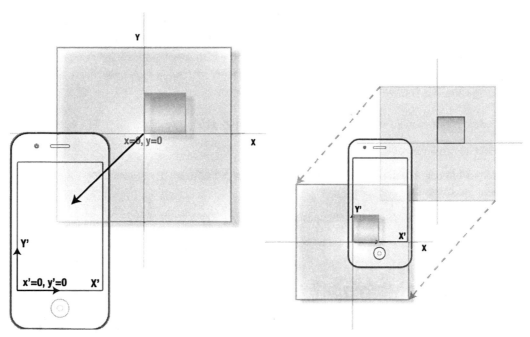

**Figure 2–12.** *Projecting x and y onto the device's screen. You can visualize this as either translating your device to the object's coordinates (left) or translating the object to the device's coordinates (right).*

And when the pixel dust settles, we have a nice matrixy form:

$$
\begin{bmatrix} x' \\ y' \\ z' \\ 1 \end{bmatrix} = \begin{bmatrix} d & 0 & 0 & T_x \\ 0 & d & 0 & T_y \\ 0 & 0 & 0 & 0 \\ 0 & 0 & 1 & d \end{bmatrix} \begin{bmatrix} x \\ y \\ z \\ 1 \end{bmatrix}
$$

Usually some final scaling is required—if, for example, the viewport is normalized. But that is left up to you.

# Now Do it Backward and in High Heels

Such was a quote allegedly given by Ginger Rogers on how she felt about dancing with the great Fred Astaire. The response was that although he was very good, she had to do everything he did *and* do it backward and in high heels. (Rogers apparently never actually said that, as its use has been traced back to a gag line from the comic strip Frank and Ernest.)

So, what does this have to do with transformations? Say you wanted to tell whether someone picked one of your objects by touching the screen. How do you know which of your objects has been selected? You must be able to do inverse transformations to "unmap" the screen coordinates back into something recognizable within your 3D space. But since the z-value gets dropped in the process, it will be necessary to search through your object list to find which was the most likely target. Untransforming something requires you to do everything backward (and in high heels if you like that sort of thing). And this is done in the following way:

1.   Multiply your modelview matrix with your Projection matrix.

2.   Invert the results.

3.   Convert the screen coordinates of the touch point into the frame of reference for your viewport.

4.   Take the results of that and multiply it by the inverted matrix from step 2.

Don't worry, that will be covered in more detail later in the book.

## What About Quaternions?

Quaternions are hyper-complex numbers that can store the RPY information in a four-dimensional vector-type thingie. They are very efficient in both performance and space and are commonly used to model the instantaneous heading of an aircraft or spacecraft in flight simulation. They are a curious creature with great properties but are reserved for later, because OpenGL doesn't support them directly.

## Summary

In this chapter, you learned the basics of 3D mathematics. First the chapter covered 2D transformations (rotation, translation, and scaling) and then 3D, with projection covered as well. Although you will not likely need to code any transformations yourself, being familiar with this chapter is key to understanding much of the OpenGL terminology later. My head hurts.

# From 2D to 3D: Adding One Extra Dimension

In the first two chapters, we covered the cool stuff and the math stuff (which could be either cool or boring). Here in Chapter 3 we'll move the bouncing cube example beyond a mere 2D version to a 3D version (4D hypercubes are beyond the scope of this work). And during the process, more 3D theory about projections, rotations, and the like will be slipped in for good measure. However, note that OpenGL is not just for 3D but can easily be used to place 2D controls in front of your 3D visualization.

## First, a Little More Theory

Remember that OpenGL ES objects are a collection of points in 3D space; that is, their location is defined by three values. These values are joined together to form faces, which are flat surfaces that look remarkably like triangles. The triangles are then joined together to form objects or pieces of objects.

To get a bunch of numbers that form vertices, other numbers that form colors, and still other numbers that combine the vertices and colors on the screen, it is necessary to tell the system about its graphic environment. Such things as the location of the viewpoint, the window (or viewport) that will receive the image, aspect ratios, and other bits of digital flotsam of sorts are needed to complete the 3D circuit. More specifically, I'll cover OpenGL's coordinates, how they relate to the frustum, how objects are clipped or culled from the scene, and the drawing to your device's display.

> **NOTE:** You're probably wondering when we get to the cool planetary stuff. Soon, Grasshopper, soon.

# OpenGL Coordinates

If you've done any sort of graphics at all on any system, you'll be acquainted with the run-of-the-mill X-Y coordinate system. X is always the horizontal axis, with right being positive, while Y is always the vertical axis, with down being positive, placing the origin in the upper-left corner. Known as *screen coordinates*, they are easily confused with *math coordinates,* which place the origin at the lower-left corner and where, for Y, up is positive.

Now jumping to OpenGL 3D coordinates, we have a slightly different system using *Cartesian* coordinates, the standard of expressing locations in space. Typically, for screen coordinates on 2D displays, the origin is in the upper-left corner with +X going right and +Y going down. However, OpenGL has the origin in the lower-left corner, with +Y going up. But now we add a third dimension, expressed as Z. In this case, +Z is pointing toward you, as shown in Figure 3–1.

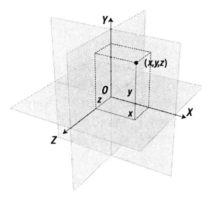

**Figure 3–1.** *OpenGL ES 3D Cartesian coordinate system (image by Jorge Stolfi)*

In fact, we have several kinds of coordinate systems, or *spaces*, in OpenGL, with each space being transformed to the next:

- *Object* space, which is relative to each of your objects.

- Camera, or *eye*, space, local to your viewpoint.

- Projection, or *clip*, space, which is the 2D screen or viewport that displays the final image.

- *Tangent* space, used for more advanced effects such as bump-mapping, which will be covered later.

- Normalized device coordinates (NDCs), which express the xyz values *normalized* from -1 to 1. That is, the value (or set of values) is normalized such that it fits inside a cube 2 units on a side.

■ Windows, or *screen*, coordinates, which are the final locations of your scene when displayed in the actual screen (no doubt to wild applause).

Naturally the previous can be expressed in pipeline form, as shown in Figure 3–2.

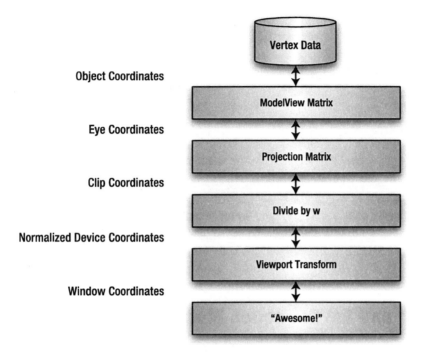

**Figure 3–2.** *Vertex transformation pipeline*

Object, eye, and clip space are the three you usually have to worry about. For example, object coordinates are generated with a local origin and then moved and rotated to *eye space*. If you have a bunch of airplanes for a combat game, for example, each will have their own local origin. You should be able to move the planes to any part of your world by moving, or *translating*, just the origin and letting the rest of the geometry follow along. At this point, the visibility of objects is tested against the viewing frustum, which is the volume of space that defines what the virtual camera can actually see. If they lay outside the frustum, they are considered invisible and so are clipped, or culled out, so that no further operations are done on them. As you may remember in Chapter 1, much of the work in graphics engine design focuses on the clipping part of the engine, so as to dump as many of the objects as early as possible to yield faster and more efficient systems.

And finally, after all of that, the screen-oriented portions of OpenGL are ready to convert, or *project*, the remaining objects. And those objects are your planes, zeppelins, missiles, trucks on the road, ships at sea, trebuchets, and anything else you want to stuff into your application.

> **NOTE:** OpenGL doesn't really define anything as "world space." However, the eye coordinates are the next best thing in that you can define everything in relation to your location.

## Eye Coordinates

There is no magical eyepoint object in OpenGL. So, instead of moving your eyepoint, you move all of the objects in relation to your eyepoint. And yes, that is easy to get confused, and you will find yourself constantly changing the signs of values, drawing funny diagrams, and holding out your hand in weird ways trying to figure out why your trebuchet is upside-down. While in eyepoint relative coordinates, instead of moving away from an object, the object, in effect, is moving away from you. Imagine you are making a video of a car rushing by. Under OpenGL, the car would be standing still; you and everything around you would be moving by it. This is done largely with the `glTranslate*()` and `glRotate*()` calls, as you will see later. It is at this point where OpenGL's modelview matrix that was referenced in the previous chapter comes into play. You may recall that the ModelView matrix handles the basic 3D transformations (as opposed to the Projection matrix, which *projects* the 3D view onto the 2D space of your screen, or the Texture matrix, which helps apply images to your object). You will refer to it frequently.

## Viewing Frustum and the Projection Matrix

In geometry, a *frustum* is that portion of (typically) a pyramid or cone that results after being cut by two parallel planes. In other words, think of the great Pyramid of Giza with the top third lopped off (not that I am condoning the destruction of Egyptian antiquities). In graphics, the viewing frustum defines the portion of the world that our virtual camera can actually see, as shown in Figure 3–3.

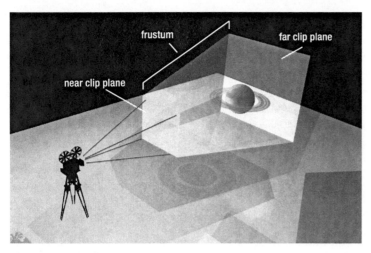

**Figure 3–3.** *Viewing frustum*

Unlike a number of things in OpenGL, the definition of the viewing frustum is very straightforward and follows the conceptual figures closely by simply defining a volume, the viewing pyramid, in space. Any objects that are whole or in part within the frustum may eventually find their way to the screen as long as it is not obscured by anything closer.

The frustum also is used to specify your field-of-view (FOV), like your camera's wide-angle vs. telephoto lens. The larger the angle that the side planes form when compared to the center axis (that is, how they fan out), the larger the FOV. And a larger FOV will allow more of your world to be visible but can also result in lower frame rates.

Up to this point, the translations and rotations use the ModelView matrix, easily set using the call gl.glMatrixMode(GL_MODELVIEW);. But now at this stage of the rendering pipeline, you will define and work with the Projection matrix. This is done largely via the frustum definitions spelled out in the section "Picture This" in Chapter 2. And it is also a surprisingly compact means of doing a lot of operations.

The final steps to convert the transformed vertices to a 2D image are as follows:

1.  A 3D point inside the frustum is mapped to a normalized cube to convert the XYZ values to NDC. NDC stands for normalized device coordinates, which is an intermediate system describing the coordinate space that lays inside the frustum and is resolution independent. This is useful when it comes to mapping each vertex and each object to your device's screen, no matter what size or how many pixels it has, be it a phone, tablet, or something new with completely different screen dimesions. Once you have this form, the coordinates have "moved" but still retain their relative relationships with each other. And of course, in NDC, they now fall into values between -1 and 1. Note that internally the Z value is flipped. Now –Z is coming toward you, while +Z is going away, but thankfully that great unplesantness is all hidden.

2.  These new NDCs are then mapped to the screen, taking into account the screen's aspect ratio and the "distance" the vertices are from the screen as specified by the near clipping plane. As a result, the further things are, the smaller they are. Most of the math is used for little more than determining the proportions of this or that within the frustum.

The previous steps describe *perspective projection*, which is the way we normally view the world. That is, the further things are, the smaller they appear. When those inherent distortions are removed, we get *orthographic projection*. At that point, no matter how far an object is, it still displays the same size. Orthographic renderings are typically used in mechanical drawings when any perspective distortion would corrupt the intent of the original artwork.

> **NOTE:** You will often need to directly address which matrix you are dealing with. The call to gl.glMatrixMode() is used to specify the current matrix, which all subsequent operations apply to until changed. Forgetting which matrix is the current one is an easy error to make.

# Back to the Fun Stuff: Going Beyond the Bouncy Square

Now we can go back to the example that was used in Chapter 1. Now that we're getting seriously 3D, several things will need to be added to handle the Z-dimension, including a larger dataset for the cube's geometry and color, methods of handing off that data to OpenGL, a more complex frustum definition, any face-culling techniques if needed, and rotations instead of just the translations.

> **NOTE:** *Translation* means to move an object around in your world up/down, left/right, and forward/backward, while *rotation* means to rotate the object around any arbitrary axis. And both are considered *transformations*.

## Adding the Geometry

From Chapter 1, you'll remember the data as defined in Listing 3–1. First is the location of the four corners, the vertices, how the vertices connect together, and how they are colored.

**Listing 3–1.** *Defining the 2D Square*

```
float vertices[] =
      {
                  -1.0f, -1.0f,
                   1.0f, -1.0f,
                  -1.0f,  1.0f,
                   1.0f,  1.0f
      };

      byte maxColor=(byte)255;

      byte colors[] =
      {
                  maxColor,maxColor,                0,maxColor,
                  0,                maxColor, maxColor,maxColor,
                  0,                              0,            0,maxColor,
                  maxColor,                0, maxColor, maxColor
      };

      byte indices[] =
      {
            0, 3, 1,
            0, 2, 3
      };
```

Now this can be extended to include the z-components, starting with the extra vertices, as shown in line 1 of Listing 3–2. Additional details of the code will be discussed after the listing.

**Listing 3–2.** *Defining the 3D Cube*

```
      float vertices[] =
      {
                  -1.0f,  1.0f, 1.0f,                                    //1
```

```
                    1.0f,  1.0f, 1.0f,
                    1.0f, -1.0f, 1.0f,
                   -1.0f, -1.0f, 1.0f,

                   -1.0f,  1.0f,-1.0f,
                    1.0f,  1.0f,-1.0f,
                    1.0f, -1.0f,-1.0f,
                   -1.0f, -1.0f,-1.0f
};

byte maxColor=(byte)255;

byte colors[] =                                                    //2
{
          maxColor,maxColor,       0,maxColor,
          0,       maxColor,maxColor,maxColor,
          0,              0,       0,maxColor,
          maxColor,       0,maxColor,maxColor,

          maxColor,       0,       0,maxColor,
          0,       maxColor,       0,maxColor,
          0,              0,maxColor,maxColor,
          0,              0,       0,maxColor
};


byte tfan1[] =
{
          1,0,3,
          1,3,2,
          1,2,6,
          1,6,5,
          1,5,4,
          1,4,0

};

byte tfan2[] =
{
          7,4,5,
          7,5,6,
          7,6,2,
          7,2,3,
          7,3,0,
          7,0,4
};
```

Line 1 extends the vertices to three dimensions, while the colors array, lines 2ff, do the same with color.

Figure 3–4 shows the way the vertices are ordered. Under normal situations, you will never have to define geometry in this fashion. You'll likely load your objects from a file stored in one of the standard 3D data formats, such as those used by 3D Studio or Modeler 3D. And considering how complicated such files can be, it is not recommended that you write your own because importers for most of the major formats are available.

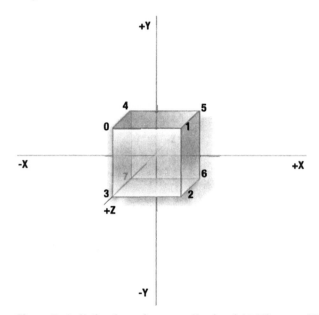

**Figure 3–4.** *Notice the various axes: X going right, Y is up, and Z is toward the viewer.*

The size of color array, as shown in line 2 of Listing 3–2, has been doubled because of the doubling of the number of vertices; otherwise, they are identical to the ones in the first example except with some different colors on the back faces.

Some new data is now needed to tell OpenGL in what order the vertices are to be used. With the square, it was a no-brainer to order, or *sequence*, the data by hand so that the four vertices could represent the two triangles. The cube makes this considerably more complicated. We could have defined each of the six faces of the cube by separate vertex arrays, but that wouldn't scale well for more complex objects. And it would be less efficient than having to shove six sets of data through the graphics hardware. Keeping all the data in a single array is the most efficient from both a memory and a speed standpoint. So, then, how do we tell OpenGL the layout of the data? In this case, we'll use the drawing mode called *triangle fans,* as shown in Figure 3–5.

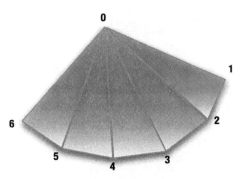

**Figure 3–5.** *A triangle fan has one common point with all triangles.*

There are many different ways data can be stored and presented to OpenGL ES. One format may be faster but uses more memory, while another may use less memory but at the cost of a little extra overhead. If you were to import data from one of the 3D files, chances are it is already optimized for one of the approaches, but if you really want to hand-tune the system, you may at some point have to repack the vertices into the format you prefer for your application.

Besides triangle fans, you will find other ways data can be stored or represented, called *modes*.

   ▦   Points and lines specify just that: points and lines. OpenGL ES can render your
        vertices as merely points of definable sizes or can render lines between the points
        to show the wireframe version. Use GL10.GL_POINTS and GL10.GL_LINES,
        respectively.

   ▦   Line strips, GL10.GL_LINE_STRIP, are a way for OpenGL to draw a series of lines
        in one shot, while line loops, GL10.GL_LINE_LOOP, are like line strips but will
        always connect the first and last vertices together.

   ▦   Triangles, triangle strips, and triangle fans round out the list of OpenGL ES
        primitives: GL10.GL_TRIANGLES, GL10.GL_TRIANGLE_STRIP, and
        GL10.GL_TRIANGLE_FAN. OpenGL itself can handle additional modes such as
        quads (faces with four vertices/sides), quad strips, and polygons.

---

**NOTE:** The term *primitive* denotes a fundamental shape or form of data in graphics systems.
Examples of primitives include cubes, spheres, and cones. The term can also be used for even
simpler shapes such as points, lines, and, in the case of OpenGL ES, triangles and triangle fans.

---

When using these low-level objects, you may recall that in the first example in Chapter 1, there was an *index*, or *connectivity*, array to tell which vertices matched which triangle. When defining the triangle arrays, called tfan1 and tfan2 in Listing 3–2, you use a similar approach except all sets of indices start with the same vertex. So, for example, the first three numbers in the array tfan1 are 1, 0, and 3.

That means the first triangle is made up of vertices 1, 0, and 3, in that order. And so, back in the array *vertices*, vertex 1 is located at x=1.0f, y=1.0f, and z=1.0f. Vertex 0 is the point at x=-1.0f, y=1.0f, and z=1.0f, while the third corner of our triangle is located at x=-1.0, y=-1.0, and z=1.0. The upside is that this makes it a lot easier to create the datasets because the actual order is now irrelevant, while the downside is that it uses up a little more memory to store the additional information.

The cube can be divided up into two different triangle fans, which is why there are two index arrays. The first incorporates the front, right, and top faces, while the second incorporates the back, bottom, and left faces, as shown in Figure 3–6.

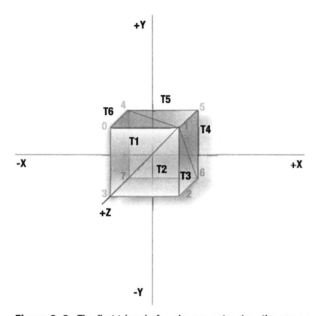

**Figure 3–6.** *The first triangle fan shares vertex 1 as the common vertex.*

## Stitching It All Together

Now the rendering code must be modified to handle the new data. Listing 3–3 shows the rest of the new `constructor` method, right under the data definitions in Listing 3–2. This will replicate much of the Chapter 1 example except for using the triangle fans instead of the connectivity array and the two calls to `gl.glDrawArray()`. This is needed because the cube is in two pieces that must be drawn separately, one each for three faces or six triangles that define the two triangle fans.

**Listing 3–3.** *The Rest of the Constructor Method*

```
ByteBuffer vbb = ByteBuffer.allocateDirect(vertices.length * 4);
vbb.order(ByteOrder.nativeOrder());
mFVertexBuffer = vbb.asFloatBuffer();
mFVertexBuffer.put(vertices);
```

```
                    mFVertexBuffer.position(0);

                    mColorBuffer = ByteBuffer.allocateDirect(colors.length);
                    mColorBuffer.put(colors);
                    mColorBuffer.position(0);

                    mTfan1 = ByteBuffer.allocateDirect(tfan1.length);
                    mTfan1.put(tfan1);
                    mTfan1.position(0);

                    mTfan2 = ByteBuffer.allocateDirect(tfan2.length);
                    mTfan2.put(tfan2);
                    mTfan2.position(0);
```

> **NOTE:** You'll note that many of the OpenGL ES calls end in an *f*, such as gl.glScalef(),
> gl.glRotatef(), and so on. The *f* means that the parameters passed are floats. The only other
> parameter types in OpenGL ES that require their own special calls are fixed-point values, so
> glScale would now be gl.glScalex(). Fixed point was useful for the older and slower
> devices, but with more current hardware the floating-point calls are recommended. You will
> notice that color arrays and other attributes can be collected as bytes, ints, longs, and so on. But
> they don't factor in to having a suite of dedicated API calls.

Listing 3–4 shows the updated draw method from the previous example. This is fundamentally the
same as the one in Chapter 1, but naturally it has our new friends, the triangle fans, instead of the
index array.

**Listing 3–4**. *Updated draw Method*

```
public void draw(GL10 gl)
        {
                gl.glVertexPointer(3, GL11.GL_FLOAT, 0, mFVertexBuffer);
                gl.glColorPointer(4, GL11.GL_UNSIGNED_BYTE, 0, mColorBuffer);

                gl.glDrawElements( gl.GL_TRIANGLE_FAN, 6 * 3, gl.GL_UNSIGNED_BYTE, mTfan1);
                gl.glDrawElements( gl.GL_TRIANGLE_FAN, 6 * 3, gl.GL_UNSIGNED_BYTE, mTfan2);
        }
```

Listing 3–5 shows a tweaked onDrawFrame from CubeRenderer.java.

**Listing 3–5.** *The Mildly Revised onDrawFrame*

```
public void onDrawFrame(GL10 gl)
        {
                gl.glClear(GL10.GL_COLOR_BUFFER_BIT | GL10.GL_DEPTH_BUFFER_BIT);
```

```
        gl.glClearColor(0.0f,0.5f,0.5f,1.0f);                          //1

        gl.glMatrixMode(GL10.GL_MODELVIEW);
        gl.glLoadIdentity();
        gl.glTranslatef(0.0f,(float)Math.sin(mTransY), -7.0f);         //2
        gl.glEnableClientState(GL10.GL_VERTEX_ARRAY);
        gl.glEnableClientState(GL10.GL_COLOR_ARRAY);

        mCube.draw(gl);

        mTransY += .075f;
    }
```

No real dramatic changes here:

■ In line 1, I've added gl.glClearColor to the mix. This specifies what color should be used when the frame is cleared. The color here is a fetching shade of teal blue.

■ In line 2, the z-value in the translation has been upped to -7 just to make the cube's depiction is little more natural looking.

One final set of changes is shown in Listing 3–6, which defines the viewing frustum. There is somewhat more information here so as to handle varying display sizes as well as making the code a little more easily understood.

**Listing 3–6.** *The New Frustum Code*

```
public void onSurfaceChanged(GL10 gl, int width, int height)
    {
        gl.glViewport(0, 0, width, height);

        float aspectRatio;
        float zNear =.1f;
        float zFar =1000;
        float fieldOfView = 30.0f/57.3f;                               //1
        float size;

        gl.glEnable(GL10.GL_NORMALIZE);

        aspectRatio=(float)width/(float)height;                        //2

        gl.glMatrixMode(GL10.GL_PROJECTION);                           //3

        size = zNear * (float)(Math.tan((double)(fieldOfView/2.0f)));  //4

        gl.glFrustumf(-size, size, -size /aspectRatio,                 //5
                           size /aspectRatio, zNear, zFar);
```

```
        gl.glMatrixMode(GL10.GL_MODELVIEW);                                    //6
    }
```

Here is what is happening:

- Line 1 defines the frustum with a given FOV, making a little more intuitive when choosing values. The field of 30 degrees is converted to radians as the Java Math libraries require, whereas OpenGL sticks to degrees.

- The aspect ratio in line 2 is based on the width divided by the height. So if the width is 1024x768, the aspect ratio would be 1.33. This helps ensure that the proportions of the image scale properly. Otherwise, were the view not to take care of the aspect ratio, its objects would look plenty squashed.

- Next, line 3 ensures that the current matrix mode is set as the projection matrix.

- Line 4 has the duty of calculating a size value needed to specify the left/right and top/bottom limits of the viewing volume, as shown in Figure 3–3. This can be thought of as your virtual window into the 3D space. With the center of the screen being the origin, you need to go from –size to +size in both dimensions. That is why the field is divided by two—so for a 60-degree field, the window will go from -30 degrees to +30 degrees. Multiplying size by zNear merely adds a scaling hint of sorts. Finally, divide the bottom/top limits by the aspect ratio to ensure your square will really be a square.

- Now we can feed those numbers into gl.glFrustum(), as shown in line 5, followed by resetting the current matrix back to GL10.GL_MODELVIEW.

If it works right, you should see something that looks exactly like the original bouncy cube! Wait, you're not impressed? OK, if you're going to be that way, let's add some rotations to the thing.

## Taking 'er Out for a Spin

Now it's time to add some more interesting animation to the scene. We're going to be spinning this slowly besides bouncing it up and down. Add the following line to the bottom of gl.onDrawFrames():

```
        mAngle+=.4;
```

Right *before* the gl.glTranslatef() call, add the following:

```
            gl.glRotatef(mAngle, 0.0f, 1.0f, 0.0f);
            gl.glRotatef(mAngle, 1.0f, 0.0f, 0.0f);
```

And naturally add private float mAngle; to the bottom of the file with the other definitions.

Now run again. "Hey! Huh?" will be the mostly likely response. The cube doesn't seem to be spinning, but instead it's rotating around your viewpoint (while bouncing at the same time), as shown in Figure 3–7. This illustrates one of the most confusing elements in basic 3D animation: getting the order of the translations and rotations correct. (Remember the discussion in Chapter 2?)

Consider our cube. If you want to have a cube spinning in front of your face, which would be the proper order? Rotate and then translate? Or translate and then rotate? Reaching way back to fifth-grade math, you might remember learning something about addition and multiplication being *commutative*. That is, the order of operations was not critical: a+b=b+a, or a*b=b*a. Well, 3D transformations are *not* commutative (finally, a use for something I'd never thought I'd need!). That is, rotation*translation is not the same as translation*rotation. See Figure 3–8.

The right side is what you are seeing right now in the rotating cube example. The cube is being translated first and then rotated, but because the rotation takes place around the "world" origin (the viewpoint's location), you see it as if it's spinning around your head.

Now to the obvious does-not-compute moment: are the rotations not placed *before* the translations in the example code anyway?

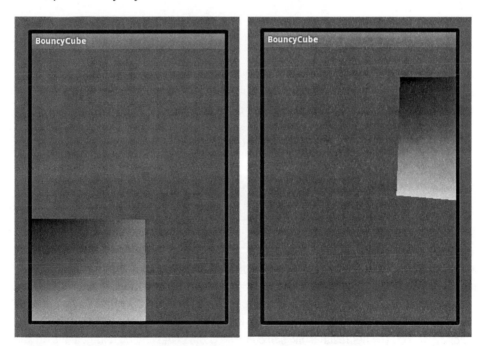

**Figure 3–7.** *Translation first, rotation second*

So, this is what should be causing the sudden outbreak of furrowed brows across the land:

```
gl.glRotatef(mAngle, 0.0f, 1.0f, 0.0f);
```

```
gl.glRotatef(mAngle, 1.0f, 0.0f, 0.0f);

gl.glTranslatef(0.0f, (float)(sinf(mTransY)/2.0f), z);
```

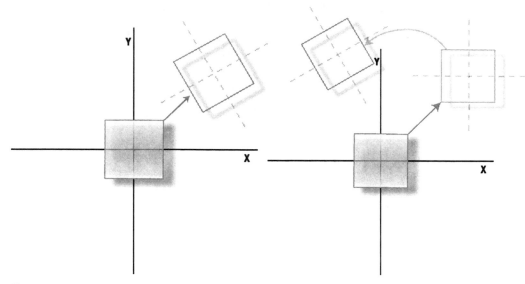

**Figure 3–8.** *Rotation first or translation first?*

However, in reality, the order of transformations is actually applied from *last to first.* Now put gl.glTranslatef() *ahead* of the two rotations, and you should see something like Figure 3–9, which is exactly what we wanted in the first place. Here is the code needed to do that:

```
gl.glTranslatef(0.0f, (float)(sinf(mTransY)/2.0f), z);

gl.glRotatef(mAngle, 0.0f, 1.0f, 0.0f);
gl.glRotatef(mAngle, 1.0f, 0.0f, 0.0f);
```

There are two different ways to visualize transformation ordering: the local coordinate and the world coordinate approach. Seeing things in the former, you move the objects to their final resting place and *then* perform the rotations. Since the coordinate system is local, the object will rotate around its own origin, making the previous sequence make sense when going from top to bottom. If you choose the world approach, which is in effect what OpenGL is doing, you must perform the rotations first around the object's local axis before performing the translation. In that way, the transformations actually happen from bottom to top. The net result is the same and so is the code, and both are confusing and easily can get out of sequence. That is why you'll see many a 3D guy or gal holding something at arm's length while moving themselves all around to help them figure out why their great-looking catapult model is flying below the ground. I call this the *3D shuffle.*

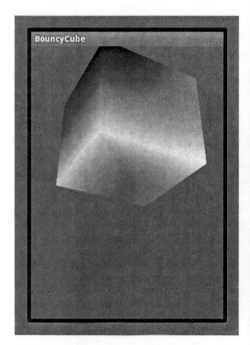

**Figure 3–9.** *Making the cube spin*

One final transformation command to be aware of right now is gl.glScale(), used for resizing the model along all three axes. Let's say you need to double the height of the cube. You would use the line glScalef(1,2,1). Remember that the height is aligned with the Y-axis, while width and depth are X and Z, which we don't want to touch.

Now the question is, where would you put the line to ensure that the geometry of the cube is the only thing affected, as in the left image In Figure 3–10, before or after the calls to gl.glRotatef() in onDrawFrame()?

If you said after, such as this:

```
gl.glTranslatef(0.0f, (GLfloat)(sinf(mTransY)/2.0f), z);

gl.glRotatef(mAngle, 0.0, 1.0, 0.0);
gl.glRotatef(mAngle, 1.0, 0.0, 0.0);

gl.glScalef(1,2,1);
```

you'd be right. The reason why this works is that since the last transformation in the list is actually the first to be executed, you must put scaling ahead of any other transformations if all you want to resize the object's geometry. Put it anywhere else, and you could end up with something like the image on the right in Figure 3–10. So, what's happening there? This was generated with the code snippet:

```
gl.glTranslatef(0.0f, (float)(sinf(mTransY)/2.0f), z);

gl.glScalef(1,2,1);

gl.glRotatef(mAngle, 0.0f, 1.0f, 0.0f);
gl.glRotatef(mAngle, 1.0f, 0.0f, 0.0f);
```

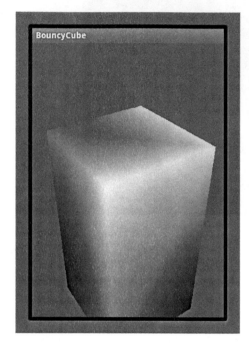 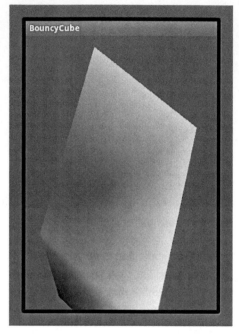

**Figure 3–10**. *Scaling before the rotations have been executed (left) and scaling after the rotations (right)*

The geometry is rotated first, and then the cube's local axis is rotated, which no longer aligns with the origin's axis. Following that with scale, it is stretched out along the world's Y-axis, instead of its own. This would be as if you already started with a vertex list of a cube rotated partway and scaled it with nothing else. So if you make the scaling at the very end, your entire world is scaled.

## Tweaking the Values

Now some more fun comes when we can start playing with various values. This section will demonstrate a number of the various principles that are not just relevant to OpenGL ES but found in nearly every 3D toolkit you're likely to stumble across.

## Clipping Regions

With a working demo, we can have fun by tweaking some of values and observing the changes. First we'll change the far clipping plane in the frustum by changing the value of zFar from 1000 down to 6.0. Why? Remember that the cube's local origin is 7.0 and its size is 2.0. So when facing straight at us, the closest point would be 6.0 because each of the sides would straddle the origin with 1.0 on each side. So, by changing the value of zFar to 6.0, the cube would be hidden when it is exactly facing us. But portions will peek through, looking something like a piece of flotsam poking above the water. The reason is that when it rotates, the corners are naturally going to be a little closer to the viewing plane, as shown in Figure 3–11.

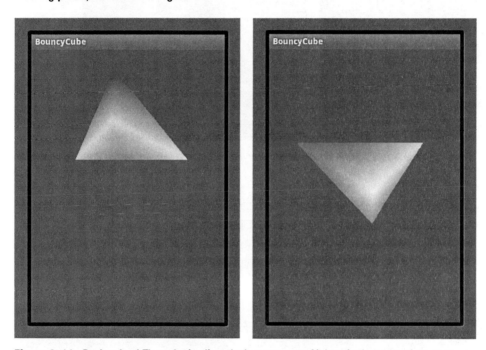

**Figure 3–11.** *Peek-a-boo! The cube is clipped when any part of it lays farther away than zFar.*

So, what happens when I move the near clipping plane farther away? Reset zFar to 1000 (a number that is arbitrarily large enough to ensure we can see everything in our exercises), and set zNear from .1 to 6.0. What do you think it will look like? It will be the opposite of the previous example. See Figure 3–12 for the results.

 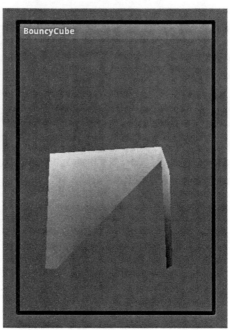

**Figure 3–12**. *The zFar plane is reset, while the zNear plane is moved back to clip any part of the cube that is too close.*

Z-clipping such as this is very helpful when dealing with large and complicated worlds. You'd likely not want all objects you might be "looking at" to be rendered, because most would likely be too far away to really see. Setting zFar and zNear to limit the visibility distance could speed up the system. However, this would not be the best substitute for preculling your objects before they get into the pipeline.

### Field of View

Remember that the viewer's FOV can also be changed in the frustum settings. Go back to our bouncy friend again and make sure your zNear and zFar settings are back to the normal values of .1 and 1000. Now change the z value in gl.onDrawFrame() to -20 and run again. The leftmost image in Figure 3–13 is what you should see.

Next we're going to zoom in. Go to setClipping() and change fieldOfView=10 degrees from 30 degrees. The results are depicted in the center image in Figure 3–13. Notice how the cube has no apparent vanishing point or no perspective when compared to the rightmost image. You'll see the same effect when using a zoom lens on a camera, because the foreshortening effect is nonexistent, making things look like an orthogonal projection.

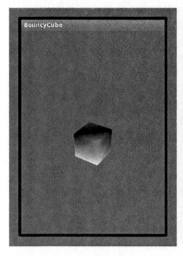  

**Figure 3–13**. *Moving the object away (left) and then zooming in on it with a 10° FOV (center). The rightmost image has the default FOV value set to 50°with the cube at only 4 units away.*

## Face Culling

Let's go back to a line of code you might remember from a few pages ago:

```
gl.glEnable(GL_CULL_FACE);
```

This enables backface culling, covered in Chapter 1, which means that the faces on the rear of an object won't be drawn, because they would never be seen anyway. It works best for convex objects and primitives such as spheres or cubes. The system calculates the face normals for each triangle, which serve as a means to tell whether a face is aimed toward us or away. By default, face windings are counterclockwise. So if a CCW face is aimed toward us, it will be rendered while all others would be culled out. You can change this behavior in two different ways should your data be nonstandard. You can specify that front-facing triangles have clockwise ordering or that culling dumps the front faces instead of the rear ones. To see this in action, add the following line to the onSurfaceCreated() method: gl.glCullFace(GL10.GL_FRONT);.

Figure 3–14 shows the results by removing the front facing triangles to show only the back ones.

> **NOTE:** gl.glEnable() is a frequent call and is used to change various states from eliminating back faces, as shown earlier, to smoothing points (GL10.GL_POINT-SMOOTH) to performing depth tests (GL10.GL_DEPTH_TEST).

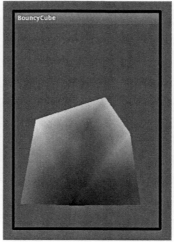

**Figure 3–14.** *The back faces are now visible, while the front ones are culled.*

# Building a Solar System

With these basic tools in our 3D arsenal, we can actually start in the main project of building a small solar-system model. What makes a solar system so ideal is that it has a very basic simple shape, several objects that must all move around each other, and a single light source. The reason why the cube example was used at first is that the shape is about as elementary as you can get for 3D, so the code was not full of extraneous geometry. When you get to something such as a sphere, much of the code will go to creating just the object, as you will see.

Although OpenGL is a great low-level platform, it still leaves a lot to be desired when it comes to anything remotely high level. As you saw in Chapter 1, when it comes to modeling tools, many available third-party frameworks could ultimately be used to do the job, but for now we're just going to be sticking with basic OpenGL ES.

> **NOTE:** Besides OpenGL itself, a popular helper toolkit called GL Utility Toolkit (GLUT) is available. GLUT provides a portable API support for basic windowing UI tasks and management functions. It can construct some basic primitives, including a sphere, so it can be very handy when doing small projects. Unfortunately, as of this writing, there is no official GLUT library for Android, or iOS for that matter, although a couple of efforts are currently in the works.

The first thing to do is to create a new project or import a previous one that establishes the usual OpenGL framework that includes the renderer and geometric object. In this case, it is a sphere described by Listing 3–7.

**Listing 3–7.** *Building Our 3D Planet*

```java
package book.SolarSystem;

import java.util.*;
import java.nio.*;
import javax.microedition.khronos.opengles.GL10;


public class Planet
{
    FloatBuffer m_VertexData;
    FloatBuffer m_NormalData;
    FloatBuffer m_ColorData;

    float m_Scale;
    float m_Squash;
    float m_Radius;
    int m_Stacks, m_Slices;

    public Planet(int stacks, int slices, float radius, float squash)
    {
        this.m_Stacks = stacks;                                          //1
        this.m_Slices = slices;
        this.m_Radius = radius;
        this.m_Squash=squash;

        init(m_Stacks,m_Slices,radius,squash,"dummy");
    }

    private void init(int stacks,int slices, float radius, float squash, String textureFile)
    {
            float[] vertexData;
            float[] colorData;                                          //2
            float colorIncrement=0f;

            float blue=0f;
            float red=1.0f;
            int numVertices=0;
            int vIndex=0;                         //vertex index
            int cIndex=0;                         //color index

            m_Scale=radius;
            m_Squash=squash;

            colorIncrement=1.0f/(float)stacks;                          //3

        {
            m_Stacks = stacks;
```

```
            m_Slices = slices;

            //vertices

                    vertexData = new float[ 3*((m_Slices*2+2) * m_Stacks)];        //4

            //color data

                    colorData = new float[ (4*(m_Slices*2+2) * m_Stacks)];        //5

            int phiIdx, thetaIdx;

            //latitude

            for(phiIdx=0; phiIdx < m_Stacks; phiIdx++)                            //6
        {
                //starts at -90 degrees (-1.57 radians) goes up to +90 degrees
                        (or +1.57 radians)

                //the first circle
                                                                                  //7
                float phi0 = (float)Math.PI * ((float)(phiIdx+0) *
                        (1.0f/(float)(m_Stacks)) - 0.5f);

                //the next, or second one.
                                                                                  //8
                float phi1 = (float)Math.PI * ((float)(phiIdx+1) *
                        (1.0f/(float)(m_Stacks)) - 0.5f);

                float cosPhi0 = (float)Math.cos(phi0);                            //9
                float sinPhi0 = (float)Math.sin(phi0);
                float cosPhi1 = (float)Math.cos(phi1);
                float sinPhi1 = (float)Math.sin(phi1);

                float cosTheta, sinTheta;

                //longitude

            for(thetaIdx=0; thetaIdx < m_Slices; thetaIdx++)                      //10
            {
                //increment along the longitude circle each "slice"

                float theta = (float) (-2.0f*(float)Math.PI * ((float)thetaIdx) *
                    (1.0/(float)(m_Slices-1)));
                cosTheta = (float)Math.cos(theta);
                sinTheta = (float)Math.sin(theta);

                //we're generating a vertical pair of points, such
```

```
                    //as the first point of stack 0 and the first point of stack 1
                    //above it. This is how TRIANGLE_STRIPS work,
                    //taking a set of 4 vertices and essentially drawing two triangles
                    //at a time. The first is v0-v1-v2 and the next is v2-v1-v3. Etc.

                    //get x-y-z for the first vertex of stack

                    vertexData[vIndex+0] = m_Scale*cosPhi0*cosTheta;                    //11
                            vertexData[vIndex+1] = m_Scale*(sinPhi0*m_Squash);
                            vertexData[vIndex+2] = m_Scale*(cosPhi0*sinTheta);

                    vertexData[vIndex+3] = m_Scale*cosPhi1*cosTheta;
                    vertexData[vIndex+4] = m_Scale*(sinPhi1*m_Squash);
                    vertexData[vIndex+5] = m_Scale*(cosPhi1*sinTheta);

                    colorData[cIndex+0] = (float)red;                                   //12
                    colorData[cIndex+1] = (float)0f;
                    colorData[cIndex+2] = (float)blue;
                    colorData[cIndex+4] = (float)red;
                    colorData[cIndex+5] = (float)0f;
                    colorData[cIndex+6] = (float)blue;
                    colorData[cIndex+3] = (float)1.0;
                    colorData[cIndex+7] = (float)1.0;

                    cIndex+=2*4;                                                        //13
                            vIndex+=2*3;                                                //14
            }

            blue+=colorIncrement;                                                       //15
        red-=colorIncrement;

    // create a degenerate triangle to connect stacks and maintain winding order

                                                                                        //16
        vertexData[vIndex+0] = vertexData[vIndex+3] = vertexData[vIndex-3];
        vertexData[vIndex+1] = vertexData[vIndex+4] = vertexData[vIndex-2];
        vertexData[vIndex+2] = vertexData[vIndex+5] = vertexData[vIndex-1];
            }

        }
            m_VertexData = makeFloatBuffer(vertexData);                                 //17
            m_ColorData = makeFloatBuffer(colorData);
}
```

OK, so it takes a lot of code to create something as basic as a sphere. Using the triangle lists is more involved than using the quads in standard OpenGL, but that's what we have to work with.

The basic algorithm is to calculate the boundaries of the *stacks*, two at a time as partners. Stacks are parallel to the ground, the X-Z plane, and they form the boundaries of the triangle strip. So, stack A and B are calculated and subdivided into triangles based on the number of slices around the circle. The next time through will take stacks B and C and then rinse and repeat. Two boundary conditions apply:

- The first and last stacks contain the two poles of our pseudo-planet, in which case they are more of a triangle fan as opposed to a strip. However, we'll treat them as strips to simplify the code.

- The end of each strip must connect with the beginning to form a contiguous set of triangles.

So, let's break this down:

- In line 1 you see that the initialization routine uses the notion of stacks and slices to define the resolution of the sphere. Having more slices and stacks means a much smoother sphere but uses much more memory not to mention additional processing time. Think of a slice as similar to an apple wedge, representing a piece of the sphere from bottom to top. A stack is a slice that is lateral, defining sections of latitude. See Figure 3–15.

  The *radius* parameter is a form of a scaling factor. You could opt to normalize all your objects and use glScalef(), but that does add extra CPU overhead, so in this case *radius* is used as a form of prescaling. *Squash* is used to create a flattened sphere necessary for Jupiter and Saturn. Since they both have very high rates of revolution, they are flattened out a bit. Jupiter's day is only about ten hours, while its diameter is more than ten times the Earth's. As a result, its polar diameter is about 93 percent of the equatorial diameter. And Saturn is even more flattened, with the polar diameter only 90 percent of the equatorial. The squash value is the polar diameter as measured against the equatorial diameter. A value of 1.0 means the object is perfectly spherical, whereas Saturn would have a squash value of .90, or 90 percent.

- In line 2 I introduce a color array. Since we want something interesting to look at until we get to the cool texture stuff in Chapter 5, let's vary the colors from top to bottom. The top is blue, and the bottom is red. The color increment calculated in line 3 is merely the color deltas from stack to stack. Red starts at 1.0 and goes down, while blue starts at 0.0 and goes up.

**Figure 3–15.** *Stacks go up and down, slices go round and round, and faces are subdivided into triangle strips.*

- Lines 4 and 5 allocate the memory for both the vertices and the colors. Later other arrays will be needed to hold the texture coordinates and face normals needed for lighting, but for now let's keep things simple. Notice that we're doing 32-bit colors, as with the cube. Three values form the RGB triplet while the fourth is for *alpha* (translucency) but is not needed in this example. The m_Slices*2 value takes into account the fact that two triangles are needed for each face bound by the slice and stack borders. Normally, this would be one square, but here it must be two triangles. The +2 handles the fact that the first two vertices are also the last vertices, so are duplicated. And of course, we need m_Stacks worth of all this stuff.

- Line 6 starts the outer loop, going from the bottom-most stack (or the southern polar regions of our planet or altitude of -90 degrees) and up to the northern pole, at +90°.

  Some Greek identifiers are used here for spherical coordinates. *Phi* is commonly used for the latitude-like values, while *theta* is used for longitude.

- Lines 7 and 8 generate the latitude for the boundaries of a specific strip. For starters, when phiIdx is 0, we want phi0 to be -90°, or -1.57 radians. The -.5 shoves everything down by 90°; otherwise, our values would go from 0 to 180°.

- In lines 9ff, some values are precalculated to minimize the CPU load.

- Lines 10ff form the inner loop, going from 0 to 360°, and defines the slices. The math is similar, so there's no need to go into extreme detail, except that we are calculating the points on a circle via lines 11ff. Both m_Scale and m_Squash come into play here. But for now, just assume that they are both 1.0 normalizing the data.

Notice that vertex 0 and vertex 2 are addressed here. vertexData[0] is *x*, while vertexData[2] is *z*—that handles the two components that are parallel to the ground. Since vertex 1 is the same as *y*, it remains constant for each loop and is consistent with it representing the latitude. Since we're doing the loops in pairs, the vertex specified by array elements 3, 4, and 5 covers the next higher stack boundary.

In effect, we are generating pairs of points, namely, each point and its mate immediately above it. And this is the format that OpenGL expects for the triangle strips, as shown in Figure 3–16.

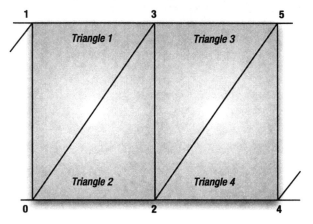

**Figure 3–16.** *A triangle strip of six vertices*

▨ In lines 12ff, the color array is generated, and as with the vertices, they are generated in pairs. The red and blue components are stashed into the array here, with no green for the time being. Line 13 increments the color index, taking into account that we generating two four-element colors entries per loop.

▨ As with the color index, the vertex index is also incremented, as in line 14, but this time only for three components.

▨ In lines 15ff, we increment the blue and decrement the red colors ensuring that the bottom "pole" is solid red, while the top is solid blue.

▨ At the end of each strip, we need to create some "degenerate" triangles, as shown in lines 16ff. The term *degenerate* specifies that the triangle actually consists of three identical vertices. Practically, it is but a single point; logically, it is a triangle that serves to connect the current stack.

▨ And finally, when all is said and done, the vertex and color data at lines 17f are converted to byte arrays that OpenGL can understand at render time. Listing 3–8 is the helper function to do this.

**Listing 3–8.** *Helper Function to Generate an Array of Floats That OpenGL Can Understand*

```
protected static FloatBuffer makeFloatBuffer(float[] arr)
{
    ByteBuffer bb = ByteBuffer.allocateDirect(arr.length*4);
    bb.order(ByteOrder.nativeOrder());
    FloatBuffer fb = bb.asFloatBuffer();
    fb.put(arr);
    fb.position(0);
    return fb;
}
```

Now that the geometry is out of the way, we need to concentrate on the draw method. See Listing 3–9.

**Listing 3–9.** *Rendering the Planet*

```
public void draw(GL10 gl)
{

    gl.glFrontFace(GL10.GL_CW);                                           //1
    gl.glVertexPointer(3, GL10.GL_FLOAT, 0, m_VertexData);               //2
    gl.glEnableClientState(GL10.GL_VERTEX_ARRAY);

    gl.glColorPointer(4, GL10.GL_FLOAT, 0, m_ColorData);
    gl.glEnableClientState(GL10.GL_COLOR_ARRAY);

                                                                         //3
    gl.glDrawArrays(GL10.GL_TRIANGLE_STRIP, 0, (m_Slices+1)*2*(m_Stacks-1)+2);
}
```

You should now recognize many of the elements from the cube examples:

- ■ First in line 1, we specify that the clockwise faces are to be the front ones.

- ■ Lines 2ff submit the color and vertex data to the renderer, ensuring that it is enabled to accept it.

- ■ And finally (!!) we can now draw our little sphere.  Oops, well, not quite yet, it is still necessary to allocate it.

Now that the planet object is complete enough for this example, let's do the driver. You can repurpose the bouncing cube renderer by renaming it to something like SolarSystemRenderer, which would be an instance of the GLSurfaceView.Renderer interface. Change the constructor to look like Listing 3–10. This will allocate the planet to a fairly coarse resolution of ten stacks and ten slices, with a radius of 1.0 and a squash value of 1.0 (i.e., perfectly round). Make sure to declare mPlanet as well and, of course, import the GL10 library.

**Listing 3–10.** *Constructor to SolarSystemRenderer*

```
public SolarSystemRenderer()
{
    mPlanet=new Planet(10,10,1.0f, 1.0f);
}
```

The top level refresh method, gl.onDrawFrame(), isn't much different from the cube one, as shown in Listing 3–11.

**Listing 3–11.** *The Main Drawing Method, Located in SolarSystemRenderer*

```
private float mTransY;
private float mAngle;

public void onDrawFrame(GL10 gl)
{
    gl.glClear(GL10.GL_COLOR_BUFFER_BIT | GL10.GL_DEPTH_BUFFER_BIT);
    gl.glClearColor(0.0f,0.0f,0.0f,1.0f);
    gl.glMatrixMode(GL10.GL_MODELVIEW);
    gl.glLoadIdentity();

    gl.glTranslatef(0.0f,(float)Math.sin(mTransY), -4.0f);

    gl.glRotatef(mAngle, 1, 0, 0);
    gl.glRotatef(mAngle, 0, 1, 0);

    mPlanet.draw(gl);

    mTransY+=.075f;
    mAngle+=.4;
}
```

There's nothing to exotic here as it is virtually identical to the counterpart for rendering the cube. Copy over onSurfaceChanged() and onSurfaceCreated() from the cube's code, while commenting out initLighting() and initGeometry() for the time being. You should now be able to compile and run it. Figure 3–17 should be the result.

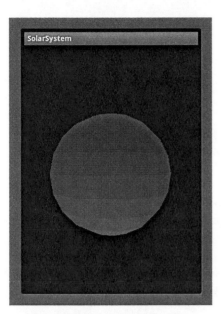

**Figure 3–17.** *The future planet Earth*

While it is rotating, having no features at all, you'll be hard-pressed to see the motion.

As with the previous examples, let's play around with some of the parameters and see what happens. First let's change the number of stacks and slices, from 10 to 20, in the SolarSystemRenderer constructor. You should see something like Figure 3–18.

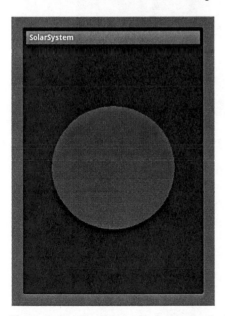

**Figure 3–18.** *The planet with double the stacks and slices*

If you want your curved objects to look smoother, there are generally three ways to accomplish it:

- Have as many triangles as possible.

- Use some special lighting and shading tools built into OpenGL.

- Use textures.

The next chapter will cover the second option. But for now, see how many slices and stacks it takes to make a really smooth sphere. (It works best with an equal number of both.) It really starts looking good at 100 each. For now, go back to 20 each.

If you want to look at the actual wireframe structure of the sphere, change GL10.GL_TRIANGLE_STRIP in the planet's draw method to GL10.GL_LINE_STRIP. And you may want to change the background color to a medium gray to make the lines stand out better (Figure 3–19, left). As an exercise, see what it takes to get the image on the right in Figure 3–19. Now ask yourself why we're not seeing triangles there but instead that funky spiral pattern. It is simply the way OpenGL draws and connects line strips. We could have it render triangle outlines by specifying a connectivity array. But for our ultimate goal, that is not necessary.

**Figure 3–19.** *The planet in wireframe mode*

On your own, change GL10.GL_LINE_STRIP to GL10.GL_POINTS. There you'll see each of the vertices rendered as a single dot.

Then try the frustum again. Set zNear from .1 to 3.2. (Why not 4? The distance of the object?) And you'll get Figure 3–20.

**Figure 3–20.** *Someone is setting the* zNear *clipping plane too close.*

And one final exercise: what would it take to get something that looks like Figure 3–21? (This is what you would need for Jupiter and Saturn; because they spin so fast, they're not spherical but rather oblate-spheroids.)

**Figure 3–21.** *What does it take to get this?*

And lastly, for extra credit, make it bounce like the cube.

# Summary

In this chapter, we started by turning the 2D cube into a 3D cube and then learned how to rotate and translate it. We also learned about the viewing frustum and how it can be used to cull out objects and zoom in and out of our scene. Lastly, we constructed a much more complicated object that will be the root of the solar-system model. The next chapter will cover shading, lighting, and materials, and a second object will be added.

# Chapter 4

# Turning On the Lights

*You must be strong now. You must never give up. And when people [or code] make you cry and you are afraid of the dark, don't forget the light is always there.*

—Author Unknown

*Light is the first of painters. There is no object so foul that intense light will not make it beautiful.*

—Ralph Waldo Emerson

*Everything's shiny, Cap'n. Not to fret.*

—Kaylee Frye, *Firefly*

This chapter will cover one of the single biggest topics for OpenGL ES: the process of illuminating, shading, and coloring the virtual landscape. We touched on color in the previous chapter, but because it is so integral to both lighting and shading, we will cover it more in depth here.

## The Story of Light and Color

Without light, the world would be a dark place (duh). Without color, it would be hard to tell the difference between stoplights.

We all take for granted the wondrous nature of light—from the soft and gentle illumination off the morning mist to the ignition of a space shuttle's main engines to the shy pale radiance of a full moon on a snowy field in mid-winter. A lot has been written about the physics of light and its nature and perception. It might take an artist a lifetime to fully understand how to take colored pigments suspended in oil and to apply them on a canvas to create a believable rainbow at the base of a waterfall. Such is the task of OpenGL ES when it comes to turning on the lights in our scenes.

Sans poetry, light is merely a portion of the full electromagnetic spectrum that our eyes are sensitive to. The same spectrum also includes radio signals that our iPhones use, X-rays to aid a physician, gamma rays sent out from a dying star billions of years ago, and microwaves that can be used to reheat some pizza left over from Wii Bowling Night last Thursday.

Light is said to have four main properties: wavelength, intensity, polarization, and direction. The wavelength determines the color that we perceive, or whether we can actually see anything in the first place. The visible spectrum starts in the violet range, with wavelengths of around 380 nanometers, on up to red, with a wavelength of around 780 nanometers. Immediately below is ultraviolet, and right above the visible range you'll find infrared, which we can't directly see but can detect indirectly in the form of heat.

The way we perceive colors from objects has to do with what wavelengths the object or its material absorbs or otherwise *interferes* with the oncoming light. Besides absorption, it could be scattered (giving us the blue of the sky or the red of the sunset), reflected, and refracted.

If someone says that their favorite color is white, they must mean that all colors are their favorite because white is a summation of all colors of the visible spectrum. If it is black, they don't like any colors, because black is the absence of color. In fact, that is why you shouldn't wear black on a nice warm sunny day. Your clothing absorbs so much energy and reflects so little (in the form of light and infrared) that some of that ultimately turns into heat.

> **NOTE:** When the sun is straight overhead, it can deliver an *irradiance* of about 1 kilowatt for every square meter. Of that, a little more than half is infrared, sensed as a very warm day, while a little less than half is visible light, and a measly 32 watts are devoted to UV.

It is said that Aristotle developed the first known color theory. He considered four colors, each corresponding to one of the four elements of air, earth, water, and fire.

However, as we look at the visible spectrum, you will notice a nice contiguous spread from violet on one end to red on the other that has neither water nor fire in it. Nor will you see discrete values of red, green, or blue, typically used nowadays to define the individual shades. In the early 19th century, British polymath Thomas Young developed the tricolor model that uses three colors to simulate all visible hues. Young proposed that the retina was made up of bundles of nerve fibers, which would respond to varying intensities of red, green, or violet light. German scientist Hermann von Helmholtz later expanded this theory in the mid-19th century.

**NOTE:** Young was a particularly colorful fellow. (Someone had to say it.) Not only was he the founder of the field of *physiological optics*, in his spare time he developed the wave theory of light, including the invention of the classic double-slit experiment, which is a college physics staple. But wait! There's more! He also proposed the theory of capillary phenomena, was the first to use the term *energy* in the modern sense, partially deciphered some of the Egyptian portion of the Rosetta Stone, and devised an improved means of tuning musical instruments. The laddie must have been seriously sleep-deprived.

Today, colors are most frequently described via red-green-blue (RGB) triplets and their relative intensity. Each of the colors fades to black with zero intensity and shows varying hues as the intensity increases, ultimately perceived as white. Because the three colors need to be added together to produce the entire spectrum, this system is an *additive* model.

Besides the RGB model, printers use a subtractive mode known as CMYK, for cyan-magenta-yellow-black (the *key*). Because the three colors cannot produce a really deep black, black is added as an accent for deep shadows or graphic details.

Another common model is HSV for hue-saturation-value, and you will frequently find it as an alternative to RGB in many graphics packages or color pickers. Developed in the 1970s specifically for computer graphics, HSV depicts color as a 3D cylinder (Figure 4–1). Saturation goes from the inside out, value goes from bottom to top, and hue goes around the edge. A variant on this is HSL, substituting value for lightness. Figure 4–2 shows the Mac OS X color picker in its many versions.

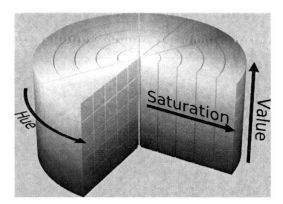

**Figure 4–1**. *HSV color wheel or cylinder (source: Wikipedia Commons)*

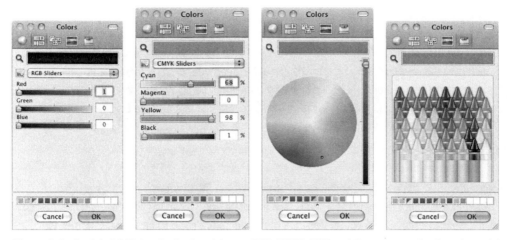

**Figure 4-2.** *Apple's OS-X standard color pickers—RGB, CMYK, HSV, and the ever-popular Crayola model*

# Let There Be Light

In the real world, light comes at us from all sides and with all colors and, when combined, can create the details and rich scenes of everyday life. OpenGL doesn't attempt to duplicate anything like the real-world lighting models, because those are very complex and time-consuming and generally reserved for Disney's rendering farms. But it can approximate it in a way that is certainly good enough for real-time gaming action.

The lighting model used in OpenGL ES permits us to place several lights of varying types around our scene. We can switch them on or off at will, specifying direction, intensity, colors, and so on. But that's not all, because we also need to describe various properties of our model and how it interacts with the incoming light. *Lighting* defines the way light sources interact with objects and the materials those objects are created with. *Shading* specifically determines the coloring of the pixel based on the lighting and material. Notice that a white piece of paper will reflect light completely differently than a pink, mirrored Christmas ornament. Taken together, these properties are bundled up into an object called a *material*. Blending the material's attributes and the light's attributes together generates the final scene.

The colors of OpenGL lights can consist of up to three different components:

- Diffuse
- Ambient
- Specular

Diffuse light can be said to come from one direction such as the sun or a flashlight. It hits an object and then scatters off in all directions, producing a pleasant soft quality. When a diffuse light hits a surface, the reflected amount is largely determined by the angle of incidence. It will be at its brightest when directly facing the light but drops as it tilts further and further away.

Ambient light is that which comes from no particular direction, having been reflected off all the surfaces that make up the environment. Look around the room you are in, and the light that is bouncing off the ceiling, walls, and your furniture all combine to form the ambient light. If you are a photographer, you know how important ambient lighting is to make a scene much more realistic than a single point source can, particularly in portrait photography where you would have a soft "fill light" to offset the brighter main light.

Specular light is that which is reflected off a shiny surface. It comes from a specific direction but bounces off a surface in a much more directed fashion. It makes the hot spot that we'd see on a disco ball or a newly cleaned and waxed car. It is at its brightest when the viewpoint is directly in line with the source and falls off quickly as we move around the object.

When it comes to both diffuse and specular lighting, they are typically the same colors. But even though we're limited to the eight light objects, having different colors for each component actually means that a single OpenGL "light" can act like three different ones at the same time. Out of the three, you might consider having the ambient light be a different color, usually one that is opposing the main coloring so as to make the scene more visually interesting. In the solar-system model, a dim blue ambient light helps illuminate the dark side of a planet and lends a greater 3D quality to it.

> **NOTE:** You don't have to specify all three types for a given light. Diffuse usually works just fine in simple scenes.

## Back to the Fun Stuff (for a While)

We're not done with the theory yet, but let's get back to coding for a while. After that, I'll cover more on light and shading theory.

You saw in the previous examples how colors defined with the standard RGB version on a per-vertex basis would let us see it without any lighting at all. Now we will create lights of various types and position them around our so-called planet. OpenGL ES must support at least eight lights total, which is the case for Android. But of course you can create more and add or remove them as needed. If you are really picky, you can check at runtime for just how many lights a particular implementation of OpenGL supports by using one of the many variants of glGet* to retrieve the values of this:

```
ByteBuffer byteBuffer = ByteBuffer.allocateDirect( 4 );
byteBuffer.order( ByteOrder.LITTLE_ENDIAN );
IntBuffer intBuffer = byteBuffer.asIntBuffer();
drawable.getGL().glGetIntegerv( GL10.GL_MAX_LIGHTS, intBuffer);
```

> **NOTE:** OpenGL ES has a number of utility functions, with glGet*() being one of the most commonly used families. The glGet* calls let you inquire about the states of various parameters, such as the current modelview matrix to the current line width. The exact call depends on the type of data requested.

Let's go back to the example code from Chapter 3, where you had a squashed red and blue planet bouncing up and down, and make the following changes:

1.  Change the earth's squash value from the solar-system controller's method initGeometry(), from .7f to 1.0f to round out the sphere again, and change the resolution (stacks and slices) to 20.

2.  In Planet.java, comment out the line blue+=colorIncrment at the end of the init() method.

What should you see? C'mon, no peeking. Cover up Figure 4–3 and guess. Got it? Now you can compile and run. The image on the left in Figure 4–3 is what you should see. Now go back to the initGeometry method and increase the number of slices and stacks to 100 each. That should yield the image on the right. So, by simply changing a few numbers around, we have a crude lighting and shading scheme. But this is only a fixed lighting scheme that breaks down the moment you want to start moving things around. That's when we let OpenGL do the heavy lifting.

Unfortunately, the process of adding lights is a little more complicated than just calling something like glMakeAwesomeLightsDude(), as we will see.

**Figure 4–3.** *Simulated lighting from below (left) and a higher polygon count to simulate shading (right)*

3.  Go back to the `onSurfaceCreated` method in the solar-system renderer from Chapter 3 and modify it to look like this:

```
public void onSurfaceCreated(GL10 gl, EGLConfig config) {
        gl.glDisable(GL10.GL_DITHER);
        gl.glHint(GL10.GL_PERSPECTIVE_CORRECTION_HINT, GL10.GL_FASTEST);
        gl.glEnable(GL10.GL_CULL_FACE);
        gl.glCullFace(GL10.GL_BACK);
        gl.glShadeModel(GL10.GL_SMOOTH);
        gl.glEnable(GL10.GL_DEPTH_TEST);
        gl.glDepthMask(false);
        initGeometry(gl);
        initLighting(gl);
    }
```

4.  And add to the renderers:

```
public final static int SS_SUNLIGHT = GL10.GL_LIGHT0;
```

5.  Then add the code in Listing 4–1 to switch on the lights.

**Listing 4–1.** *Initializing the Lights*

```
private void initLighting(GL10 gl)
{
    float[] diffuse = {0.0f, 1.0f, 0.0f, 1.0f};                              //1
    float[] pos = {0.0f, 10.0f, -3.0f, 1.0f};                               //2
    gl.glLightfv(SS_SUNLIGHT, GL10.GL_POSITION, makeFloatBuffer(pos));      //3
    gl.glLightfv(SS_SUNLIGHT, GL10.GL_DIFFUSE, makeFloatBuffer(diffuse));   //4
    gl.glShadeModel(GL10.GL_FLAT);                                          //5
    gl.glEnable(GL10.GL_LIGHTING);                                         //6
    gl.glEnable(SS_SUNLIGHT);                                              //7
}
```

This is what's going on:

■   The lighting components are in the standard RGBA normalized form. So in this case, there is no red, no full green, and no blue. The final value of alpha should be kept at 1.0 for now, because it will be covered in more detail later.

■   Line 2 is the position of the light. It is at a y of +10 and a z of -3, the same for the planet. So, it will be hovering above our sphere.

■   In lines 3 and 4, we set the light's position and the diffuse component to the diffuse color. `glLightfv()` is a new call and is used to set various light-related parameters. You can retrieve any of this data at a later time using `glGetLightfv()`, which retrieves any of the parameters from a specific light.

- In line 5 we specify a shading model. Flat means that a face is a single solid color, while setting it to GL_SMOOTH will cause the colors to blend smoothly across the face and from face to face.

- And finally, line 6 tells the system we want to use lighting, while line 7 enables the one light we've created.

> **NOTE:** The final parameter of glLightfv() takes an array of four GLfloat values; the *fv* suffix means "float-vector." There is also a glLightf() call to set single-value parameters.

Now compile and run. Eh? What's that, you say? You see only a black thing about the size of the super-massive black hole at the center of the galaxy M31? Oh yes, we forgot something, sorry. As previously mentioned, OpenGL in all of its varieties still remains a relatively low-level library, so it is up to the programmer to handle all sorts of housekeeping tasks that you'd expect a higher-level system to manage (and it gets much worse on OpenGL ES 2.0). And once the lights are turned on, the predefined vertex colors are ignored, so we get black. With that in mind, our sphere model needs an extra layer of data to tell the system just how to light its facets, and that is done through an array of *normals* for each vertex.

What is a vertex normal? *Face* normals are normalized vectors that are *orthogonal* (perpendicular) to a plane or face. But in OpenGL, vertex normals are used instead because they provide for better shading down the road. It sounds odd that a vertex can have a "normal" of its own. After all, what is the "direction" of a vertex? It is actually quite simple conceptually, because vertex normals are merely the normalized sum of the normals of the faces adjacent to the vertex. See Figure 4–4.

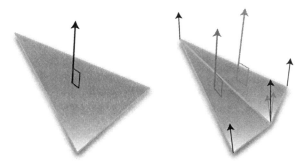

**Figure 4–4**. *A face normal is illustrated on the right, while vertex normals for a triangle fan are on the left.*

OpenGL needs all of this information to tell what "direction" the vertex is aiming at so it can calculate just how much illumination is falling on it, if at all. It will be its brightest when aiming directly at the light source and dim as it starts tilting away. This means we need to modify our planet generator to create a normal array along with the vertex and color arrays, as shown in Listing 4–2.

**Listing 4–2.** Adding the Normal Generator to *Planet.java*

```
private void init(int stacks,int slices, float radius, float squash, String textureFile)
{
        float[] vertexData;
        float[] colorData;
        float[] normalData;
        float   colorIncrement=0f;

        float blue=0f;
        float red=1.0f;
        int numVertices=0;
        int vIndex=0;                                    //Vertex index
        int cIndex=0;                                    //Color index
        int nIndex =0;                                   //Normal index

        m_Scale=radius;
        m_Squash=squash;

        colorIncrement=1.0f/(float)stacks;
        m_Stacks = stacks;
        m_Slices = slices;

        //Vertices
                vertexData = new float[ 3*((m_Slices*2+2) * m_Stacks)];

        //Color data
                colorData = new float[ (4*(m_Slices*2+2) * m_Stacks)];

        // Normalize data
                normalData = new float [ (3*(m_Slices*2+2)* m_Stacks)];       //1

        int phiIdx, thetaIdx;

        //Latitude
        for(phiIdx=0; phiIdx < m_Stacks; phiIdx++)
{
        //Starts at -90 degrees (-1.57 radians) and goes up to +90 degrees
            (or +1.57 radians).
        //The first circle
           float phi0 = (float)Math.PI * ((float)(phiIdx+0) * (1.0f/(float)
               (m_Stacks)) - 0.5f);

        //The next, or second one.
           float phi1 = (float)Math.PI * ((float)(phiIdx+1) * (1.0f/(float)
               (m_Stacks)) - 0.5f);

           float cosPhi0 = (float)Math.cos(phi0);
```

```
float sinPhi0 = (float)Math.sin(phi0);
float cosPhi1 = (float)Math.cos(phi1);
float sinPhi1 = (float)Math.sin(phi1);

float cosTheta, sinTheta;

//Longitude
for(thetaIdx=0; thetaIdx < m_Slices; thetaIdx++)
{

    //Increment along the longitude circle each "slice."

    float theta = (float) (2.0f*(float)Math.PI * ((float)thetaIdx) *
        (1.0/(float)(m_Slices-1)));
    cosTheta = (float)Math.cos(theta);
    sinTheta = (float)Math.sin(theta);

    //We're generating a vertical pair of points, such
    //as the first point of stack 0 and the first point of stack 1
    //above it. This is how TRIANGLE_STRIPS work,
    //taking a set of 4 vertices and essentially drawing two triangles
    //at a time. The first is v0-v1-v2 and the next is v2-v1-v3, etc.

    //Get x-y-z for the first vertex of stack.

    vertexData[vIndex+0] = m_Scale*cosPhi0*cosTheta;
    vertexData[vIndex+1] = m_Scale*(sinPhi0*m_Squash);
    vertexData[vIndex+2] = m_Scale*(cosPhi0*sinTheta);

    vertexData[vIndex+3] = m_Scale*cosPhi1*cosTheta;
    vertexData[vIndex+4] = m_Scale*(sinPhi1*m_Squash);
    vertexData[vIndex+5] = m_Scale*(cosPhi1*sinTheta);


    colorData[cIndex+0] = (float)red;
    colorData[cIndex+1] = (float)0f;
    colorData[cIndex+2] = (float)blue;
    colorData[cIndex+4] = (float)red;
    colorData[cIndex+5] = (float)0f;
    colorData[cIndex+6] = (float)blue;
    colorData[cIndex+3] = (float)1.0;
    colorData[cIndex+7] = (float)1.0;


    // Normalize data pointers for lighting.
    normalData[nIndex + 0] = cosPhi0*cosTheta;              //2
    normalData[nIndex + 1] = sinPhi0;
    normalData[nIndex + 2] = cosPhi0*sinTheta;

    normalData[nIndex + 3] = cosPhi1*cosTheta;              //3
```

```
                    normalData[nIndex + 4] = sinPhi1;
                    normalData[nIndex + 5] = cosPhi1*sinTheta;

                    cIndex+=2*4;
                    vIndex+=2*3;                    nIndex+=2*3;
                }

                //Blue+=colorIncrement;
                  red-=colorIncrement;

            //Create a degenerate triangle to connect stacks and maintain winding order.
            vertexData[vIndex+0] = vertexData[vIndex+3] = vertexData[vIndex-3];
            vertexData[vIndex+1] = vertexData[vIndex+4] = vertexData[vIndex-2];
            vertexData[vIndex+2] = vertexData[vIndex+5] = vertexData[vIndex-1];
            }
        m_VertexData = makeFloatBuffer(vertexData);
        m_ColorData = makeFloatBuffer(colorData);
        m_NormalData = makeFloatBuffer(normalData);

}
```

▨ In line 1, the normal array is allocated the same as the vertex memory, a simple array containing 3-components-per normal.

▨ Sections 2 and 3 generate the normal data. It doesn't look like any fancy-schmancy normal averaging scheme covered earlier, so what gives? Since we're dealing with a very simple symmetrical form of a sphere, the normals are identical to the vertices without any scaling values (to ensure they are unit vectors—that is, of length 1.0). Notice that the calculations for the vPtr values and the nPtrs are virtually the same as a result.

> **NOTE:** You'll rarely need to actually generate your own normals. If you do any real work in OpenGL ES, you'll likely be importing models from third-party applications, such as 3D-Studio or Strata. They will generate the normal arrays along with the others for you.

There's one final step, and that is to modify the draw() method in Planet.java to look like Listing 4–3.

**Listing 4–3.** *The New draw Routine*

```
public void draw(GL10 gl)
    {
            gl.glMatrixMode(GL10.GL_MODELVIEW);
            gl.glEnable(GL10.GL_CULL_FACE);
            gl.glCullFace(GL10.GL_BACK);
```

```
gl.glNormalPointer(GL10.GL_FLOAT, 0, m_NormalData);                          //1
gl.glEnableClientState(GL10.GL_NORMAL_ARRAY);                                //2

gl.glVertexPointer(3, GL10.GL_FLOAT, 0, m_VertexData);
gl.glEnableClientState(GL10.GL_VERTEX_ARRAY);

gl.glColorPointer(4, GL10.GL_FLOAT, 0, m_ColorData);
gl.glEnableClientState(GL10.GL_COLOR_ARRAY);

gl.glDrawArrays(GL10.GL_TRIANGLE_STRIP, 0, (m_Slices+1)*2*(m_Stacks-1)+2);
}
```

It's not much different than the original, except with the addition of lines 1 and 2 for sending the normal data to the OpenGL pipeline alongside the color and vertex information. If you have a very simple model in which many of the vertices all share the same normal, you can dump the normal array and use glNormal3f() instead, saving a little memory and CPU overhead in the process.

Let's make one final tweak. For this example, ensure that the planet is allocated with the stack and slice values set back to 10 (from 100 used at the end of Chapter 3). This makes it easier to see how some of the lighting works. Now you can compile and run it for real, and if you get something similar to Figure 4–5, relax and take a pause for a cool refreshing beverage.

**Figure 4–5.** *Flat lighting*

Now that you're back, I am sure you've spotted something a little odd. Supposedly the geometry is based on strips of triangles, so why are the faces those weird four-sided triangle things?

When set for flat shading, OpenGL picks up its illumination cue from only a single vertex, the last one of the respective triangle. Now, instead of the strips being drawn from triangles in horizontal pairs, think of them loosely coupled in vertical pairs, as you see in Figure 4–6.

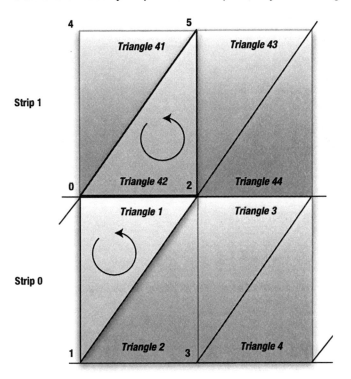

**Figure 4–6.** *"Stacked" triangle pairs*

In Strip 0, Triangle 1 will be drawn using vertices 0, 1, and 2, with vertex 2 used for the shading. Triangle 2 will use 2, 1, and 3. Lather, rinse, and repeat for the rest of the strip. Next for Strip 1, Triangle 41 will be drawn with vertices 4, 0, and 5. But Triangle 42 will use vertices 5, 0, and 2, with the same vertex as Triangle 1 for its shading. That is why the vertical pairs combine to form a "bent" quadrilateral.

There are few reasons nowadays to use flat shading, so in initLighting(), swap out GL_FLAT for GL_SMOOTH, and in glShadeModel(), change the light's position by changing the following:

```
float[] pos = {0.0f, 10.0f, -3.0f, 1.0f};
```

   to this:

```
float[] pos = {0.0f, 5.0f, 0.0f, 1.0f};
```

This will show more of the illuminated side. And now you probably know the drill: compile, run, and compare. Then for fun, decrease the sphere's resolution from 20 slices and segments down to 5. Go back to flat shading on this one, and then compare to smooth shading. See Figure 4–7. The rightmost image in Figure 4–7 is particularly interesting, because the shading model starts to break down, showing some artifacting along the face edges.

**Figure 4–7.** *From left to right: smooth shading a sphere with 20 stacks and 20 slices; flat shading on a sphere of only 5 stacks and slices; smooth shading*

## Fun with Light and Materials

Now, since we have a nice smooth sphere to play with, we can start tinkering with the other lighting models and materials. But first a thought experiment: say you have a green sphere as shown earlier but your diffuse light is red. What color will the sphere be? (Pause for the *Jeopardy* theme.) Ready? Well, in the real world what would it be? Reddish green? Greenish red? A mauvy shade of pinky-russet? Let's try it and find out. Modify initLighting() again, as shown in Listing 4–4. Note that the light vectors have been renamed to their specific colors to make it a little more readable.

**Listing 4–4.** *Adding Some More Light Types and Materials*

```
private void initLighting(GL10 gl)
{
    float[] diffuse = {0.0f, 1.0f, 0.0f, 1.0f};
    float[] pos = {0.0f, 5.0f, -3.0f, 1.0f};
    float[] white = {1.0f, 1.0f, 1.0f, 1.0f};
    float[] red={1.0f, 0.0f, 0.0f, 1.0f};
    float[] green={0.0f,1.0f,0.0f,1.0f};
```

```
    float[] blue={0.0f, 0.0f, 1.0f, 1.0f};
    float[] cyan={0.0f, 1.0f, 1.0f, 1.0f};
    float[] yellow={1.0f, 1.0f, 0.0f, 1.0f};
    float[] magenta={1.0f, 0.0f, 1.0f, 1.0f};
    float[] halfcyan={0.0f, 0.5f, 0.5f, 1.0f};

    gl.glLightfv(SS_SUNLIGHT, GL10.GL_POSITION, makeFloatBuffer(pos));
    gl.glLightfv(SS_SUNLIGHT, GL10.GL_DIFFUSE, makeFloatBuffer(green));

    gl.glMaterialfv(GL10.GL_FRONT_AND_BACK, GL10.GL_DIFFUSE, makeFloatBuffer(red));  //1

    gl.glShadeModel(GL10.GL_SMOOTH);
    gl.glEnable(GL10.GL_LIGHTING);
    gl.glEnable(SS_SUNLIGHT);
    gl.glLoadIdentity();                                                              //2
}
```

If you see our old friend, the supermassive black hole from M31, you've done well. So, why is it black? That's simple; remember the discussion at the start of this chapter on colors and reflectance? A red object looks red only when the lighting hitting it has a red component, precisely the way our green light doesn't. If you had a red balloon in a dark room and illuminated it with green light on it, it would look black, because no green would come back to you. And if someone asks you what you're doing with a red balloon in a dark room, just growl "Physics!" Then tell them that they just wouldn't understand in a dismissive tone.

So, with this understanding, replace the red diffuse material with green in line 1. What should you get? Right, the green sphere is illuminated again. But you may notice something really interesting. The green now looks a little bit brighter than before adding the material. The image on the left in Figure 4–8 shows it without any material specified, and the image on the right shows it with the green diffuse material added.

**Figure 4–8.** *Without green material defined (left) and with it defined (right)*

Let's do one more experiment. Let's make the diffuse light be a more traditional white. What should now happen with the green? Red? How about blue? Since the white light has *all* those components, the colored materials should all show up equally well. But if you see the black ball again, you changed the material's color, not the lighting.

## Specular Lighting

Well, how about the specular stuff? Add the following line to the lights section:

```
gl.glLightfv(SS_SUNLIGHT,GL10.GL_SPECULAR, makeFloatBuffer(red));
```

To the material section, add this:

```
gl.glMaterialfv(GL10.GL_FRONT_AND_BACK, GL10.GL_SPECULAR, makeFloatBuffer(red));
```

And change the light's position to the following:

```
float[] pos={10.0f,0.0f,3.0f,1.0f};
```

> **NOTE:** The first value to `glMaterial*` must always be GL_FRONT_AND_BACK. In normal
> OpenGL, you're permitted to have different materials on both sides of a face, but not so in
> OpenGL ES. However, you still must use the front and back values in OpenGL ES, or materials
> will not work properly.

Reset the diffuse material back to green. You should see something that looks like a big mess of
something yellowish-reddish. Shorthand for what's happening is that there's yet another value we can
use to play with the lighting. Called *shininess*, it specifies just how shiny the object's surface is and
ranges from 0 to 128. The higher the value, the more focused the reflection will be, and hence the
shinier it appears. But since it defaults to 0, it spreads the specular wealth across the entire planet. It
overpowers the green so much that when mixed with the red, it shows up as yellow. So, in order to get
control of this mess, add this line:

```
gl.glMaterialf(GL10.GL_FRONT_AND_BACK,GL10.GL_SHININESS, 5);
```

I'll explain shortly the real math behind this, but for right now see what happens with the value of 5.
Next try 25, and compare it with Figure 4–9. Shininess values from 5 to 10 correspond roughly to
plastics; greater than that, and we get into serious metal territory.

**Figure 4–9.** *Shininess set to 0, 5.0, and 25.0, respectively*

## Ambient Lighting

It's time for some fun with the ambient lighting. Add the following line to `initLighting()`; then
compile and run:

```
gl.glLightfv(SS_SUNLIGHT, GL10.GL_AMBIENT, makeFloatBuffer(blue));
```

Does it look like the image on the left in Figure 4–10? And what should you do to get the image on the right? You need to add the following line:

```
gl.glMaterialfv(GL10.GL_FRONT_AND_BACK, GL10.GL_AMBIENT, makeFloatBuffer(blue));
```

 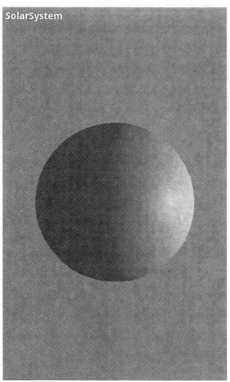

**Figure 4–10.** *Blue ambient light only (left), both ambient light and ambient material (right)*

Besides the ambient attribute for each light, you can also set a world ambient value. The light-based values are variables, as are all of light parameters, so they vary as a function of the distance, attenuation, and so on. The world value is a constant across your entire OpenGL ES universe and can be set by adding the following to your `initLighting()` routine:

```
float[] colorVector={r, g, b, a};
gl.glLightModelfv(GL10.GL_LIGHT_MODEL_AMBIENT, makeFloatBuffer(colorVector));
```

The default value is a dim gray formed by a color with red=.2f, green=.2f, and blue=.2f. This helps ensure that your objects are always visible no matter what. And while we're at it, there is one other value for `glLightModelfv()`, and that is defined by the parameter of GL_LIGHT_MODEL_TWO_SIDE. The parameter is actually a boolean float. If it is 0.0, only one side will be illuminated; otherwise, both will. The default is 0.0. And if for any reason you wanted to change which faces were front ones, you may use `glFrontFace()` and specify the triangles ordered clockwise or counterclockwise represent the front face. CCW is the default.

## Taking a Step Back

So, what is actually happening here? Quite a lot, actually. There are three general shading models in use for real-time computer graphics. OpenGL ES 1.1 uses two of those, both of which we've seen. The first, the flat model, simply shades each triangle with one constant value. You've seen what that looks like in Figure 4–5. And in the good ol' days, this was a valid option, considering it was much faster than any others. However, when the iPhone in your pocket is roughly the equivalent of a handheld Cray-1, those kinds of speed tricks are really a thing of the past. The smooth model uses *interpolative* shading, calculating the colors at each vertex and then interpolating them across the faces. The actual kind of shading OpenGL uses is a special form of this called *Gouraud shading*. This is where the vertex normals are generated based on normals of all the adjacent faces.

The third kind of shading is called *Phong* and is not used in OpenGL because of high CPU overhead. Instead of interpolating color values across the face, it interpolates normals, generating a normal for each fragment (that is, pixel). This helps remove some of the artifacting along edges defined by high curvatures, which produce very sharp angles. Phong can diminish that effect, but so can using more triangles to define your object.

There are numerous other models. Jim Blinn of the JPL/Voyager animations in the 1970s created a modified form of Phong shading, now called the Blinn-Phong model. If the light source and viewer can be treated as if they are at infinity, it can be less computationally intensive.

The Minnaert model tends to add a little more contrast to diffuse materials. Oren-Nayer adds a "roughness" component to the diffuse model in order to match reality just a little bit better.

## Emissive Materials

Still another significant parameter we need to cover here that factors into the final color is `GL_EMISSION`. Unlike the diffuse, ambient, and specular bits, `GL_EMISSION` is for materials only and specifies that a material is *emissive* in quality. An emissive object has its own internal light source such as the sun, which will come in handy in the solar-system model. To see this in action, add the following line to the other material code in `initLighting()` and remove the ambient material:

```
gl.glMaterialfv(GL10.GL_FRONT_AND_BACK, GL10.GL_EMISSION, makeFloatBuffer(yellow));
```

Because the yellow is at full intensity, what do you expect to see? Probably like the image on the left in Figure 4–11. Next cut the values down by half so you have this:

```
float[] yellow={.5f, .5f, 0.0f, 1.0f};
```

Now what do you see? I'll bet it looks something like the image on right in Figure 4–11.

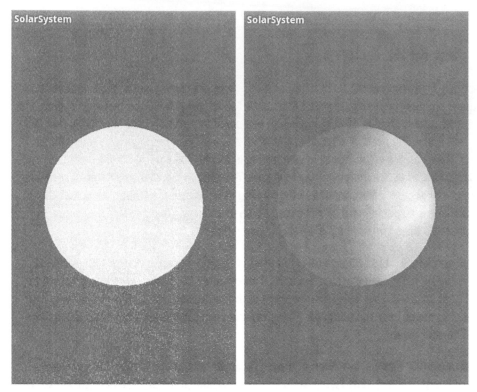

**Figure 4–11**. *A body with emissive material set to full intensity for the yellow (left); the same scene but with just 50 percent intensity (right)*

Superficially, emissive materials may look just like the results of using ambient lighting. But unlike ambient lights, only a single object in your scene will be affected. And as a side benefit, they don't use up additional light objects. However, if your emissive objects do represent real lights of any sort such as the sun, putting a light object inside definitely adds another layer of authenticity to the scene.

One further note regarding materials: if your object has had the color vertices specified, like both our cube and sphere have, those values can be used instead of setting materials. You must use `gl.glEnable(GL10.GL_COLOR_MATERIAL);`. This will apply the vertex colors to the shading system, instead of those specified by the `glMaterial*` calls.

## Attenuation

In the real world, of course, light decreases the farther an object is from the light source. OpenGL ES can model this factor as well using one or more of the following three attenuation factors:

- GL_CONSTANT_ATTENUATION

- GL_LINEAR_ATTENUATION

- GL_QUADRATIC_ATTENUATION

All three are combined to form one value that then figures into the total illumination of each vertex of your model. They are set using gLightf (GLenum light, GLenum pname, GLfloat param), where light is your light ID such as GL_LIGHT0, pname is one of the three attenuation parameters listed earlier, and the actual value is passed using param.

Linear attenuation can be used to model attenuation caused by factors such as fog. The quadratic attenuation models the natural  falloff of light as the distance increases, which changes exponentially. As the distance of the light doubles, the illumination is cut to one quarter of the previous amount.

Let's just look at one, GL_LINEAR_ATTENUATION, for the time being. The math behind all three will be unveiled in a moment. Add the following line to initLighting():

```
gl.glLightf(SS_SUNLIGHT, GL10.GL_LINEAR_ATTENUATION, .025f);
```

And just to make things a little clearer visually, ensure that the emissive material is turned off. What do you see? Now increase the distance down the x-axis from 10 to 50 in the pos vector. Figure 4–12 illustrates the results.

**Figure 4–12.** *The light's x distance is 10 (left) and 50 (right), with a constant attenuation of 0.025.*

## Spotlights

The standard lights default to an isotropic model; that is, they are like a desk light without a shade, shining equally (and blindingly) in all directions. OpenGL provides three additional lighting parameters that can turn the run-of-the-mill light into a directional light:

- GL_SPOT_DIRECTION
- GL_SPOT_EXPONENT
- GL_SPOT_CUTOFF

Since it is a directional light, it is up to you to aim it using the GL_SPOT_DIRCTION vector. It defaults to 0,0,-1, pointing down the –z-axis, as shown in Figure 4–13. Otherwise, if you want to change it, you would use a call similar to the following that aims it down the +x-axis:

```
GLfloat direction[]={1.0,0.0,0.0};

gl.glLightfv(GL10.GL_LIGHT0, GL10.GL_SPOT_DIRECTION, direction);
```

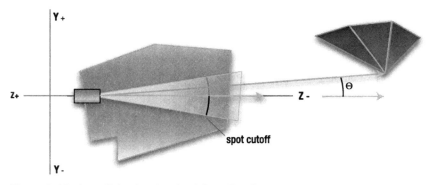

**Figure 4–13.** *A spotlight aimed at the default direction*

GL_SPOT_CUTOFF specifies the angle at which the spotlight's beam fades to 0 intensity from the center of the spotlight's cone and is naturally half the angular diameter of the full beam. The default value is 45 degrees, for a beam width of 90 degrees. And the lower the value, the narrower the beam.

The third and final spotlight parameter, GL_SPOT_EXPONENT, establishes the rate of drop-off of the beam's intensity, which is still another form of attenuation. OpenGL ES will take the cosine of the angle formed by the beam's center axis and that of an arbitrary vertex, $\Theta$, and raise it to the power of GL_SPOT_EXPONENT. Because its default is 0, the light's intensity will be the same across all parts of the illuminated region until the cutoff value is reached, and then it drops to zero.

## Light Parameters in Play

Table 4–1 summarizes the various light parameters covered in this section.

**Table 4–1.** *All of the Possible Lighting Parameters for* glLight* *Calls in OpenGL ES 1.1*

| Name | Purpose |
| --- | --- |
| GL_AMBIENT | Sets the ambient component of a light |
| GL_DIFFUSE | Sets the diffuse component of a light |
| GL_SPECULAR | Sets the specular component of a light |
| GL_POSITION | Sets the x,y,z coordinates of the light |
| GL_SPOT_DIRECTION | Aims a spotlight |
| GL_SPOT_EXPONENT | Specifies the rate of falloff from the center of a spotlight's beam |
| GL_SPOT_CUTOFF | Specifies the angle from the center of a spotlight's beam drops to 0 intensity |
| GL_CONSTANT_ATTENUATION | Specifies the constant attenuation factor |
| GL_LINEAR_ATTENUATION | Specifies the linear component of the attenuation factor; simulates fog or other natural phenomena |
| GL_QUADRATIC_ATTENUATION | Specifies the quadratic portion of the attenuation factor, simulating the normal decrease in intensity as a function of distance |

# The Math Behind Shading

The diffuse shading model gives a very smooth look to objects, as you have seen. It uses something called the *Lambert lighting model*. Lambert lighting states simply that the more directly aimed a specific face is to the light source, the brighter it will be. The ground beneath your feet is going to be brighter the higher the sun is in the sky. Or in the more obscure but precise technical version, the reflective light increases from 0 to 1 as the angle, $\Theta$, between the incident light, *I*, and the face's normal, *N*, decrease from 90 to 0 degrees based on cos $(\Theta)$. See Figure 4–14. Here's a quickie thought experiment: when $\Theta$ is 90 degrees, it is coming from the side; cos(90) is 0, so the reflected light along N is naturally going to be 0. When it is coming straight down, parallel to N, cos(0) will be 1, so the maximum amount will be reflected back. And this can be more formally expressed as follows:

$$I_d = k_d I_i \cos(\Theta)$$

$I_d$ is the intensity of the diffuse reflection, $K_i$ is the intensity of the incoming ray of light, and $k_d$ represents the *diffuse reflectance* that is loosely coupled to the roughness of the object's material. *Loosely* means that in a lot of real-world materials, the actual surface may be somewhat polished but yet translucent, while the layers immediately underneath perform the scattering. Materials such as this may have both strong diffuse and specular components. Also, each color band may have its own *k* value in real life, so there would be one for red, green, and blue.

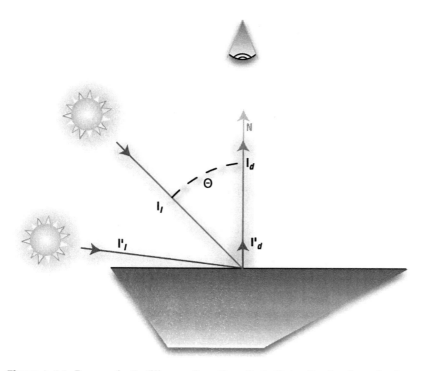

*Figure 4–14. For a perfectly diffuse surface, the reflected intensity of an incoming beam will be the vertical component of that beam, or cosine of the angle between the incoming beam and the surface normal.*

## Specular Reflections

As referenced earlier, specular reflections serve to give your model a shiny appearance besides the more general diffuse surface. Few things are perfectly flat or perfectly shiny, and most lay somewhere in between. In fact, the earth's oceans are good specular reflectors, and on images of the earth from long distances, the sun's reflection can clearly be seen in the oceans.

Unlike a diffuse "reflection," which is equal in all directions, a specular reflection is highly dependent on the viewer's angle. We've been taught that the *angle of incidence=angle of reflectance*. This is true enough for the perfect reflector. But with the exception of mirrors, the nose of a '51 Studebaker, or the nicely polished forehead of that Cylon centurion right before he blasts you 150,000 years into the past, few things are perfect reflectors. And as such, there will be a slight scattering of the incoming ray; see Figure 4–15.

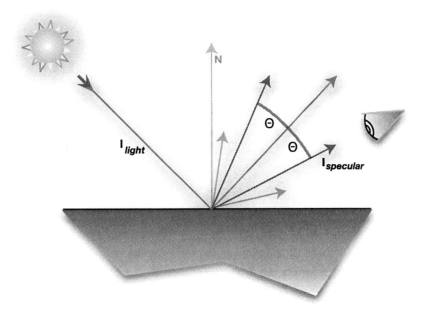

**Figure 4–15.** *For a specular reflection, the incoming ray is scattered but only around the center of its reflected counterpart.*

The equation of the specular component can be expressed as follows:

$$I_{specular} = W(q)I_{light}\cos^n \Theta$$

where:

$I_{light}$ is the intensity of the incoming ray.

$W(q)$ is how reflective the surfaces is based on the angle of $I_{light}$.

*n* is the *shininess factor* (sound familiar?).

$\Theta$ is the angle between the reflected ray and the ray hitting the eye.

This is actually based on what's called the Fresnel Law of Reflection, which is where the W(q) value comes from. Although W(q) is not directly used OpenGL ES 1.1 because it varies with the angle of incidence and is therefore a little more complicated than the specular lighting model, it could be used in a shader for version OpenGL ES 2.0. In that case, it would be particularly useful in doing reflections off the water, for example. In its place is a constant that is based on the specular values from the material setting.

The shininess factor, also called the *specular exponent*, is what we played with earlier. However, in real life *n* can go far higher than the max of 128.

## Attenuation

Now back to the three kinds of attenuation listed earlier: constant, linear, and quadratic. The total attenuation is calculated as follows, where $k_c$ is the constant, $k_l$ is the linear value, $k_q$ is the quadratic component, and $d$ stands for the distance from the light and an arbitrary vertex:

$$k_l = \frac{1}{\left(k_c + k_l d + k_q d^2\right)}$$

## Summing It All Up

So, now you can see that there are many factors in play to merely generate the color and intensity of that color for any of the vertices of any models in our scene. These include the following:

- Attenuation because of distance
- Diffuse lights and materials
- Specular lights and materials
- Spotlight parameters
- Ambient lights and materials
- Shininess
- Emissivity of the material

You can think of all of these as acting on the entire color vector or on each of the individual R, G, and B components of the colors.

So, to spell it all out, the final vertex color will be as follows:

$$color = ambient_{world\ model}\ ambient_{material} + emissive_{material} + intensity_{light}$$

where:

$$intensity_{light} = \sum_{i=0}^{n-1} (attenuation \ \ factor)_i (spotlight \ \ factor)_i$$

$$\left[ ambient_{light} ambient_{material} + \cos(\Theta)^{shininess} specular_{light} specular_{material} \right]$$

In other words, the color is equal to the some of the things not controlled by the lights added to the intensity of all the lights once we take into account the attenuation, diffuse, specular, and spotlight elements.

When calculated, these values act individually on each of the R, G, and B components of the colors in question.

## So, What's This All For?

One reason why it is handy to understand what's going on beneath the hood is that it helps make OpenGL and related tools less mysterious. Just like when you learn a foreign language, say Klingon (and if you, dear reader, are Klingon, *majQa' nuqDaq 'oH puchpa' 'e'!*), it ceases to be the mystery that it once was; where growls were growls and snarls were snarls, now you might recognize them as a lovely poem about fine tea.

And another reason is, as mentioned early on, all of these nice "high-level" tools are absent in OpenGL ES 2.0. Most any of the earlier shading algorithms will have to be implemented by you in little bits o' code that are called *shaders*. Fortunately, information on the most common shaders is available on the Internet and, replicating the previous information, relatively straightforward.

# More Fun Stuff

Now, armed with all of this photonic goodness, it's time to get back to coding and introduce more than one light. Secondary lights can make a surprisingly large difference in the authenticity of the scene for little effort.

Go back to `initLighting()` and make it look like Listing 4–5. Here we add two more lights, named `SS_FILLLIGHT1` and `SS_FILLLIGHT2`, respectively. Add their definitions to the renderer's class:

```
public final static int SS_SUNLIGHT1 = GL10.GL_LIGHT1;

public final static int SS_SUNLIGHT2 = GL10.GL_LIGHT2;
```

Now compile and run. Do you see the image on the left in Figure 4–16? Here is where the Gouraud shading model breaks down, as mentioned earlier, exposing the edges of the triangles. And what is the solution? At this point, simply increase the number of slices and stacks from 20 to 50 each, and you'll get the much more pleasing image, shown on the right in Figure 4–16.

**Listing 4–5.** *Adding Two Fill Lights*

```
private void initLighting(GL10 gl)
{
        float[] posMain={5.0f,4.0f,6.0f,1.0f};
        float[] posFill1={-15.0f,15.0f,0.0f,1.0f};
        float[] posFill2={-10.0f,-4.0f,1.0f,1.0f};

        float[] white={1.0f,1.0f,1.0f,1.0f};
        float[] red={1.0f,0.0f,0.0f,1.0f};
        float[] dimred={.5f,0.0f,0.0f,1.0f};

        float[] green={0.0f,1.0f,0.0f,0.0f};
        float[] dimgreen={0.0f,.5f,0.0f,0.0f};
        float[] blue={0.0f,0.0f,1.0f,1.0f};
        float[] dimblue={0.0f,0.0f,.2f,1.0f};

        float[] cyan={0.0f,1.0f,1.0f,1.0f};
        float[] yellow={1.0f,1.0f,0.0f,1.0f};
        float[] magenta={1.0f,0.0f,1.0f,1.0f};
        float[] dimmagenta={.75f,0.0f,.25f,1.0f};

        float[] dimcyan={0.0f,.5f,.5f,1.0f};

        //Lights go here.

        gl.glLightfv(SS_SUNLIGHT, GL10.GL_POSITION, makeFloatBuffer(posMain));
        gl.glLightfv(SS_SUNLIGHT, GL10.GL_DIFFUSE, makeFloatBuffer(white));
        gl.glLightfv(SS_SUNLIGHT, GL10.GL_SPECULAR, makeFloatBuffer(yellow));

        gl.glLightfv(SS_FILLLIGHT1, GL10.GL_POSITION, makeFloatBuffer(posFill1));
        gl.glLightfv(SS_FILLLIGHT1, GL10.GL_DIFFUSE, makeFloatBuffer(dimblue));
        gl.glLightfv(SS_FILLLIGHT1, GL10.GL_SPECULAR, makeFloatBuffer(dimcyan));

        gl.glLightfv(SS_FILLLIGHT2, GL10.GL_POSITION, makeFloatBuffer(posFill2));
        gl.glLightfv(SS_FILLLIGHT2, GL10.GL_SPECULAR, makeFloatBuffer(dimmagenta));
        gl.glLightfv(SS_FILLLIGHT2, GL10.GL_DIFFUSE, makeFloatBuffer(dimblue));

        gl.glLightf(SS_SUNLIGHT, GL10.GL_QUADRATIC_ATTENUATION, .005f);

        //Materials go here.

        gl.glMaterialfv(GL10.GL_FRONT_AND_BACK, GL10.GL_DIFFUSE, makeFloatBuffer(cyan));
```

```
        gl.glMaterialfv(GL10.GL_FRONT_AND_BACK, GL10.GL_SPECULAR,
    makeFloatBuffer(white));

        gl.glMaterialf(GL10.GL_FRONT_AND_BACK, GL10.GL_SHININESS, 25);


        gl.glShadeModel(GL10.GL_SMOOTH);
        gl.glLightModelf(GL10.GL_LIGHT_MODEL_TWO_SIDE, 1.0f);

        gl.glEnable(GL10.GL_LIGHTING);
        gl.glEnable(SS_SUNLIGHT);
        gl.glEnable(SS_FILLLIGHT1);
        gl.glEnable(SS_FILLLIGHT2);

        gl.glLoadIdentity();
}
```

 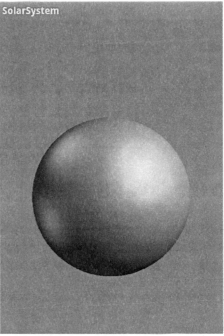

**Figure 4–16.** *Three lights, one main and two fill. The left image has a low-resolution sphere, while the right image is high-resolution.*

In the previous examples, a number of new API calls were covered, which are summarized in Table 4–2. Get to know them—they are your friends, and you'll be using them a lot.

**Table 4–2.** *New API Calls Covered*

| Name | Purpose |
|------|---------|
| glGetLight | Retrieves any of the parameters from a specific light |
| glLight* | Sets the parameters for the lights |
| glLightModel | Specifies the light model, either GL_LIGHT_MODEL_AMBIENT or GL_LIGHT_MODEL_TWO_SIDE |
| glMaterialfv | Defines the attributes for the current material |
| glNormal | Assigns a single normal to an array of faces |
| glNormalPointer | Specifies the current normal array for an object in the execute method |
| glShadeModel | Either GL_FLAT or GL_SMOOTH |
| glPopMatrix | Pops a matrix off the current stack |
| glPushMatrix | Pushes a matrix on the current stack |

# Back to the Solar System

Now we have enough tools to get back to the solar-system project. Hold on, there is a lot of material to cover here. In particular are some other aspects of OpenGL that have nothing to do with lighting or materials but need to be addressed before the solar-system model gets much more complex.

First we need to add some new method declarations and instance variables to renderer class. See Listing 4–6.

**Listing 4–6.** *Preparing for the sun and earth.*

```
public final static int X_VALUE = 0;

public final static int Y_VALUE = 1;

public final static int Z_VALUE = 2;

Planet m_Earth;
```

```
Planet m_Sun;
float[] m_Eyeposition = {0.0f, 0.0f, 0.0f};
```

Next, a second object, in this case, our sun, needs to be generated, sized, and placed. And while we're at it, change the size of the earth to make it smaller than the sun. So, replace the initialization code in the renderer's constructor with Listing 4–7.

**Listing 4–7.** *Add a second object and Initialize the Viewer's Position*

```
m_Eyeposition[X_VALUE] = 0.0f;                                    //1
m_Eyeposition[Y_VALUE] = 0.0f;
m_Eyeposition[Z_VALUE] = 5.0f;

m_Earth = new Planet(50, 50, .3f, 1.0f);                         //2
m_Earth.setPosition(0.0f, 0.0f, -2.0f);                         //3

m_Sun = new Planet(50, 50,1.0f, 1.0f);                          //4
m_Sun.setPosition(0.0f, 0.0f, 0.0f);                           //5
```

Here's what's going on:

- Our eyepoint, line 1, now has a well-defined location of +5 on the z-axis.

- In line 2, the earth's diameter is reduced to .3.

- Initialize the earth's location to be behind the sun from our standpoint, at z=-2, line 3.

- Now we can create the sun and place it at the exact center of our relatively fake solar system, line 4 and 5.

initLighting() needs to look like in Listing 4–8, cleaned up from all of the mucking around in the previous examples.

**Listing 4–8.** *Expanded Lighting for the Solar System Model*

```
private void initLighting(GL10 gl)
{
    float[] sunPos={0.0f, 0.0f, 0.0f, 1.0f};
    float[] posFill1={-15.0f, 15.0f, 0.0f, 1.0f};
    float[] posFill2={-10.0f, -4.0f, 1.0f, 1.0f};
    float[] white={1.0f, 1.0f, 1.0f, 1.0f};
    float[] dimblue={0.0f, 0.0f, .2f, 1.0f};
    float[] cyan={0.0f, 1.0f, 1.0f, 1.0f};
    float[] yellow={1.0f, 1.0f, 0.0f, 1.0f};
    float[] magenta={1.0f, 0.0f, 1.0f, 1.0f};
    float[] dimmagenta={.75f, 0.0f, .25f, 1.0f};
    float[] dimcyan={0.0f, .5f, .5f, 1.0f};

    //Lights go here.
```

```
gl.glLightfv(SS_SUNLIGHT, GL10.GL_POSITION, makeFloatBuffer(sunPos));
gl.glLightfv(SS_SUNLIGHT, GL10.GL_DIFFUSE, makeFloatBuffer(white));
gl.glLightfv(SS_SUNLIGHT, GL10.GL_SPECULAR, makeFloatBuffer(yellow));

gl.glLightfv(SS_FILLLIGHT1, GL10.GL_POSITION, makeFloatBuffer(posFill1));
gl.glLightfv(SS_FILLLIGHT1, GL10.GL_DIFFUSE, makeFloatBuffer(dimblue));
gl.glLightfv(SS_FILLLIGHT1, GL10.GL_SPECULAR, makeFloatBuffer(dimcyan));

gl.glLightfv(SS_FILLLIGHT2, GL10.GL_POSITION, makeFloatBuffer(posFill2));
gl.glLightfv(SS_FILLLIGHT2, GL10.GL_SPECULAR, makeFloatBuffer(dimmagenta));
gl.glLightfv(SS_FILLLIGHT2, GL10.GL_DIFFUSE, makeFloatBuffer(dimblue));

//Materials go here.

gl.glMaterialfv(GL10.GL_FRONT_AND_BACK, GL10.GL_DIFFUSE, makeFloatBuffer(cyan));
gl.glMaterialfv(GL10.GL_FRONT_AND_BACK, GL10.GL_SPECULAR, makeFloatBuffer(white));

gl.glLightf(SS_SUNLIGHT, GL10.GL_QUADRATIC_ATTENUATION,.001f);
gl.glMaterialf(GL10.GL_FRONT_AND_BACK, GL10.GL_SHININESS, 25);
gl.glShadeModel(GL10.GL_SMOOTH);
gl.glLightModelf(GL10.GL_LIGHT_MODEL_TWO_SIDE, 0.0f);

gl.glEnable(GL10.GL_LIGHTING);
gl.glEnable(SS_SUNLIGHT);
gl.glEnable(SS_FILLLIGHT1);
gl.glEnable(SS_FILLLIGHT2);
}
```

Naturally, the top-level execute method has to be completely overhauled, along with the addition of a small utility function, as shown in Listing 4–9.

**Listing 4–9.** *New rendering Methods*

```
static float angle = 0.0f;

private void onDrawFrame(GL10 gl)
{
    float paleYellow[]={1.0f, 1.0f, 0.3f, 1.0f};                              //1
    float white[]={1.0f, 1.0f, 1.0f, 1.0f};
    float cyan[]={0.0f, 1.0f, 1.0f, 1.0f};
    float black[]={0.0f, 0.0f, 0.0f, 0.0f};                                  //2

    float orbitalIncrement= 1.25f;                                           //3
    float[] sunPos={0.0f, 0.0f, 0.0f, 1.0f};

    gl.glEnable(GL10.GL_DEPTH_TEST);
    gl.glClear(GL10.GL_COLOR_BUFFER_BIT | GL10.GL_DEPTH_BUFFER_BIT);
```

```
gl.glClearColor(0.0f,0.0f,0.0f,1.0f);
gl.glPushMatrix();                                                    //4

gl.glTranslatef(-m_Eyeposition[X_VALUE], -m_Eyeposition[Y_VALUE],-
m_Eyeposition[Z_VALUE]);
                                                                      //5

gl.glLightfv(SS_SUNLIGHT, GL10.GL_POSITION, makeFloatBuffer(sunPos));  //6
gl.glMaterialfv(GL10.GL_FRONT_AND_BACK, GL10.GL_DIFFUSE, makeFloatBuffer(cyan));
gl.glMaterialfv(GL10.GL_FRONT_AND_BACK, GL10.GL_SPECULAR, makeFloatBuffer(white));

gl.glPushMatrix();                                                    //7
angle+=orbitalIncrement;                                              //8
gl.glRotatef(angle, 0.0f, 1.0f, 0.0f);                                //9
executePlanet(m_Earth, gl);                                           //10
gl.glPopMatrix();                                                     //11

gl.glMaterialfv(GL10.GL_FRONT_AND_BACK, GL10.GL_EMISSION, makeFloatBuffer(paleYellow));
                                                                      //12
gl.glMaterialfv(GL10.GL_FRONT_AND_BACK, GL10.GL_SPECULAR, makeFloatBuffer(black)); //13
executePlanet(m_Sun, gl);                                             //14


gl.glMaterialfv(GL10.GL_FRONT_AND_BACK, GL10.GL_EMISSION, makeFloatBuffer(black)); //15

gl.glPopMatrix();                                                     //16

}

    private void executePlanet(Planet m_Planet, GL10 gl)
{

        float posX, posY, posZ;
        posX = m_Planet.m_Pos[0];                                     //17
        posY = m_Planet.m_Pos[1];
        posZ = m_Planet.m_Pos[2];

        gl.glPushMatrix();
        gl.glTranslatef(posX, posY, posZ);                            //18
        m_Planet.draw(gl);                                            //19
        gl.glPopMatrix();
}
```

Here's what's going on:

- Line 1 creates a lighter shade of yellow. This just colors the sun a slightly more accurate hue.

- We need a black color to "turn off" some of the material characteristics if needed, as in line 2.

- In line 3, the orbital increment is needed to get the earth to orbit the sun.

- glPushMatrix() in line 4 is a new API call. When combined with glPopMatrix(), it helps isolate the transformations for one part of the world from another part. In this case, the first glPushMatrix actually prevents the following call to glTranslate() from adding new translations upon itself. You could dump the glPush/PopMatrix pair and put the glTranslate out of onDrawFrame(), into the initialization code, just as long as it is called only once.

- The translation in line 5 ensures that the objects are "moved away" from our eyepoint. Remember that everything in an OpenGL ES world effectively revolves around the eyepoint. I prefer to have a common origin that doesn't rely on viewer's location, and in this case, it is the position of the sun, as expressed in offsets from the eyepoint.

- Line 6 merely enforces the sun's location as being at the origin.

- Ooh! Another glPushMatrix() in line 7. This ensures that any transformations on the earth don't affect the sun.

- Lines 8 and 9 get the earth to orbit the sun. How? In line 10, a little utility function is called. That performs any transitions and moves an object away from the origin if need be. As you recall, the transformations can be thought of being last called/first used. So, the translation in executePlanets() is actually performed first, followed by the glRotation. Note that this method will have the earth orbiting in a perfect circle, whereas in reality, no planets will have a perfectly circular orbit, so glTranslation will be used.

- glPopMatrix() in line 11 dumps any of the transformations unique to the earth.

- Line 12 sets the sun's material to be emissive. Note that the calls to glMaterialfv are not bound to any specific object. They set the current material used by all following objects only until the next calls are made. Line 13 turns off any specular settings used for the Earth.

- Line 14 calls our utility again, this time with the sun.

▓ The emissive material attribute is switched off, here in line 15, followed by another `glPopMatrix()`. Note that every time you do use a push matrix, it must be paired with a pop. OpenGL ES can handle stacks up to 16 deep. Also, since there are three kinds of matrices in use in OpenGL (the Modelview, Projection, and Texture), make sure that you are pushing/popping the proper stack. You can ensure this by remembering to use `glMatrixMode()`.

▓ Now in `executePlanet()`, line 17 gets the planet's current position so line 18 can translate the planet to the proper position. In this case, it never actually changes, because we're letting `glRotatef()` handle the orbital duties. Otherwise, the xyz would constantly change as a factor of time.

▓ Finally, call the planet's own `drawing` routine in line 19.

To Planet.java, add the following line to the instance variables:

```
public float[] m_Pos = {0.0f, 0.0f, 0.0f};
```

And after the `execute` method, add the code in Listing 4–10, defining the new methods.

**Listing 4–10.** *The Setter for m_Pos*

```
public void setPosition(float x, float y, float z)
{
    m_Pos[0] = x;
    m_Pos[1] = y;
    m_Pos[2] = z;
}
```

And while you're at it, let's turn down the gray in the background. It's supposed to be space, and space isn't gray. Go back to the renderer, onDrawFrame(), and change the call to `glClearColor` to read as follows:

```
gl.glClearColor(0.0f,0.0f, 0.0f, 1.0f);
```

Now compile and run. You should see something like Figure 4–17.

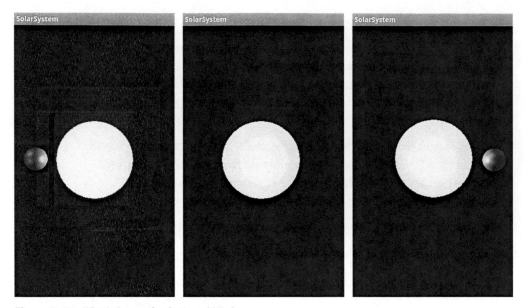

**Figure 4–17.** *What's happening in the middle?*

There's something odd here. When running, you should see the earth come out from behind the sun on the left side, orbit toward us to cross in front of the sun, and then move away to repeat the orbit again. So, why don't we see the earth in front of the sun in the middle image (Figure 4–17)?

In all graphics, computer or otherwise, the order of drawing plays a big role. If you're painting a portrait, you draw the background first. If you are generating a little solar system, well, the sun should be drawn first (er, maybe not…or not always).

Rendering order, or *depth sorting,* and how to determine what objects occlude other objects has always been a big part of computer graphics. Before the sun was added, render order was irrelevant, because there was only a single object. But as the world gets a lot more complicated, you'll find that there are two general ways this problem is solved.

The first is called the *painter's algorithm.* This means simply to draw the farthest objects first. This is very easy in something as simple as one sphere orbiting another. But what happens when you have very complicated 3D immersive worlds like World of Warcraft or Second Life? These would actually use a variant of painter's algorithm, but with some precomputed information ahead of time that determines all possible orders of occlusion. That information is then used to form a *binary space partitioning* (BSP) tree. Any place in the 3D world can be mapped to an element in the tree, which can then be traversed to fetch the optimum order for viewer's location. This is very fast in execution but complicated to set up. Fortunately, it is way overkill for our simple universe. The second means of depth sorting isn't sorting at all but actually uses the z component of each individual pixel. A pixel on the screen has an x and y value, but it can also have a z value as well, even though the Viewsonic in front of me is a flat 2D surface. As one pixel is ready to draw on top of another, the z values are compared, and the closer of the two wins out. Called *z-buffering*, it is very simple and straightforward but can chew up extra CPU time and graphics memory for very complicated scenes. I prefer the latter, and OpenGL makes z-buffering very easy to implement.

In method OnSurfaceCreated, find:

```
gl.glDepthMask(false);
```

and replace with

```
gl.glDepthMask(true);
```

If it works right, you should now see the earth eclipsing the sun when in front or being hidden while in back. See Figure 4–18.

**Figure 4–18.** *Using the z-buffer*

# And the Banding Played On

Under Android, the GLSurfaceView object  does not default to "true" 32-bit color—that is, 8 bits each for red, green, blue, and alpha. Instead, it chooses a somewhat lower-quality mode called "RGB565," which uses only 16 bits per pixel, or 5 bits for red, 6 for green, and 5 for blue. With a lower-resolution color mode such as this, you will likely get the "banding" artifacts on smoothly shaded objects, as illustrated by the image on the left in Figure 4–19. This happens simply because not enough colors are available. However, you can direct GLSurfaceView to use higher resolution modes, resulting in the image on the right in Figure 4–19. Use the following code in the onCreate() handler in the activity object:

```
GLSurfaceView view = new GLSurfaceView(this);
view.setEGLConfigChooser(8,8,8,8,16,0);                      //The new line
view.setRenderer(new SolarSystemRenderer());
setContentView(view);
```

The new line (view.setEGLConfigChooser(8,8,8,8,16,0) tells the view to use 8 bits per color, in addition to 16 bits for depth, or z-buffering, which was described above. The final value is for a stencil that will be covered in Chapter 7.

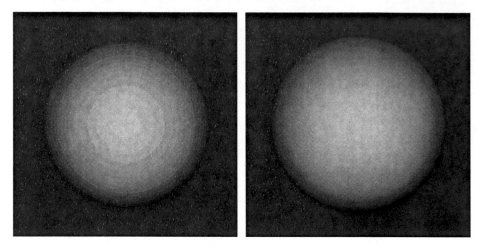

**Figure 4–19.** *16-bit color on the left, 32-bit color on the right.*

Be careful about automatically using the 32-bit color modes because some older devices do not support them and could crash as a result. It is advised that you check for which modes are available before using anything other than the default. This can be done by creating a custom "ColorChooser" object that will enumerate all possible modes. And yes, it is a pain, and a lot of code. An example will be available on the web site.

# Summary

This chapter covered the various approaches to lighting and shading the scene, along with the mathematical algorithms used to determine the color at each vertex. You also studied diffuse, specular, emissive, and ambient lighting along with various parameters having to do with turning the lights into spotlights. The solar-system model was updated to support multiple objects and to use z-buffering to handle object occlusion properly.

# Chapter 5

# Textures

*The true worth of a man is not to be found in man himself, but in the colours and textures that come alive in others.*

—Albert Schweitzer

People would be a rather dull bunch without texture to their lives. Removing those interesting little foibles and eccentricities would remove a little of the sheen in our daily wanderings, be they odd but beguiling little habits or unexpected talents. Imagine the high-school janitor who happens to be an excellent ballroom dancer, the famous comedian who must wear only new white socks every day, the highly successful game engineer who's afraid to write letters by hand—all can make us smile and add just a little bit of wonder through the day. And so it is when creating artificial worlds. The visual perfection that computers can generate might be pretty, but it just doesn't feel right if you want to create a sense of authenticity to your scenes. That's where texturing comes in.

Texture makes that which is perfect become that which is real. The American Heritage Dictionary describes it this way: "The distinctive physical composition or structure of something, especially with respect to the size, shape, and arrangement of its parts." Nearly poetic, huh?

In the world of 3D graphics, texturing is as vital as lighting in creating compelling images and can be incorporated with surprisingly little effort nowadays. Much of the work in the graphics chip industry is rooted in rending increasingly detailed textures at higher rates than each previous generation of hardware.

Because texturing in OpenGL ES is such a vast topic, this chapter will be confined to the basics, with more advanced topics and techniques reserved for the next chapter. So with that in mind, let's get started.

# The Language of Texturing

Say you wanted to create an airstrip in a game you're working on. How would you do that? Simple, take a couple of black triangles, stretch them really long. Bang! Now you've got your landing strip! Not so fast there, sport. What about the lines painted down the center of the strip? How about a bunch of small white faces? That could work. But don't forget those yellow chevrons at the very end. Well, add a bunch of additional faces, and color them yellow. And don't forget about the numbers. How about the curved lines leading to the tarmac? Pretty soon you might be up to hundreds of triangles, but that still wouldn't help with the oil spots, repairs, skid marks, or roadkill. Now it starts getting complicated. Getting all of the fine detail could require thousands if not tens of thousands of faces. Meanwhile, your buddy, Arthur, is also creating a strip. You are comparing notes, telling him about polygon counts and that you haven't even gotten to the roadkill yet. And Arthur says all he needed was a couple of triangles and one image. You see, he used texturemaps, and using texturemaps can create a highly detailed surface such as an airstrip, brick walls, armor, clouds, creaky weathered wooden doors, a cratered terrain on a distant planet, or a the rusting exterior of a '56 Buick.

In the early days of computer graphics, texturing, or *texture mapping*, used up two of the most precious resources: CPU cycles and memory. It was used sparingly, and all sorts of little tricks were done to save on both resources. With memory now virtually free (when compared to 20 years ago) and with modern chips having seemingly limitless speed, using textures is no longer a decision one should ever have to stay up all night and struggle with.

## All About Textures (Mostly)

Textures come in two broad types: *procedural* and *image*. Procedural textures are generated on the fly based on some algorithm. There are "equations" for wood, marble, asphalt, stone, and so on. Nearly any kind of material can be reduced to an algorithm and hence drawn onto an object, as shown in Figure 5–1.

**Figure 5–1.** *The chalice on the left is polished gold, while on the right uses a procedural texture to look like gold ore, while the cone looks like marble.*

Procedural textures are very powerful because they can produce an infinite variety of scalable patterns that can be enlarged to reveal increasingly more detail, as shown in Figure 5–2. Otherwise, this would require a massive static image.

**Figure 5–2.** *Close-up on the goblet at the right in Figure 5–1. Notice the fine detailing that would need a very large image to accomplish.*

The 3D rendering application Strata Design 3D-SE, which was used for the previous images, supports both procedural and image-based textures. Figure 5–3 shows the dialog used to specify the parameters of the gold ore texture depicted in Figure 5–2.

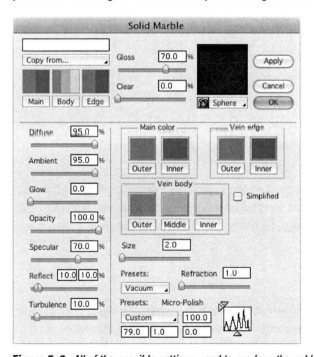

**Figure 5–3.** *All of the possible settings used to produce the gold ore texture in Figure 5–2*

Procedural textures, and to a lesser degree, image textures, can be classified in a spectrum of complexity from random to structured. Random, or *stochastic* textures, can be thought of as "looking like noise," like a fine-grained material such as sand, dust, gravel, the grain in paper, and so on. Near stochastic could be flames, grass, or the surface of a lake. On the other hand, structured textures have broad recognizable features and patterns. A brick wall, wicker basket, plaid, or herd of geckos would be structured.

## Image Textures

As referenced earlier, image textures are just that. They can serve duty as a surface or material texture such as mahogany wood, steel plating, or leaves scattered across the ground. If done right, these can be seamlessly tiled to cover a much larger surface than the original image would suggest. And because they come from real life, they don't need the sophisticated software used for the procedural variety. Figure 5–4 shows the chalice scene, but this time with wood textures, mahogany for the chalice, and alder for the cone, while the cube remains gold.

**Figure 5–4.** *Using real-world image textures*

Besides using image textures as materials, they can be used as pictures themselves in your 3D world. A rendered image of a Galaxy Tab can have a texture dropped into where the screen is. A 3D city could use real photographs for windows on the buildings, for billboards, or for family photos in a living room.

## OpenGL ES and Textures

When OpenGL ES renders an object, such as the mini-solar system in Chapter 4, it draws each triangle and then lights and colorizes it based on the three vertices that make up each face. Afterward, it merrily goes about to the next one. A texture is nothing more than an image. As you learned earlier, it can be generated on the fly to handle context-sensitive details (such as cloud patterns), or it can be a .jpg, .png, or anything else. It is made up of pixels, of course, but when operating as a texture, they are called *texels*. You can think of an OpenGL ES texture as a bunch of little colored "faces" (the texels), each of the same size and stitched together in one sheet of, say, 256 such "faces" on a side. Each face is the same size as each other one and can be stretched or squeezed so as to work on surfaces of any size or shape. They don't have corner geometry to waste memory storing xyz values, can come in a multitude of lovely colors, and give a lot of bang for the buck. And of course they are extraordinarily versatile.

Like your geometry, textures have their own coordinate space. Where geometry denotes locations of its many pieces using the trusty Cartesian coordinates known as *x, y*, and *z*, textures use *s* and *t*. The process that applies a texture to some geometric object is called *UV mapping*. (*s* and *t* are used only for OpenGL world, whereas others use *u* and *v*. Go figure.)

So, how is this applied? Say you have a square tablecloth that you must make fit a rectangular table. You need to attach it firmly along one side and then tug and stretch it along the other until it just barely covers the table. You can attach just the four corners, but if you really want it to "fit," you can attach other parts along the edge or even in the middle. That's a little how a texture is fitted to a surface.

Texture coordinate space is *normalized*; that is, both *s* and *t* range from 0 to 1. They are unitless entities, abstracted so as not to rely on either the dimensions of the source or the destination. So, the face to be textured will carry around with its vertices *s* and *t* values that lay between 0.0 to 1.0, as shown in Figure 5–5.

**Figure 5–5.** *Texture coordinates go from 0 to 1.0, no matter what the texture is.*

In the most elementary example, we can apply a rectangular texture to a rectangular face and be done with it, as illustrated in Figure 5–5. But what if you wanted only part of the texture? You could supply a .png that had only the bit you wanted, which is not very convenient if you wanted to have many variants of the thing. However, there's another way. Merely change the *s* and *t* coordinates of the destination face. Let's say all you wanted was the upper-left quarter of the Easter Island statue I call Hedly. All you need to do is to change the coordinates of the destination, and those coordinates are based on the proportion of the image section you want, as shown in Figure 5–6. That is, because you want the image to be cropped halfway down the *S*-axis, the *s* coordinate will no longer go from 0 to 1 but instead from 0 to .5. And the *t* coordinate would then would go from .5 to 1.0. If you wanted the lower-left corner, you'd use the same 0 to .5 ranges as the *s* coordinate.

Also note that the texture coordinate system is resolution independent. That is, the center of an image that is 512 on a side would be (.5,.5), just as it would be for an image 128 on a side.

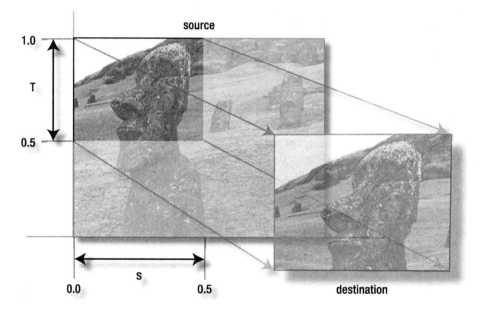

**Figure 5–6.** *Clipping out a portion of the texture by changing the texture coordinates*

Textures are not limited to rectilinear objects. With careful selections of the *st* coordinates on your destination face, you can do some of the more colorful shapes depicted in Figure 5–7.

**Figure 5–7.** *Mapping an image to unusual shapes*

If you keep the image coordinates the same across the vertices of your destination, the image's corners will follow those of the destination, as shown in Figure 5–8.

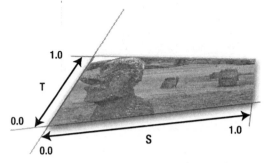

**Figure 5–8.** *Distorting images can give a 3D effect on 2D surfaces.*

Textures can also be *tiled* so as to replicate patterns that depict wallpaper, brick walls, sandy beaches, and so on, as shown in Figure 5–9. Notice how the coordinates actually go beyond the upper limit of 1.0. All that does is to start the texture repeating so that, for example, an *s* of .6 equals an *s* of 1.6, 2.6, and so on.

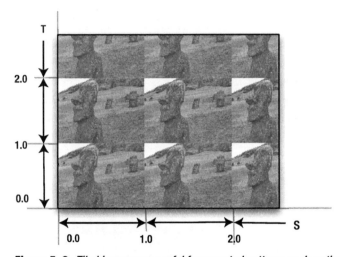

**Figure 5–9.** *Tiled images are useful for repeated patterns such as those used for wallpaper or brick walls.*

Besides the tiling model shown in Figure 5–9, texture tiles can also be "mirrored," or clamped. Both are mechanisms for dealing with s and *t* outside of the 0 to 1.0 range.

Mirrored tiling is like repeat but merely flips columns/rows of alternating images, as shown in Figure 5–10a. Clamping an image means that the last row or column of texels repeats, as shown in Figure 5–10b. Clamping looks like a total mess with my sample image but is useful when the image has a neutral border. In that case, you can prevent any image repetition on either or both axes if *s* or *v* exceeds its normal bounds.

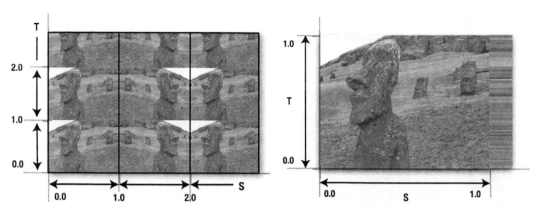

**Figure 5–10.** *The left (a) shows a mirrored-repeat for just the S axis, while the right texture (b) is clamped.*

**NOTE:** The problem with the right edge on the image at the right in Figure 5–10 suggests that textures designed to be clamped should have a 1-pixel-wide border to match the colors of the object to which they are bound—unless you think it's really cool, then of course, that trumps nearly everything.

OpenGL ES, as you know by now, doesn't do *quadrilaterals*—that is, faces with four sides (as opposed to its big desktop brother). So, we have to fabricate them using two triangles, giving us structures such as the triangle strips and fans that we experimented with in Chapter 3. Applying textures to this "fake" quadrilateral is a simple affair. One triangle has texture coordinates of (0,0), (1,0), and (0,1), while the other has coordinates of (1,0), (1,1), and (0,1). It should make more sense if you study Figure 5–11.

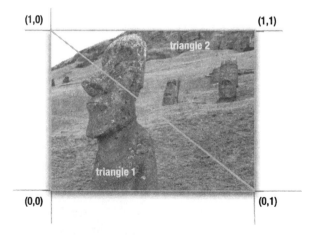

**Figure 5–11.** *Placing a texture across two faces*

And finally, let's take a look at how a single texture can be stretched across a whole bunch of faces, as shown in Figure 5–12, and then we can do the fun stuff and see whether it's for real.

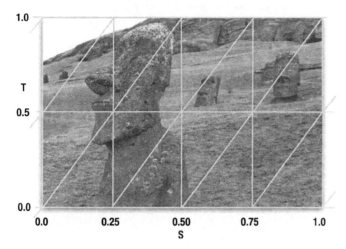

**Figure 5–12.** *Stretching a texture across many faces*

# Image Formats

OpenGL ES supports many different image formats, and I'm not talking about .png vs. .jpg, but I mean the form and layout in memory. The standard is 32 bits, which assigns 8 bits of memory each for red, green, blue, and alpha. Referred to as RGBA, it is the standard used for most of the exercises. It is also the "prettiest" because it provides more than 16 million colors and translucency. However, you can often get away with 16-bit or even 8-bit images. In doing that, you can save a lot of memory and crank up the speed quite a bit, with careful selection of images. See Table 5–1 for some of the more popular formats.

**Table 5–1.** *Some of the More Popular Image Formats*

| Format | Details |
| --- | --- |
| RGBA | 8 bits/channel, including alpha. |
| RGB | 8 bits/channel, no alpha. |
| ALPHA | A single 8-bit channel used for stencils. |
| LUMINANCE | A single 8-bit channel for grayscale images. |
| RGB565 | 16 bits total: 5 for red, 6 for green, and 5 for blue. The green is given a little more color fidelity because the eye is more sensitive to that than to either red or blue. |

| RGBA4444 | 16 bits, 4 for each channel. |
| --- | --- |
| RGBA5551 | 5 bits per color channel, and 1 for alpha. |

Also a format requirement of sorts is that, generally, OpenGL can use only texture images that are power-of-two on a side. Some systems can get around that, such as iOS with certain limitations, but for the time being, just stick with the standard.

So, with all of this stuff out of the way, time to start coding.

# Back to the Bouncy Square One

Let's take a step back and create the generic bouncy square again, which we first did in Chapter 1. We'll apply a texture to it and then manipulate it to show off some of the tricks detailed earlier, such as repeating, animating, and distortion.

Feel free to recycle that first project.

Next comes the actual creation of the texture. This will read in an image file of any type that Android supports and convert it to a format that OpenGL can use.

Before we start, one additional step is required. Android needs to be notified about the image file that will be used as the texture. This can be accomplished by adding the image file hedly.png to /res/drawable folder. If the drawable folder doesn't exist, you may create it now and add it to the project. We will be storing texture information in integer array. Add the following line to Square.java:

```
private int[] textures = new int[1];
```

Add the following imports:

```
import android.graphics.*;celar
import android.opengl.*;
```

Next add the Listing 5–1 to Square.java to create texture.

**Listing 5–1.** *Creating an OpenGL Texture*

```
public int createTexture(GL10 gl, Context contextRegf, int resource)

    {
        Bitmap image = BitmapFactory.decodeResource(contextRegf.getResources(),
            resource);                                                          // 1
        gl.glGenTextures(1, textures, 0);                                       // 2
        gl.glBindTexture(GL10.GL_TEXTURE_2D, textures[0]);                      // 3
```

```
    GLUtils.texImage2D(GL10.GL_TEXTURE_2D, 0, image, 0);          // 4

    gl.glTexParameterf(GL10.GL_TEXTURE_2D, GL10.GL_TEXTURE_MIN_FILTER,
        GL10.GL_LINEAR);                                          // 5a

    gl.glTexParameterf(GL10.GL_TEXTURE_2D, GL10.GL_TEXTURE_MAG_FILTER,
        GL10.GL_LINEAR;                                           // 5b

    image.recycle();                                             //6
    return resource;
}
```

So let's break this down:

- Line 1 loads the Android bitmap, letting the loader handle any image format that Android can read in. Table 5–2 lists the supported formats.

- glGenTextures() in line 2 gets an unused texture "name," which in reality is just a number. This ensures that each texture you use has a unique identifier. If you want to reuse identifiers, then you'd call glDeleteTextures().

- After that, the texture is *bound* to the current 2D texture in the next line, exchanging the new texture for the previous one. In OpenGL ES, there is only one of these texture targets, so it must always be GL_TEXTURE_2D, whereas grown-up OpenGL has several. See Table 5–3 for all available parameters. Binding also makes this texture active, because only one texture is active at a time. This also directs OpenGL where to put any of the new image data. See table 5–2.

- Here in line 4, GLUtils an Android utility class that binds OpenGL ES, and the Android APIs is used. This utility specifies the 2D texture image for the bitmap that we created in line 1. The image (texture) is created internally in its native format based on the bitmap created.

- Finally, lines 5a and 5b, set some parameters that are required on the Android. Without them, the texture has a default "filter" value that is unnecessary at this time. The min and max filters tell the system how to handle a texture under certain circumstances where it has to be either shrunk down or enlarged to fit a given polygon. Table 5–3 shows the available types of parameters in OpenGL ES.

- And to be a good neighbor, line 6 tells Android to explicitly recycle the bitmap because bitmaps can take up a whopping lot of memory.

**Table 5–2.** *The Image Formats Supported by Android*

| Format | Extensions |
| --- | --- |
| Portable Network Graphic | `.png` |
| Joint Photographic Experts Group (JPEG) | `.jpg`, `.jpeg` |
| Graphic Interchange Format (GIF) | `.gif` |
| Windows Bitmap Format (DIB) | `.bmp`, `.BMP`f |

**Table 5–3.** *All of the* `GL_TEXTURE` *Parameters for* `glTexParameter*` *Calls in OpenGL ES 1.1*

| Name | Purpose |
| --- | --- |
| `GL_TEXTURE_MIN_FILTER` | Sets the minification type (see Table 5–4) |
| `GL_TEXTURE_MAG_FILTER` | Sets the magnification type (see Table 5–5) |
| `GL_TEXTURE_WRAP_S` | Specifies how textures are to be *wrapped* in the S direction, `GL_CLAMP` or `GL_REPEAT` |
| `GL_TEXTURE_WRAP_T` | Specifies how textures are to be *wrapped* in the T direction, `GL_CLAMP` or `GL_REPEAT` |

Before we call `createTexture` method, we need to get the context and the resource ID of the image (`headly.png`). To get the context, modify the `onCreate()` method in `BouncySquareActivity.java` from this:

```
view.setRenderer(new SquareRenderer(true));
```

to the following:

```
view.setRenderer(new SquareRenderer(true, this.getApplicationContext()));
```

This will also require changing the constructor definition in `SquareRenderer.java` to the following:

```
public SquareRenderer(boolean useTranslucentBackground, Context context) {
    mTranslucentBackground = useTranslucentBackground;
    this.context = context;                                              //1
    this.mSquare = new Square();
}
```

You'll need to add the following import:

```
import android.content.Context;
```

And add an instance variable to support the new context. The context is used a little later when the image is loaded and converted to an OpenGL-compatible texture.

Now, to get the resource ID, add following to in the onSurfaceCreated() method in SquareRenderer.java:

```
int resid = book.BouncySquare.R.drawable.hedly;          //1

mSquare.createTexture(gl, this.context, resid);          //2
```

- Line 1 gets the resource of the image (hedly.png) that we added in the drawable folder. Of course, you can use any image you want.

- In Line 2, we use the object of Square class and call the createTexture() method with the correct context and the resource ID of the image.

And then adding the following to the interface's instance variables in Square.java:

```
public FloatBuffer mTextureBuffer;
float[] textureCoords =
{
    0.0f, 0.0f,
    1.0f, 0.0f,
    0.0f, 1.0f,
    1.0f, 1.0f
};
```

This defines the texture coordinates. Now create the textureBuffer similar to vertBuffer we created in Chapter 1 in the square's constructor.

```
ByteBuffer tbb = ByteBuffer.allocateDirect(textureCoords.length * 4);

tbb.order(ByteOrder.nativeOrder());

mTextureBuffer = tbb.asFloatBuffer();

mTextureBuffer.put(textureCoords);

mTextureBuffer.position(0);
```

My image, hedly.png, is the photo of one of the mysterious huge stone heads on Easter Island in the Pacific. For ease of testing, use a power-of-two (POT) image that is 32 bits and RGBA.

**NOTE:** By default, OpenGL requires each row of texels in the image data to be aligned on a 4-byte boundary. Our RGBA textures adhere to that; for other formats, consider using the call

> glPixelStorei(GL_PACK_ALIGNMENT,x), where x can be 1, 2, 4, or 8 bytes for alignment. Use 1 to cover all cases.

Note that there is usually a size limitation for textures, which depends on the actual graphics hardware used. You can find out how big a texture a particular platform can use by calling the following, where maxSize is an integer that compensates at runtime:

```
gl.glGetIntegerv(GL10.GL_MAX_TEXTURE_SIZE,maxSize);
```

Finally, the draw() routine needs to be modified, as shown in Listing 5–2. Most of this you have seen before. I've migrated the glEnableClientState() calls from the renderer module down here to make the square object now more contained.

**Listing 5–2.** *Render the Geometry with the Texture*

```
public void draw(GL10 gl)
    {
            gl.glVertexPointer(2, GL10.GL_FLOAT, 0, mFVertexBuffer);
            gl.glEnableClientState(GL10.GL_VERTEX_ARRAY);
            gl.glColorPointer(4, GL10.GL_UNSIGNED_BYTE, 0, mColorBuffer);
            gl.glEnableClientState(GL10.GL_COLOR_ARRAY);

            gl.glEnable(GL10.GL_TEXTURE_2D);                              //1
            gl.glEnable(GL10.GL_BLEND);                                   //2

            gl.glBlendFunc(GL10.GL_ONE, GL10.GL_SRC_COLOR);              //3
            gl.glBindTexture(GL10.GL_TEXTURE_2D, textures[0]);           //4

            gl.glTexCoordPointer(2, GL10.GL_FLOAT,0, mTextureBuffer);     //5
            gl.glEnableClientState(GL10.GL_TEXTURE_COORD_ARRAY);         //6

            gl.glDrawArrays(GL10.GL_TRIANGLE_STRIP, 0, 4);              //7

            gl.glDisableClientState(GL10.GL_COLOR_ARRAY);
            gl.glDisableClientState(GL10.GL_VERTEX_ARRAY);
            gl.glDisableClientState(GL10.GL_TEXTURE_COORD_ARRAY;         //8
    }
```

So, what's going on here?

■ In line 1, the GL_TEXTURE_2D target is enabled. Desktop OpenGL supports 1D and 3D textures but not ES.

■ Here in line 2 is where blending can be enabled. Blending is where color and the destination color are blended (mixed) according to some equation that is switched on in line 3.

- The blend function determines how the source and destination pixels/fragments are mixed together. The most common form is where the source overwrites the destination, but others can create some interesting effects. Since this is such a large topic, it will be covered a little later.

- Line 4 ensures that the texture we want is the current one.

- Here in line 5 is where the texture coordinates are handed off to the hardware.

- And just as you had to tell the client to handle the colors and vertices, you need to do the same for the texture coordinates here in line 6.

- Line 7 you'll recognize, but this time besides drawing the colors and the geometry, it now takes the information from the current texture (the `texture_2d`), matches up the four texture coordinates to the four corners specified by the `vertices[]` array (each vertex of the textured object needs to have a texture coordinate assigned to it), and blends it using the values specified in line 3.

- Finally, disable the client state for texture in the same way it was disabled for color and vertices.

If everything works right, you should see something like the image on the left in Figure 5–13. Notice how the texture is also picking up the colors from the vertices? Comment out the line `glColorPointer(4, GL10.GL_UNSIGNED_BYTE, 0, mColorBuffer)`, and you should now see the image on the right in Figure 5–13. If you don't see any image, double-check your file and ensure that it really is a power-of-two in size, such as 128x128 or 256x256.

**Figure 5–13.** *Applying texture to the bouncy square. The left uses the vertex colors; the right does not.*

What's that you say? The texture is upside-down? This could very well be a problem depending on how the respective OS treats bitmaps. OpenGL wants the lower-left corner to be the origin, whereas some image formats or drivers elect to have the upper-left corner instead. There are two main ways to get around this: You can elect to change the code, or you can supply a preflipped image. Because this is a very simple project, I'd elect just to flip the graphic with an image editor.

So now we can replicate some of the examples in the first part of this chapter. The first is to pick out only a portion of the texture to display. Change `textureCoords` to the following:

```
float[] textureCoords =

{
        0.0f, 0.0f,
        0.5f, 0.0f,
        0.0f, 0.5f,
        0.5f, 0.5f
};
```

Did you get Figure 5–14?

**Figure 5–14.** *Cropping the image using s and t coordinates*

The mapping of the texture coordinates to the real geometric coordinates looks like Figure 5–15. Spend a few minutes to understand what is happening here if you're not quite clear yet. Simply put, there's a one-to-one mapping of the texture coordinates in their array with that of the geometric coordinates.

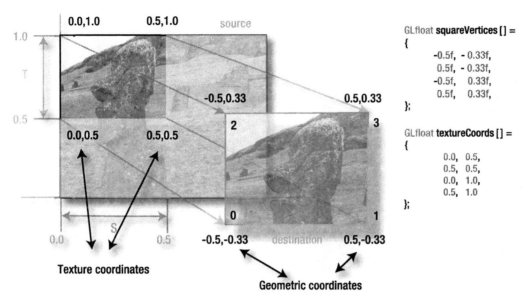

**Figure 5–15.** *The texture coordinates have a one-to-one mapping with the geometric ones.*

Now change the texture coordinates to the following. Can you guess what will happen? (Figure 5–16):

```
    float[] textureCoords =

{

        0.0f, 2.0f,
        2.0f, 2.0f,
        0.0f, 0.0f,
        2.0f, 0.0f
};
```

**Figure 5–16.** *Repeating the image is convenient when you need to do repetitive patterns such as wallpaper.*

Now let's distort the texture by changing the vertex geometry, and to make things visually clearer, restore the original texture coordinates to turn off the repeating:

```
    float  vertices[] =
{
                -1.0f, -0.7f,
                1.0f, -0.30f,
                -1.0f, 0.70f,
                1.0f,  0.30f,
};
```

This should pinch the right side of the square and take the texture with it, as shown in Figure 5–17.

**Figure 5–17.** *Pinching down the right side of the polygon*

Armed with all of this knowledge, what would happen if you changed the texture coordinates *dynamically*? Add the following code to draw( )—anywhere should work out.

```
textureCoords[0]+=texIncrease;

textureCoords[2]+=texIncrease;

textureCoords[4]+=texIncrease;

textureCoords[6]+=texIncrease;

textureCoords[1]+=texIncrease;

textureCoords[3]+=texIncrease;

textureCoords[5]+=texIncrease;

textureCoords [7] +=texIncrease;
```

And make both textureCoords and texIncrease instance variables.

This will increase the texture coordinates just a little from frame to frame. Run and stand in awe. This is a really simple trick to get animated textures. A marquee in a 3D world might use this. You could create a texture that was like a strip of movie film with a cartoon character doing something and change the *s* and *t* values to jump from frame to frame like a little flipbook. Another is to create a texture-based font. Since OpenGL has no native font support, it's up to us, the long suffering engineers of the world, to add it in ourselves. Sigh. This could be done by placing of the characters of the desired font onto a single *mosaic* texture and then selecting them by careful use of texture coordinates.

## Mipmaps

Mipmaps are a means of specifying multiple levels of detail for a given texture. That can help in two ways: it can smooth out the appearance of a textured object as its distance to the viewpoint varies, and it can save resource usage when textured objects are far away.

For example, in Distant Suns, I may use a texture for Jupiter that is 1024x512. But that would be a waste of both memory and CPU if Jupiter was so far away that it was only a few pixels across. Here is where mipmapping can come into play. So, what is a mipmap?

From the Latin phrase "multum in parvo" (literally: much in little), a *mipmap* is a family of textures of varying levels of detail. Your root image might be 128 on a side, but when a part of a mipmap, it would have textures that were also 64, 32, 16, 8, 4, 2, and 1 pixel on a side, as shown in Figure 5–18.

**Figure 5–18.** *Hedly the head, the mipmapped edition*

Go back to the original exercise for this chapter, the bouncy square with the texture, and you'll be putting mipmapping through the test.

First, create a family of textures from 1x1 on up to 256x256, making each texture twice the size of the previous while coloring them different colors. The colors enable you to easily tell when one image changes to another. Add them to your project under /res/drawable/, and then in SquareRendered.java in onSurfaceCreated(), swap out the single call to createTexture() with Listing 5–3. Note that the last parameter is finally used, which is the level of detail index. Use 0 for the default if you have only a single image as earlier. Anything above 0 will be the rest of the mipmap family of images. So, the first one is of Hedly, and the rest I used are colored squares to make it really easy to see the different images when they pop in and out. Note that if you do generate mipmaps manually like this, you need to specify images for *each and every* level, and they must be the right dimensions, so you can't skip the 1, 2, and 4 pixel images just to save a couple lines of code. Otherwise, nothing will show. And make sure the original image is 256 on a side so that there is an unbroken chain from 1 to 256 of images.

To make it easy to turn on or off mipmapping, I've added the following instance variable to Square.java.

```
public boolean m_UseMipmapping = true;
```

Add Listing 5–3 to the onSurfaceCreated() method in SquareRenderer.java.

**Listing 5–3**. *Setting Up a Custom Prefiltered Mipmap*

```
int resid = book.BouncySquare.R.drawable.hedly256;
mSquare.createTexture(gl, this.context, resid, true);

if (mSquare.m_UseMipmapping)
{
        resid = book.BouncySquare.R.drawable.mipmap128;
        mSquare.createTexture(gl, this.context, resid, false);
        resid = book.BouncySquare.R.drawable.mipmap64;
        mSquare.createTexture(gl, this.context, resid, false);
        resid = book.BouncySquare.R.drawable.mipmap32;
        mSquare.createTexture(gl, this.context, resid, false);
        resid = book.BouncySquare.R.drawable.mipmap16;
        mSquare.createTexture(gl, this.context, resid, false),
        resid = book.BouncySquare.R.drawable.mipmap8;
        mSquare.createTexture(gl, this.context, resid, false);
        resid = book.BouncySquare.R.drawable.mipmap4;
        mSquare.createTexture(gl, this.context, resid, false);
        resid = book.BouncySquare.R.drawable.mipmap2;
        mSquare.createTexture(gl, this.context, resid, false);
        resid = book.BouncySquare.R.drawable.mipmap1;
        mSquare.createTexture(gl, this.context, resid, false);
}
```

After this, createTexture() in Square.java needs to be replaced with the contents of Listing 5–4.

**Listing 5–4.** *Generate the Mipmap Chain*

```
private int[] textures = new int[1];
static int level = 0;
```

```
        public int createTexture(GL10 gl, Context contextRegf, int resource, boolean
imageID)

    {

            Bitmap tempImage = BitmapFactory.decodeResource(
                        contextRegf.getResources(), resource);          // 1

            if (imageID == true) {
                    gl.glGenTextures(1, textures, 0);
                    gl.glBindTexture(GL10.GL_TEXTURE_2D, textures[0]);
        }

            GLUtils.texImage2D(GL10.GL_TEXTURE_2D, level, tempImage, 0);     // 4
                level++;

            if (m_UseMipmapping == true) {
                    gl.glTexParameterx(GL10.GL_TEXTURE_2D,
                            GL10.GL_TEXTURE_MIN_FILTER,
                            GL10.GL_LINEAR_MIPMAP_NEAREST);
                    gl.glTexParameterx(GL10.GL_TEXTURE_2D,
                            GL10.GL_TEXTURE_MAG_FILTER,
                            GL10.GL_LINEAR_MIPMAP_NEAREST);
        } else {
                    gl.glTexParameterf(GL10.GL_TEXTURE_2D,
                            GL10.GL_TEXTURE_MIN_FILTER,
                            GL10.GL_LINEAR);
                    gl.glTexParameterf(GL10.GL_TEXTURE_2D,
                            GL10.GL_TEXTURE_MAG_FILTER,
                            GL10.GL_LINEAR);
        }

            tempImage.recycle();// 6
            return resource;
    }
```

Naturally onDrawFrame() also needs some changes as well. Add following instance variables to SquareRenderer.java:

```
float z = 0.0f;

boolean flipped=false;

float delz_value=.040f;

float delz = 0.0f;

float furthestz=-20.0f;
```

```
      static float rotAngle=0.0f;
```

Now, use Listing 5–5 in place of the current onDrawFrame(). This will causes the z value to oscillate back and forth so you can observe mipmapping in action.

**Listing 5–5.** *onDrawFrame() with Varying z Values*

```
    public void onDrawFrame(GL10 gl) {

            gl.glClear(GL11.GL_COLOR_BUFFER_BIT | GL11.GL_DEPTH_BUFFER_BIT);

            gl.glMatrixMode(GL11.GL_MODELVIEW);
            gl.glLoadIdentity();

            if(z<furthestz)
        {
                    if(!flipped)
                {
                            delz=delz_value;
                            flipped=true;
                    } else {
                            flipped=false;
                    }
            } else if(z > -.01f) {
                    if(!flipped) {
                            delz=-delz_value;
                            flipped=true;
                    } else {
                            flipped=false;
                    }
        }
            z=z+delz;

            gl.glTranslatef(0.0f, (float) (Math.sin(mTransY) / 2.0f), z);
            gl.glRotatef(rotAngle, 0, 0, 1.0f);
            rotAngle+=.5f;


            mSquare.draw(gl);

            mTransY += .15f;
    }
```

Finally, ensure that the call glColorPonter() is removed from the square's draw() method.

If that compiles and runs OK, you should see something like Figure 5–19, with the different colors popping in and out as OpenGL ES selects which one is the best for a given distance.

**Figure 5–19.** *Different images for each mipmap level pop in and out depending on the distance to the eyepoint.*

It is possible to have OpenGL generate the mipmaps for you, as illustrated in the next section.

## Filtering

An image, when used as a texture, may exhibit various artifacting depending on its content and final size when projected onto the screen. Very detailed images might be seen with an annoying shimmering effect. However, it is possible to dynamically modify an image to minimize these effects through a process called *filtering*.

Let's say you have a texture that is 128x128, but the texture face is 500 pixels on a side. What should you see? Obviously the image's original pixels, now called *texels*, are going to be much larger than any of the screen pixels. This is a process referred to as *magnification*. Conversely, you could have a case where the texels are much smaller than a pixel, and that is called *minification*. Filtering is the process used to determine how to correlate a pixel's color with the underlying texel, or texels. Tables 5–4 and 5–5 show the possible variants of this.

**Table 5–4.** *Texture Filter Types in OpenGL ES for Minification*

| Name | Purpose |
|------|---------|
| GL_LINEAR | Smooths texturing using the four nearest texels closest to the center of the pixel being textured |
| GL_LINEAR_MIPMAP_LINEAR | Similar to GL_LINEAR but uses the two nearest mipmaps closest to the rendered pixel |
| GL_LINEAR_MIPMAP_NEAREST | Similar to GL_LINEAR but uses the one nearest mipmap closest to the rendered pixel |
| GL_NEAREST | Returns the nearest texel value to the pixel being rendered |
| GL_NEAREST_MIPMAP_NEAREST | Similar to GL_NEAREST but uses the texel from the nearest mipmap |

**Table 5–5.** *Texture Filter Types in OpenGL ES for Magnification*

| Name | Purpose |
|------|---------|
| GL_LINEAR | Smooths texturing using the four nearest texels closest to the center of the pixel being textured |
| GL_NEAREST | Returns the nearest texel value to the pixel being rendered |

There are three main approaches to filtering:

- *Point sampling (called in OpenGL lingo)*: A pixel's color is based on the texel that is nearest to the pixel's center. This is the simplest, the fastest, and naturally yields the least satisfactory image.

- *Bilinear sampling, otherwise called just linear* A pixel's coloring is based on a weighted average of a 2x2 array of texels nearest to the pixel's center. This can smooth out an image considerably.

- *Trilinear sampling*: This requires mipmaps and takes the two closest mipmap levels to the final rendering on the screen, performs a bilinear selection on each, and then takes a weighted average of the two individual values.

You can see this in action by taking another look at the first exercise. To your mipmapping experiment, add the following lines to the very end of createTexture() while removing the initialization lines that created all of the previous mipmap images (except image #0, of course):

```
gl.glHint(GL11.GL_GENERATE_MIPMAP,GL10.GL_NICEST);
gl.glTexParameterf(GL10.GL_TEXTURE_2D,GL11.GL_GENERATE_MIPMAP,GL10.GL_TRUE);
```

The second call, already referenced in the previous section, will automatically create a mipmap out of your only image handed off to the renderer. And make sure that createTexture() is being called only once, because there is no need to use our own custom images for the various levels of detail. The first call to glHint() tells the system to use whatever algorithm it has to generate the nicest-looking images. You can also choose GL_FASTEST and GL_DONT_CARE. The latter will select what it thinks might be the best for this case.

In Figure 5–20, the image on the left shows a close-up of Hedly with the filtering off, while on the right, it is switched on.

**Figure 5–20.** *The left side has all filtering turned off. The right side has bilinear filtering turned on.*

## OpenGL Extensions

Even though OpenGL is a standard, it was designed with extensibility in mind, letting various hardware manufacturers add their own special sauce to the 3D soup using extension strings. In OpenGL, developers can poll for possible extensions and then use them if they exist. To get a look at this, use the following line of code:

```
String extentionList=gl.glGetString(GL10.GL_EXTENSIONS);
```

This will return a space-separated list of the various extra options in Android for OpenGL ES, looking something like this (from Android 2.3):

```
GL_OES_byte_coordinates GL_OES_fixed_point GL_OES_single_precision
GL_OES_read_format GL_OES_compressed_paletted_texture GL_OES_draw_texture
GL_OES_matrix_get GL_OES_query_matrix GL_OES_EGL_image
GL_OES_compressed_ETC1_RGB8_texture GL_ARB_texture_compression
GL_ARB_texture_non_power_of_two GL_ANDROID_user_clip_plane
GL_ANDROID_vertex_buffer_object GL_ANDROID_generate_mipmap
```

This can be helpful to find custom features that one phone might have over another. One possibility would be the use of a special image compression format called PVRTC, custom only to devices that use the PowerVR class of graphics chips. PVRTC is closely bound to the PowerVR hardware in a way that can improve both rendering and loading times. Devices such as the Samsung Galaxy S, Motorola's Droid X, the BlackBerry playbook, and the all iOS devices as of this writing can take advantage of PVRTC. Non-PowerVR devices, such as those that use the Ardreno or Tegra cores, may have their own special format as well.

You can tell whether your device supports PVRTC, should the string `GL_IMG_texture_compression_pvrtc` show up in the previous extension list. Other GPUs may have similar formats, so you would be encouraged to check in with the developer forums and SDKs if you want to go the custom route.

# Finally, More Solar System Goodness

Now we can go back to our solar-system model from the previous chapter and add a texture to the earth so that it can really look like the earth. Make the similar changes to `SolarSystemActivity.java` as we did for `BouncySquareActivity.java` earlier by modifying the setter to this:

```
view.setRenderer(new SolarSystemRenderer(this.getApplicationContext()));
```

Also modify the constructor in `SolarSystemRenderer.java` to handle the passed context.

```
import android.content.Context;

public Context myContext;
public SolarSystemRenderer(Context context)
{
    this.myContext = context;
}
```

We need to store the context in a public variable because we will be passing this to `init()` function when creating image texture. Next, examine `Planet.java`, and swap out the `init()` for Listing 5–6; the changes have been highlighted. And for the earth's texture, many examples are available. Just do a search on Google. Or you might want to check NASA first at `http://maps.jpl.nasa.gov/`.

***Listing 5–6.*** Modified Sphere Generator with Texture Support Added

```
private void init(int stacks,int slices, float radius, float squash, GL10 gl,
        Context context, boolean imageId, int resourceId)              // 1
{
        float[] vertexData;
        float[] normalData;
```

```
            float[] colorData;
            float[] textData=null;

            float colorIncrement=0f;

            float blue=0f;
            float red=1.0f;

            int vIndex=0;                            //vertex index
            int cIndex=0;                            //color index
            int nIndex=0;                            //normal index
            int tIndex=0;                            //texture index

            if(imageId == true)
            createTexture(gl, context, resourceId);                      //2

            m_Scale=radius;
            m_Squash=squash;

            colorIncrement=1.0f/(float)stacks;

            m_Stacks = stacks;
            m_Slices = slices;

             //Vertices

            vertexData = new float[ 3*((m_Slices*2+2) * m_Stacks)];

             //Color data

            colorData = new float[ (4*(m_Slices*2+2) * m_Stacks)];

             //Normal pointers for lighting

            normalData = new float[3*((m_Slices*2+2) * m_Stacks)];

                    if(imageId == true)                                  //3
                    textData = new float [2 * ((m_Slices*2+2) * (m_Stacks))];

            int      phiIdx, thetaIdx;

             //Latitude

            for(phiIdx=0; phiIdx < m_Stacks; phiIdx++)
        {
                    //Starts at -1.57 and goes up to +1.57 radians.

                    ///The first circle.

                    float phi0 = (float)Math.PI * ((float)(phiIdx+0) *
                    (1.0f/(float)(m_Stacks)) - 0.5f);

                    //The next, or second one.
```

```
    float phi1 = (float)Math.PI * ((float)(phiIdx+1) *
    (1.0f/(float)(m_Stacks)) - 0.5f);

float cosPhi0 = (float)Math.cos(phi0);
float sinPhi0 = (float)Math.sin(phi0);
float cosPhi1 = (float)Math.cos(phi1);
float sinPhi1 = (float)Math.sin(phi1);

float cosTheta, sinTheta;

//Longitude

for(thetaIdx=0; thetaIdx < m_Slices; thetaIdx++)
{

        //Increment along the longitude circle each "slice."

        float theta = (float) (2.0f*(float)Math.PI *
        ((float)thetaIdx) * (1.0/(float)(m_Slices-1)));
        cosTheta = (float)Math.cos(theta);
        sinTheta = (float)Math.sin(theta);

        //We're generating a vertical pair of points, such
        //as the first point of stack 0 and the first point of
        //stack 1 above it. This is how TRIANGLE_STRIPS work,
        //taking a set of 4 vertices and essentially drawing two
        //triangles at a time. The first is v0-v1-v2, and the next
        //is v2-v1-v3, etc.

        //Get x-y-z for the first vertex of stack.

        vertexData[vIndex]   = m_Scale*cosPhi0*cosTheta;
        vertexData[vIndex+1] = m_Scale*(sinPhi0*m_Squash);
        vertexData[vIndex+2] = m_Scale*(cosPhi0*sinTheta);

        vertexData[vIndex+3]  = m_Scale*cosPhi1*cosTheta;
        vertexData[vIndex+4] = m_Scale*(sinPhi1*m_Squash);
        vertexData[vIndex+5] = m_Scale*(cosPhi1*sinTheta);

        //Normal pointers for lighting

        normalData[nIndex+0] = (float)(cosPhi0 * cosTheta);
        normalData[nIndex+2] = cosPhi0 * sinTheta;
        normalData[nIndex+1] = sinPhi0;

        //Get x-y-z for the first vertex of stack N.

        normalData[nIndex+3] = cosPhi1 * cosTheta;
        normalData[nIndex+5] = cosPhi1 * sinTheta;
        normalData[nIndex+4] = sinPhi1;

        if(textData != null)                                //4
```

```
                {
                    float texX = (float)thetaIdx *
                (1.0f/(float)(m_Slices-1));
                    textData [tIndex + 0] = texX;
                    textData [tIndex + 1] = (float)(phiIdx+0) *
                (1.0f/(float)(m_Stacks));
                    textData [tIndex + 2] = texX;
                    textData [tIndex + 3] = (float)(phiIdx+1) *
                (1.0f/(float)(m_Stacks));
                }

            colorData[cIndex+0] = (float)red;
            colorData[cIndex+1] = (float)Of;
            colorData[cIndex+2] = (float)blue;
            colorData[cIndex+4] = (float)red;
            colorData[cIndex+5] = (float)Of;
            colorData[cIndex+6] = (float)blue;
            colorData[cIndex+3] = (float)1.0;
            colorData[cIndex+7] = (float)1.0;

            cIndex+=2*4;
            vIndex+=2*3;
            nIndex+=2*3;

            if(textData!=null)                                          //5
            tIndex+= 2*2;

            blue+=colorIncrement;
            red-=colorIncrement;

            //Degenerate triangle to connect stacks and maintain
            //winding order.

            vertexData[vIndex+0] = vertexData[vIndex+3] =
            vertexData[vIndex-3];
            vertexData[vIndex+1] = vertexData[vIndex+4] =
            vertexData[vIndex-2];
            vertexData[vIndex+2] = vertexData[vIndex+5] =
            vertexData[vIndex-1];

            normalData[nIndex+0] = normalData[nIndex+3] =
            normalData[nIndex-3];
            normalData[nIndex+1] = normalData[nIndex+4] =
            normalData[nIndex-2];
            normalData[nIndex+2] = normalData[nIndex+5] =
            normalData[nIndex-1];

        if(textData!= null)                                             //6
    {
    textData [tIndex + 0] = textData [tIndex + 2] =
        textData [tIndex -2];
    textData [tIndex + 1] = textData [tIndex + 3] =
        textData [tIndex -1];
```

```
                    }
                }
            }

            m_Pos[0]= 0.0f;
            m_Pos[1]= 0.0f;
            m_Pos[2]= 0.0f;

            m_VertexData = makeFloatBuffer(vertexData);
            m_NormalData = makeFloatBuffer(normalData);
            m_ColorData = makeFloatBuffer(colorData);

            if(textData!= null)
                m_TextureData = makeFloatBuffer(textData);
    }
```

So, here is what's happening:

- A GL object, context, image ID, and resource ID for the image are added to the end of the parameter list in line 1.

- In line 2, the texture is created.

- In lines 3ff, the coordinate array for the texture is allocated.

- Next, calculate the texture coordinates in lines 4ff. Since the sphere has x slices and y stacks and the coordinate space goes only from 0 to 1, we need to advance each value by increments of 1/m_slices for *s* and 1/m_stacks for *t*. Notice that this covers two pairs of coordinates, one above the other, matching the layout of the triangle-strips that also produces stacked pairs of coordinates.

- In line 5, advance the coordinate array to hold the next set of values.

- And finally, some loose threads are tied together in preparation for going to the next stack up in line 6.

Make sure to add the following to the instance data:

```
    FloatBuffer m_TextureData;
```

Copy over the createTexture() method from the first example to Planet.java, and make the changes as needed. Feel free to remove the mipmap support if you like, but there's no harm in leaving it in, It's just not essential for this exercise. Make sure that glTexParameterf() has GL10.GL_LINEAR as the params.

For an earth texture, note that this will wrap around the *entire* sphere model, so not just any image will do, and as such it should resemble Figure 5–21.

**Figure 5–21.** *Textures typically fill out the entire frame, edge to edge. Planets use a Mercator projection (a cylindrical map).*

Once you've found a suitable .png, add it to your project under /res/drawable-nodpi/, and hand it off to the planet object when allocated. Since you don't need a texture for the sun, you can just pass a 0 as resource ID. So we can set false as imageId for sun's planet object but true for the earth. Next we modify the planet's constructor to look like Listing 5–7.

**Listing 5–7.** *Adding Several New Parameters for Planet.java*

```
public Planet(int stacks, int slices, float radius, float squash, GL10 gl, Context
context, boolean imageId, int resourceId)
    {
    this.m_Stacks = stacks;
    this.m_Slices = slices;
    this.m_Radius = radius;
    this.m_Squash = squash;
    init(m_Stacks,m_Slices,radius,squash, gl, context, imageId, resourceId);
    }
```

Naturally, initGeometry() needs to be changed to support the extra parameters, as shown in Listing 5–8.

**Listing 5–8.** *initGeometry() Passes New Parameters to Planet.java*

```
private void initGeometry(GL10 gl) {
        int resid;
m_Eyeposition[X_VALUE] = 0.0f;
m_Eyeposition[Y_VALUE] = 0.0f;
m_Eyeposition[Z_VALUE] = 10.0f;

resid =  com.SolarSystem.R.drawable.earth_light;
m_Earth = new Planet(50, 50, .3f, 1.0f, gl, myContext, true, resid);
m_Earth.setPosition(0.0f, 0.0f, -2.0f);
```

```
m_Sun = new Planet(50, 50, 1.0f, 1.0f, gl, myContext, false, 0);
m_Sun.setPosition(0.0f, 0.0f, 0.0f);
}
```

And of course we'll need to update the `draw()` method in `Planet.java`, as shown in Listing 5–9.

**Listing 5–9.** *Ready to Handle the New Texture*

```java
    public void draw(GL10 gl)
    {
        gl.glMatrixMode(GL10.GL_MODELVIEW);
        gl.glEnable(GL10.GL_CULL_FACE);
        gl.glCullFace(GL10.GL_BACK);

        gl.glEnableClientState(GL10.GL_VERTEX_ARRAY);
        gl.glEnableClientState(GL10.GL_NORMAL_ARRAY);
        gl.glEnableClientState(GL10.GL_COLOR_ARRAY);

      if(m_TextureData != null)
    {
        gl.glEnable(GL10.GL_TEXTURE_2D);                      //1
        gl.glEnableClientState(GL10.GL_TEXTURE_COORD_ARRAY);
        gl.glBindTexture(GL10.GL_TEXTURE_2D, textures[0]);
        gl.glTexCoordPointer(2, GL10.GL_FLOAT, 0, m_TextureData);
    }

        gl.glMatrixMode(GL10.GL_MODELVIEW);
        gl.glVertexPointer(3, GL10.GL_FLOAT, 0, m_VertexData);
        gl.glNormalPointer(GL10.GL_FLOAT, 0, m_NormalData);
        gl.glColorPointer(4, GL10.GL_FLOAT, 0, m_ColorData);
        gl.glDrawArrays(GL10.GL_TRIANGLE_STRIP, 0, (m_Slices+1)*2*(m_Stacks-1)+2);

        gl.glDisable(GL10.GL_BLEND);
        gl.glDisable(GL10.GL_TEXTURE_2D);
        gl.glDisableClientState(GL10.GL_TEXTURE_COORD_ARRAY);


    }
```

In lines 1ff, you'll recognize the same calls from the example with the square. First enable texture support, then call a `glBindTexture()` to ensure the current texture is made available, then alert the system to expect an array of texture coordinates, and then hand it the data.

Compile and run, and ideally you'll see something like Figure 5–22.

**NOTE:** It is not uncommon to come across emulator bugs in the Android environment (such as when this example was being prepared). If you see something that you didn't expect and it defies any logical explanation, then try running the code on hardware and see what happens.

**Figure 5–22.** *Sun and the Earth*

# Summary

This chapter served as a basic introduction to textures and their uses. The following topics were covered: basic texture theory, how texture coordinates are expressed, mipmaps for greater fidelity, and how textures may be filtered to smooth them out. The solar-system model was updated so that the earth now really looks like the earth using a texture map. Table 5–7 summarizes all of the new API calls covered. In the next chapter, we'll continue with textures, putting to use the Android's multiple texture units, along with blending techniques.

# Chapter 6

# Will It Blend?

*Yes! It blends!*

—Tom Dickson, owner of the Blendtec blender company

In 2006, Tom Dickson posted a goofy video to YouTube illustrating how tough his company's blenders were by blending some marbles into powder. Since then his frequent videos have been viewed more than 100 million times and have featured blendings of everything from a Tiki torch and a laser pointer to a Justin Bieber doll and a new camcorder. Tom's kind of blending has nothing to do with our kind of blending, though, unless the sadistic and unmerciful pulverization of a couple of Android touchpad and phones count. After all, they are OpenGL ES devices: devices that have their own form of blending, albeit not nearly as destructive. (Yes, it's a stretch.)

Blending plays an important role in OpenGL ES applications. It is the process used to create translucent objects that can be used for something as simple as a window to something as complicated as a pond. Other uses include the addition of atmospherics such as fog or smoke, the smoothing out of aliased lines, and the simulation of various sophisticated lighting effects. OpenGL ES 2.0 has a complex mechanism that uses small modules called *shaders* to do specialized blending effects, among other things. But before shaders, there were blending functions, which are not nearly as versatile but considerably easier to use.

In this chapter, you'll learn the basics of blending functions and how to apply them for both color and alpha blending. After that, you'll use a different kind of blending involving multiple textures, used for far more sophisticated effects such as shadowing. Finally, I'll figure out how we can apply these effects in the solar-system project.

# Alpha Blending

You have no doubt noticed the color quadruplet of "RGBA." As mentioned earlier, the *A* part is the *alpha channel*, and it is traditionally used for specifying translucency in an image. In a bitmap used for texturing, the alpha layer forms an 8-bit image of sorts, which can be translucent in one section, transparent in another, and completely opaque in a third. If an object isn't using texturing but instead has its color specified via its vertices, lighting, or overall global coloring, alpha will let the entire object or scene have translucent properties. A value of 1.0 means the object or pixel is completely opaque, while 0 means it is completely invisible.

For alpha to work as with any blending model, you work with both a source and a destination image. Because this topic is best understood through examples, we're going to start with the first one now.

Grab your Chapter 1 exercise, and then use Listing 6–1 in place of the original methods. Solid squares of colors are used here first instead of textured ones, because it makes for a simpler example.

**Listing 6–1.** *The New and Improved* onDrawFrame() *Method*

```
    public void onDrawFrame(GL10 gl)
{
        gl.glClearColor(0.0f,0.0f,0.0f,1.0f);                                    //1
        gl.glClear(GL11.GL_COLOR_BUFFER_BIT | GL11.GL_DEPTH_BUFFER_BIT);

        gl.glMatrixMode(GL11.GL_MODELVIEW);
        gl.glEnableClientState(GL11.GL_VERTEX_ARRAY);

        //SQUARE 1

        gl.glLoadIdentity();
        gl.glTranslatef(0.0f,(float)Math.sin(mTransY), -3.0f);                   //2
        gl.glColor4f(0.0f, 0.0f, 1.0f, 1.0f);
        mSquare.draw(gl);

        //SQUARE 2

        gl.glLoadIdentity();                                                     //3
        gl.glTranslatef( (float)(Math.sin(mTransY)/2.0f),0.0f, -2.9f);
        gl.glColor4f(1.0f, 0.0f, 0.0f, 1.0f);
        mSquare.draw(gl);

        mTransY += .075f;
    }
```

And as before, let's take a close look at the code:

- ▓ In lines 1ff, the buffer is cleared to black, making it easier to see any blending later.

- ▓ In lines 2ff we can draw one square that is moved up and down and then back by 3 units, while given a blue color. Because there is no coloring-per-vertex, this call to glColor4f() will set the entire square to blue. However, notice the last component of 1.0. That is the *alpha*, and it will be addressed shortly. And immediately following gl.glColor4f() is the call to actually draw the square.

- ▓ Lines 3ff address the second square, coloring it red and moving it left and right. Moving it away by 2.9 instead of 3.0 units ensures that the red square will be in front of the blue one.

If all works, you should have something that looks like Figure 6–1.

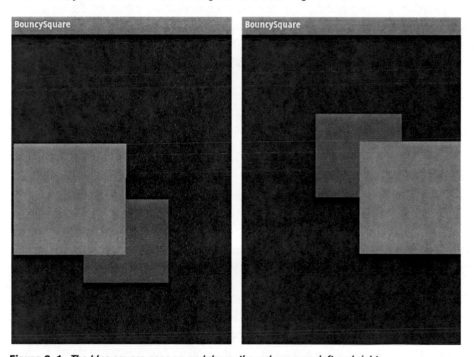

**Figure 6–1.** *The blue square goes up and down; the red one goes left and right.*

It's not much to look at, but this will be the framework for the next several experiments. The first will switch on the default blending function.

As with so many other OpenGL features, turn blending on with the call gl.glEnable(GL10.GL_BLEND). Add that anywhere before the first call to mSquare.draw(). Recompile, and what do you see? Nothing, or at least nothing has changed. It still looks like Figure 6–1. That's because there's more to blending than saying "Blend, you!" We must specify a blending *function* as well, which describes how the source colors (as expressed via its fragments, or pixels) mix with those at the destination. The default, of course, is when the source fragments always replace those at the destination, when depth cueing is off. As a matter of fact, proper blending can be assured only when z-buffering is switched off.

# Blending Functions

To change the default blending, we must resort to using `glBlendFunc()`, which comes with two parameters. The first tells just what to do with the source, and the second, the destination. To picture what goes on, note that all that ultimately happens is that each of the RGBA source components is added, subtracted, or whatever, with each of the destination components. That is, the source's red channel is mixed with the destination's red channel, the source's green with the destination's green, and so on. This is usually expressed the following way: call the source RGBA values *Rs, Gs, Bs,* and *As,* and call the destination values *Rd, Gd, Bd,* and *Ad*. But we also need both source and destination *blending factors,* expressed as *Sr, Sg, Sb, Sa*, and *Dr, Dg, Db,* and *Da*. (It's not as complicated as it seems, really). And here's the formula for the final composite color:

$$(R,G,B) = ((Rs*Sr)+(Rd*Dr),(Gs*Sg)+(Gd*Dg),(Bs*Sb)+(Bd*Db))$$

In other words, multiply the source color by its blending factor and add it to the destination color multiplied by its blending factor.

One of the most common forms of blending is to overlay a translucent face on top of stuff that has already been drawn—that is, the destination. As before, that can be a simulated windowpane, a heads-up display for a flight simulator, or other graphics that just might look nicer when mixed with the existing imagery. (The latter is used a lot in Distant Suns for a number of the elements such as the constellation names, the outlines, and so on.) Depending on the purpose, you may want the overlay to be nearly opaque, using an alpha approaching 1.0, or very tenuous, with an alpha approaching 0.0.

In this basic blending task, the source's colors are first multiplied by the alpha value, its blending factor. So, if the source red is maxed out at 1.0 and the alpha is 0.75, the result is derived by simply multiplying 1.0 by 0.75. The same would be used for both green and blue. On the other hand, the destination colors are multiplied by *1.0 minus the source's alpha*. Why? That effectively yields a composite color that can never exceed the maximum value of 1.0; otherwise, all sorts of color distortion could happen. Or imagine it this way: the source's alpha value is the proportion of the color "width" of 1.0 that the source is permitted to fill. The leftover space then becomes 1.0 minus the source's alpha. The larger the alpha, the greater the proportion of the source color that can be used, with an increasingly smaller proportion reserved for the destination color. So, as the alpha approaches 1.0, the greater the amount of the source color is copied to the frame buffer, replacing the destination color.

> **NOTE:** In these examples, normalized color values are used because they make it much easier to follow the process instead of using unsigned bytes, which would express the colors from 0 to 255.

Now we can examine that in the next example. To set up the blending functions described earlier, you would use the following call:

gl.glBlendFunc(GL10.*GL_SRC_ALPHA*, GL10.*GL_ONE_MINUS_SRC_ALPHA*);

The GL_SRC_ALPHA and GL_ONE_MINUS_SRC_ALPHA are the blending factors described earlier. And remember that the first parameter is the source's blending, the object being written at present. Place that line immediately after where you enable blending. And to the red colors, compile and run. Do you see Figure 6–2?

**Figure 6–2.** *The red square has an alpha of .5, the blue, 1.0.*

So, what's happening? The blue has an alpha of 1.0, so each blue fragment completely replaces anything in the background. Then the red with an alpha of .5 means that 50 percent of the red is written to the destination. The black area will be a dim red, but only 50 percent of the specified value of 1.0 given in glColor4f(). So far, so good. Now on top of the blue, 50 percent of the red value is mixing with a 50 percent blue value:

Blended color=Color Source*Alpha of source + (1.0-Alpha of Source)*Color of the destination. Or looking at each component based on the values in the previous example:

Red=1.0*0.5+(1.0-0.5)*0.0

Green=0.0*0.5+(1.0-0.5)*0.0

Blue=0.0*0.5+(1.0-0.5)*1.0

So, the final color of the fragment's pixels should be 0.5,0.0,0.5, or magenta. Now the red and resulting magenta are a little on the dim side. What would you do if you wanted to make this much brighter? It would be nice if there were a means of blending the full intensities of the colors. Would you use alpha values of 1.0? Nope. Why? Well, with blue as the destination and a source alpha of 1.0, the earlier blue channel equation would be 0.0*1.0+(1.0-1.0)*1.0. And that equals 0, while the red would be 1.0, or solid. What you would want is to have the brightest red when writing to the black background, and the same for the blue. For that you would use a blending function that writes both colors at full intensity, such as GL_ONE. That means the following:

```
gl.glBlendFunc(GL10.GL_ONE, GL10.GL_ONE);
```

Going back to the equations using the source triplet of red=*1, green=0, blue=0*, and destination of red=*0, green=0, blue=1* (with alpha defaulting to 1.0), the calculations would be as follows:

Red=1*1+0*1

Green=0* (1+(0-0)*1

Blue=0*1+(1-0)*1

And that yields a color in which red=1, green=0, and blue=1. And that my friends, is magenta (see Figure 6–3).

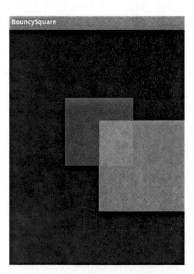

**Figure 6–3.** *Blending full intensities of red and blue*

Now it's time for another experiment of sorts. Take the code from the previous example, set both alphas to 0.5, and reset the blend function to the traditional values for transparency:

```
gl.glBlendFunc(GL10.GL_SRC_ALPHA, GL10.GL_ONE_MINUS_SRC_ALPHA);
```

After you run this modified code, take note of the combined color, and notice that the further square is blue at -4.0 away and is also the first to be rendered, with the red one as the second. Now reverse the order of the colors that are drawn, and run. What's wrong? You should get something like Figure 6–4.

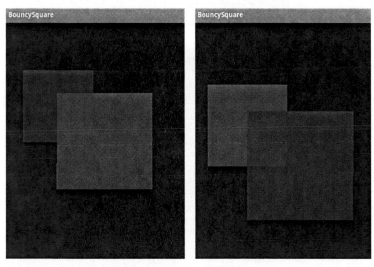

**Figure 6–4.** *The left is drawn with blue first, while the one on the right, red first.*

The intersections are slightly different colors. This shows one of the mystifying gotchas in OpenGL: as with most any 3D framework, the blending will be slightly different depending on the order of the faces and colors when rendered. In this case, it is actually quite simple to figure out what's going on. In the image on the left in Figure 6–4, the blue square is drawn first with an alpha of .5. So, even though the blue color triplet is defined as 0,0,1, the alpha value will knock that down to 0,0,.5 as it is written to the frame buffer. Now add the red square with similar properties. Naturally the red will write to the black part of the frame buffer in the same manner as the blue, so the final value will be .5,0,0. But note what happens when red writes on top of the blue. Since the blue is already at half of its intensity, the blending function will cut that down even further, to .25, as a result of the destination part of the blending function, *(1.0-Source alpha)\*blue+destination*, or (1.0-.5).5+0, or .25. The final color is then *.5,0,.25.* With the lower intensity of the blue, it contributes less to the composite color, leaving red to dominate. Now in the image on the right in Figure 6–4, the order is reversed, so the blue dominates with a final color of .25,0,.5.

Table 6–1 has all of the allowable OpenGL ES blending factors, although not all are supported by both source and destination. As you can see, there is ample room for tinkering, with no set rules of what creates the best-looking effect. This will be highly reliant on your individual tastes and needs. It is a lot of fun to try different values, though. Make sure to fill the background with a dim gray, because some of the combinations will just yield black when written to a black background.

**Table 6–1.** *The Source and Destination Blending Values; Note That Not All Are Available to Both Channels*

| Blend Factor | Description |
| --- | --- |
| GL_ZERO | Multiplies the operand by 0. |
| GL_ONE | Multiplies the operand by 1. |
| GL_SRC_COLOR | Multiplies the operand by the four components of the source color (destination only). |
| GL_ONE_MINUS_SRC_COLOR | Multiplies the operand by (1.0 - source colors) (destination only). |
| GL_DST_COLOR | Multiplies the operand by the four components of the destination color (source only). |
| GL_ONE_MINUS_DST_COLOR | Multiplies the operand by the 1.0 – destination colors (source only). |
| GL_SRC_ALPHA | Multiplies the operand by the source alpha. |
| GL_ONE_MINUS_SRC_ALPHA | Multiplies the operand by (1.0 - source alpha). |
| GL_DST_ALPHA | Multiplies the operand by the destination alpha. |
| GL_ONE_MINUS_DST_ALPHA | Multiplies the operand by (1.0-destination alpha). |
| GL_SRC_ALPHA_SATURATE | Special mode for older graphics implementations to help anti-aliasing. You'll likely never use it. (Source only.) |

And one final method here that might be really handy in some blending operations is that of glColorMask(). This function lets you block one or more color channels from being written to the destination. To see this in action, modify the red square's colors to be 1,1,0,1; set the two blend functions back to GL_ONE; and comment out the line gl.glBlendEquation(GL10.GL_FUNC_SUBTRACT);. You should see something like the image on the left in Figure 6–5 when run. The red square is now yellow and, when blended with blue, yields white at the intersection. Now add the following line:

```
gl.glColorMask(true, false, true, true);
```

The preceding line *masks*, or turns off, the green channel when being drawn to the frame buffer. When run, you should see image on the right in Figure 6–5, which looks remarkably like Figure 6–3. And as a matter of fact, logically they are identical.

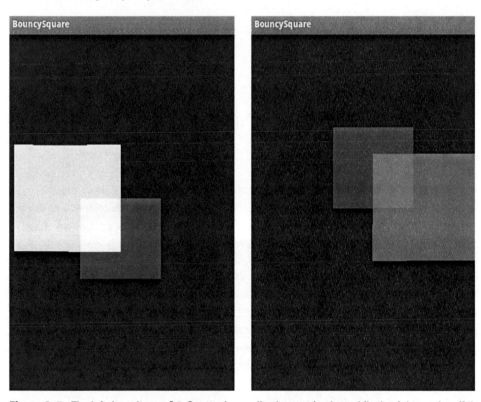

**Figure 6–5.** *The left doesn't use* glColorMask, *so all colors are in play, while the right masks off the green channel.*

# Multicolor Blending

Now we can spend a few minutes looking at the effect of blending functions when the squares are defined with individual colors for each vertex. Add in Listing 6–2 to the constructor for the square. The first color set defines yellow, magenta, and cyan. The complementary colors to the standard red-green-blue are specified in the second set.

**Listing 6–2.** *Vertex Colors for the Two Squares*

```
    float squareColorsYMCA[] =
{
            1.0f, 1.0f, 0.0f, 1.0f,
            0.0f, 1.0f, 1.0f, 1.0f,
            0.0f, 0.0f, 0.0f, 1.0f,
            1.0f, 0.0f, 1.0f, 1.0f
};

    float squareColorsRGBA[] =

{
            1.0f, 0.0f, 0.0f, 1.0f,
            0.0f, 1.0f, 0.0f, 1.0f,
            0.0f, 0.0f, 1.0f, 1.0f,
            1.0f, 1.0f, 1.0f, 1.0f
};
```

Assign the first color array to the first square (which has been the blue one up until now) and the second to the former red square. I do this in `SquareRenderer.java` and pass the color arrays in via the square's constructor. Of course, now we need two squares, one for each color set instead of just the one. And don't forget to enable the use of the color array.

You should be familiar enough now to know what to do. Also, notice that the arrays are now normalized as a bunch of floats as opposed to the previously used unsigned bytes, so you'll have to tweak the calls to `glColorPointer()`. The solution is left up to the student (I always wanted to say that). With the blending disabled, you should see the leftmost image in Figure 6–6, and when enabled using the traditional function for transparency, the middle image in Figure 6–6 should be the result. What? It isn't? You say it still looks like the first figure? Why would that be?

Look back at the color arrays. Notice how the last value in each row, alpha, is at its maximum. Remember that with this blending mode, anything of the destination values are multiplied by (1.0 – source alpha), or rather, 0.0, so that the source color reigns supreme as shown in a previous example. One solution to seeing some real transparency would be to use the following:

```
        gl.glBlendFunc(GL10.GL_ONE, GL10.GL_ONE);
```

This works because it ditches the alpha channel altogether. If you want alpha with the "standard" function, merely change the 1.0 values to something else, such as .5, and change the blend function to the following:

```
gl.glBlendFunc(GL10.GL_SRC_ALPHA, GL10.GL_ONE_MINUS_SRC_ALPHA);
```

And the result is the rightmost image in Figure 6–6.

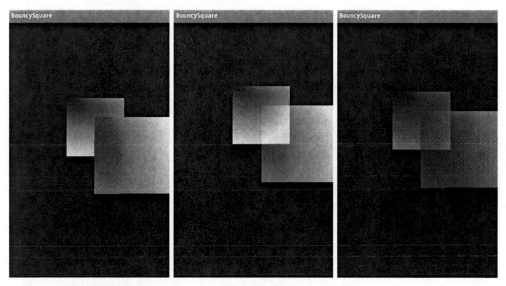

**Figure 6–6.** *No blending, GL_ONE blending, and alpha blending, respectively*

# Texture Blending

Now, with fear and trembling, we can approach the blending of textures. Initially this seems much like the alpha blending described earlier, but all sorts of interesting things can be done by using multitexturing.

First let's rework the previous code to support two textures at once and do vertex blending. You'll have to modify Square.draw() and in createImage() from the Chapter 5 examples. The square will also need to support texture coordinates as well, and each instance of the square will need their own unique texture. The rightmost image in Figure 6–7 is what you should get if you disable blending. The center one can be generated if you activate the colors from the previous exercise and enable blending using the GL_ONE functions from earlier in this chapter.

So, how was the right image generated?

Using a single bitmap and colorizing it is a common practice to save memory. If you are doing some UI components in the OpenGL layer, consider using a single image, and colorize it using these techniques. You might ask why is it a solid red as opposed to merely being tinted red, allowing for some variation in colors. What is happening here is that the vertex's colors are being multiplied by the colors of each fragment. For the red, I've used the RGB triplet of 1.0,0.0,0.0. So when each fragment is being calculated in a channel-wise multiplication, the green and blue channels are going to be multiplied by 0, so they are completely filtered out, leaving just the red. If you wanted to let some of the other colors leak through, you would specify the vertices to lean toward a more neutral tone, with the desired tint color being a little higher than the others, such as 1.0, 0.7,0.7.

**Figure 6–7**. *On the left, only the textures are displayed. In the center, they're blended with color, and in the one on the right, solid red.*

You can also add translucency to textures quite easily, Figure 6–8. To enable this, I'll introduce a small simplifying factor here. You can colorize the textured face by one single color by simply using glColor4f() and eliminate the need to create the vertex color array altogether. So, for the second square, the closest one, color it using glColor4f(1, 1, 1, .75), and make sure to reset the coloring for the first square; otherwise, it will darken with the second one. Also, ensure that blending is turned on and that the blending function uses the SRC_ALPHA/ONE_MINUS_SRC_ALPHA combination.

**Figure 6–8.** *The image on the left has an alpha of .5, while on the right, .75.*

# Multitexturing

So now we've covered blending for colors and mixed mode with textures and colors, but what about two textures together to make a third? Such a technique is called *multitexturing*. Multitexturing can be used for layering one texture on top of another while performing certain mathematical operations. More sophisticated applications include simple image processing. But let's go for the low-hanging fruit first.

Multitexturing requires the use of *texture combiners* and *texture units*. *Texture combiners* let you combine and manipulate textures that are bound to one of the hardware's texture units, the specific part of the graphics chip that wraps an image around an object. If you anticipate using combiners in a big way, you might want to verify the supported total by
`gl.glGetIntegerv(GL10.GL_MAX_COMBINED_TEXTURE_IMAGE_UNITS, numberTextureUnits)`, where `numberTextureUnits` is defined as a int.

To set up a pipeline to handle multitexturing, we need to tell OpenGL what textures to use and how to mix them together. The process isn't that much different (in theory at least) than defining the blend functions when dealing with the alpha and color blending operations previously. It does involve heavy use of the `glTexEnvf()` call, another one of OpenGL's wildly overloaded methods. (If you don't believe me, check out its official reference page on the OpenGL site.) This sets up the *texture environment* that defines each stage of the multitexturing process.

Figure 6–9 illustrates the combiner chain. Each combiner refers to the *previous* texture fragment (P0 or Pn) or the incoming fragment for the first combiner. It then takes a fragment from a "source" texture (S0 in the figure), combines it with P0, and hands it off to the next combiner if needed, C1, and the cycle repeats.

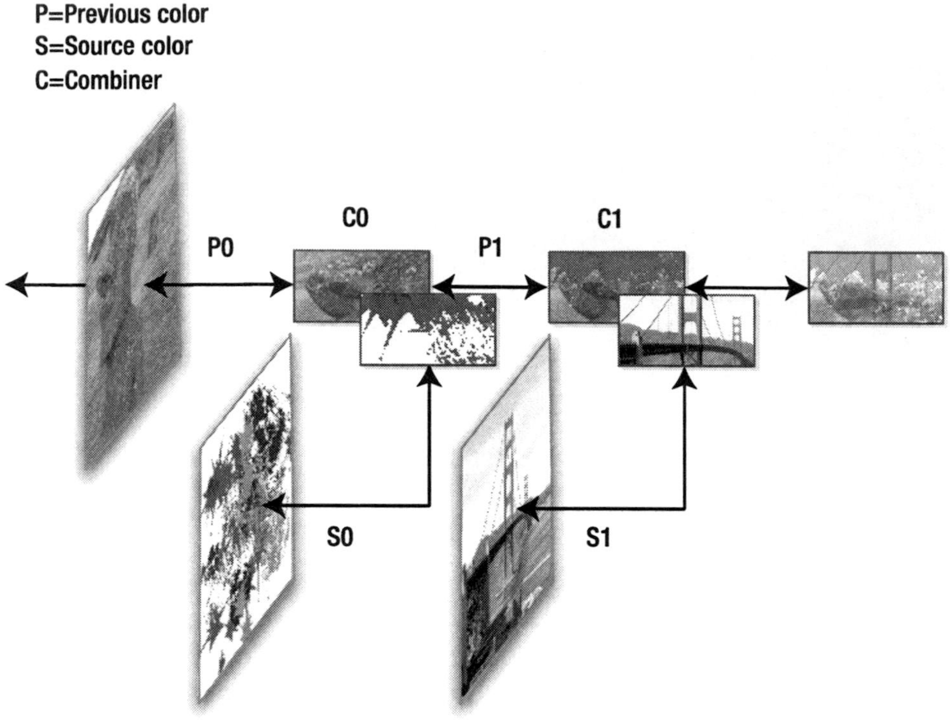

P=Previous color
S=Source color
C=Combiner

**Figure 6–9.** *The texture combiner chain*

The best way to tackle this topic is like any others: go to the code. In the following example, two textures are loaded together, bound to their respective texture units, and merged into a single output texture. Several different kinds of methods used to combine the two images are tried with the results of each shown and examined in depth.

First off, we revisit our old friend Square.draw(). We're back to only a single texture, going up and down. The color support has also been turned off. So, you should have something like Listing 6–3. And make sure you are still loading a second texture.

**Listing 6–3.** *Square.draw() Revisited, Modified for Multitexture Support*

```
    public void draw(GL10 gl)
{

        gl.glEnable(GL10.GL_TEXTURE_2D);
        gl.glBindTexture(GL10.GL_TEXTURE_2D,mTexture0);
        gl.glEnableClientState(GL10.GL_TEXTURE_COORD_ARRAY);
```

```
      gl.glFrontFace(GL11.GL_CW);
      gl.glVertexPointer(2, GL11.GL_FLOAT, 0, mFVertexBuffer);
      gl.glColorPointer(4, GL11.GL_FLOAT, 0, mColorBuffer);

      gl.glClientActiveTexture(GL10.GL_TEXTURE0);                          //1
      gl.glTexCoordPointer(2, GL10.GL_FLOAT,0,mTextureCoords);

      gl.glClientActiveTexture(GL10.GL_TEXTURE1);                          //2
      gl.glTexCoordPointer(2, GL10.GL_FLOAT,0,mTextureCoords);

      multiTexture(gl,mTexture0,mTexture1);                               //3

      gl.glDrawElements(GL11.GL_TRIANGLES, 6, GL11.GL_UNSIGNED_BYTE, mIndexBuffer);
      gl.glFrontFace(GL11.GL_CCW);
}
```

There is a new call here, shown in lines 1 and 2. It's glClientActiveTexture(), which sets what texture unit to operate on. This is on the client side, not the hardware side of things, and indicates which texture unit is to receive the texture coordinate array. Don't get this confused with glActiveTexture(), used in Listing 6–4, that actually turns a specific texture unit on. Line 3 is the call to the method that configures the texture units.

This is a very simple default case. The fancy stuff comes later.

**Listing 6–4.** *Setting Up the Texture Combiners*

```
      public void multiTexture(GL10 gl, int tex0, int tex1)
{
              float combineParameter= GL10.GL_MODULATE;                   //1

              // Set up the First Texture.
              gl.glActiveTexture(GL10.GL_TEXTURE0);                        //2
              gl.glBindTexture(GL10.GL_TEXTURE_2D, tex0);                  //3

              // Set up the Second Texture.
              gl.glActiveTexture(GL10.GL_TEXTURE1);
              gl.glBindTexture(GL10.GL_TEXTURE_2D, tex1);

              // Set the texture environment mode for this texture to combine.
              gl.glTexEnvf(GL10.GL_TEXTURE_ENV, GL10.GL_TEXTURE_ENV_MODE,
                  combineParameter);                                      //4
}
```

- Line 1 specifies what the combiners should do. Table 6–1 lists all the possible values available.

- glActiveTexture() in line 2makes active a specific hardware texture unit.

▨ Line 3 should not be a mystery, because you have seen it before. In this example, the first texture is bound a specific hardware texture unit. The following two lines do the same for the second texture.

▨ Now tell the system what to do with the textures in the final line. In the table, P is previous, S is source, subscript a is alpha, and c is color and is used only when color and alpha have to be considered separately.

**Table 6-2.** *Possible Values for* `GL_TEXTURE_ENV_MODE`

| Texture Mode | Function |
|---|---|
| `GL_ADD` | $P_n + S_n$ (component-wise addition of the RGBA values from the two texture fragments, $S$ being source, $P$ being the previous) |
| `GL_BLEND` | $P_n(1 - S_n) + S_n \times C$ (C is constant color set by `GL_TEXTURE_ENV_COLOR`) |
| `GL_COMBINE` | See the discussion after the table |
| `GL_DECAL` | $P_n \times (1 - S_{an}) + (S_{cn} \times S_{an})$ |
| `GL_MODULATE` | $P_n \times S_n$ |
| `GL_REPLACE` | Output color $= S_n$ |

Now compile and run. Your display should superficially resemble the results of Figure 6–10.

**Figure 6–10.** *Hedly is the "previous" texture on the left, while the Jackson Pollack-ish painting is the "source." When using* `GL_MODULATE`, *the results are on the right.*

Now it's time to play with other combiner settings. Try GL_ADD for the combineParameter in Listing 63 replacing GL_MODULATE. Then follow this by GL_BLEND and GL_DECAL. The results are shown in Figure 6–11. For addition, notice how the white part of the overlay texture is opaque. Because white is 1.0 for all three colors, it will always yield a 1.0 color so as to block out anything underneath. For the nonwhite shades, you should see a little of the Hedly texture poke through. GL_BLEND, in the middle image of Figure 6–11 is not quite as obvious. Why cyan splats in place of the red? Simple. Say the red value is 1.0, its highest. Consider the equation for GL_BLEND:

$$\text{Output} = P_n(1 - S_n) + S_n \times C$$

The first section would be zero for red, since red's value of 1 is subtracted by the one in the equation, and by gosh, the second one would be too, providing that the default environment color of black is used. Consider the green channel. Assume that the background image has a value of .5 for green, the "previous" color, while keeping the splat color (the source) of solid red (so no blue or green in the splat). Now the first section of the equation becomes .5*(1.0-0.0), or .5. That is, the .5 value for green in the *previous* texture, Hedly, is multiplied against "1-minus-green" in the source texture. Since both the green and blue channels in the source's red splats would be 0.0, this means that the combination of green and blue without any red gives a cyan shading because cyan is the inverse of red. And if you look really close at the middle image in Figure 6–11, you can just make out a piece of Hedly poking through. The same holds true for the magenta and yellow splats. In the rightmost image in Figure 6–11, GL_DECAL is used and can serve many of the same duties that decals for plastic models had, namely, the application of signs or symbols that would block out anything behind it. So for decals, typically the alpha channel would be set to 1.0 for the actual image part of the texture, while it would be 0.0 for any part that was not of the desired image. Typically the background would be black, and on your paint program you would have it generate an alpha channel based on luminosity or for the part of the image that has a nonzero color. In the case of the splat, because the background was white, I had to invert the colors first to turn it black, generate the mask, and merge it with the normal positive image. Some alpha that is slightly less than 1 was generated for the green channel, and as a result, you can see a little part of Hedly showing through.

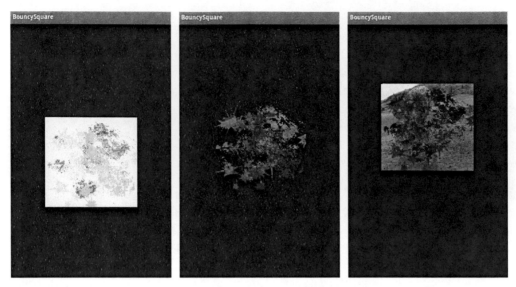

**Figure 6–11.** *On the left* GL_ADD *was used,* GL_BLEND *for the center, and* GL_DECAL *on the right*

One final task would be to animate the second texture. You will need create a duplicate set of textureCoordinates, mTextureCoods0, and mTextureCoords1, one for each texture, as we can no longer share them. Next expose the "raw" coordinates used to generate the Java byte buffers in the constructor. That way, we can modify them in the Square.draw() method. Then add the following to draw() to update only the coordinates for the decal texture:

```
    for(i=0;i<8;i++)
{
        mTextureCoordsAnimated[i]+=.01;
}

        mTextureCoords1.position(0);
      mTextureCoords1.put(mTextureCoordsAnimated);
```

mTextureCoords1.position() is called to reset the buffer's internal pointer. Otherwise, the following call to put() will append the data the next time through and overrun the buffers.

An effect like this could be used to animate rain or snow in a cartoon-like setting or a cloud layer surrounding a planet. The latter would be cool if you had two additional textures one for the upper deck of clouds and one for the lower, moving at different rates.

As mentioned earlier, the environment parameter GL_COMBINE needs an additional family of settings to get working, because it lets you operate on a much more precise level with the combiner equations. If you were to do nothing more than just use GL_COMBINE, it defaults to GL_MODULATE, so you'd see no difference between the two. The use of Arg0 and Arg1 represent the input sources, which are the texture combiners. They're are set up by using something like the following line, where GL_SOURCE0_RGB, is argument 0 or Arg0 referenced in Table 6–3:

```
gl.glTexEnvf(GL10.GL_TEXTURE_ENV, GL10.GL_SOURCE0_RGB, GL10.GL_TEXTURE);
```

And similarly you'd use GL_SOURCE1_RGB for Arg1:

```
gl.glTexEnvf(GL10.GL_TEXTURE_ENV, GL10.GL_SOURCE1_RGB, GL10.GL_TEXTURE);
```

**Table 6–3.** *Possible Values for GL_COMBINE_RGB and GL_COMBINE_ALPHA Parameters*

| GL_COMBINE_* | Function |
|---|---|
| GL_REPLACE | Arg0 |
| GL_MODULATE | Arg0 * Arg1 *(the default)* |
| GL_ADD | Arg0 + Arg1 |
| GL_ADD_SIGNED | Arg0 + Arg1-0.5 |
| GL_INTERPOLATE | Arg0 * Arg2 + Arg1 * (1-Arg2) |
| GL_SUBTRACT | Arg0 - Arg1 |
| GL_DOT3_RGB | 4*(((Arg0red-.5)*(Arg1red-.5))+((Arg0green-.5)*(Arg1green-.5))+ ((Arg0blue-.5)*(Arg1blue-.5))) *(GL_COMBINE_RGB only)* |
| GL_DOT3_RGBA | Same as above, but with alpha added (*GL_COMBINE_RGBA* only) |

# Mapping with Bumps

You can do many extremely sophisticated things with textures; bump mapping is just one. So what follows is a discussion of exactly what "bumps" are and why anyone should be concerned with mapping them.

As previously pointed out, much of the challenge in computer graphics is to make complicated-looking visuals using clever hacks behind the scene. Bump mapping is just one of those tricks, and in OpenGL ES 1.1, it can be implemented with texture combiners.

Just as textures were "tricks" to layer complexity to a simple face, bump mapping is a technique to add a third dimension to the texture. It's used to generate a roughness to the overall surface of an object, giving some surprisingly realistic highlights when illuminated. It might be used to simulate waves on a lake, the surface of a tennis ball, or a planetary surface.

Roughness of an object's surface is perceived by the way it plays with both light and shadow. For example, consider a full moon vs. a gibbous moon, as shown in Figure 6–12. The moon is full when the sun is directly in front of it, and as a result, the surface is little more than varying shades of gray.

No shadows whatsoever are visible. It's not much different from you looking at the ground facing away from the sun. Around the shadow of your head the surface looks flat. Now, if the light source is moved to the side of things, suddenly all sorts of details pop out. The image on the right in Figure 6–12 shows a gibbous moon that has the sun toward the left, the moon's eastern limb. It's a completely different story, isn't it?

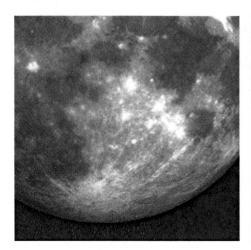 

**Figure 6–12.** *Relatively little detail shows on the left, while with oblique lighting, a lot more shows on the right.*

Understanding how highlights and shadows work together is absolutely critical to the training of fine artists and illustrators.

Adding real surface displacement to replicate the entire lunar surface would likely require many gigabytes of data and is out of the question for the current generation of small handheld devices from both a memory and CPU standpoint. Thus enters the rather elegant hack of bump mapping to the center stage.

You might remember that back in Chapter 4 that you had to add an array of "face normals" to the sphere model. Normals are merely vectors that are perpendicular to the face that show the direction the face is pointing. It is the angle of the normal to any of the light sources that largely determines just how bright or dark the face will be. And the more directly oriented the face is toward the light, the brighter it will be. So, what if you had a compact way to encode normals not on a face-by-face basis, as a model might have relatively few faces, but on, say, a pixel-by-pixel basis? And what if you could combine that encoded normal array with a real image texture and process it in a way that could brighten or darken a pixel from the image, based on the direction of incoming light?

This brings us back to the texture combiners. In Table 6–3, notice the last two combiner types: GL_DOT3_RGB and GL_DOT3_RGBA. Now, reach back, way back to your high-school geometry classes. Remember the dot product of two vectors? Both the dot products and cross products were those things that you scorned with the whine "Teacherrrrr?? Why do I need to know *this*?" Well, now you are going to get your answer.

The dot product is the length of a vector based on the angle of two other vectors. Still not following? Consider the diagram on the left in Figure 6–13. The dot product is the "amount" of the normal vector that is aiming toward the light, and that value is used to directly illuminate the face. In the diagram on the right in Figure 6–13, the face is at a right angle to the direction of the sun, so it is not illuminated.

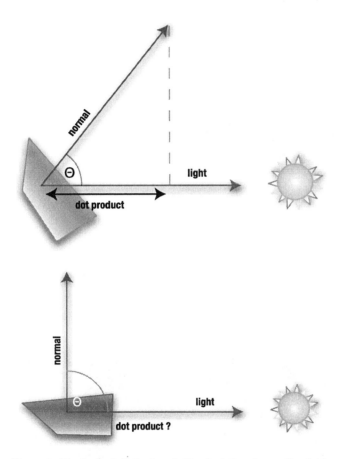

**Figure 6–13.** *On the left, the face is illuminated; not so on the right.*

With this in mind, the "cheat" that bump mapping uses is as follows. Take the actual texture you want to use, and add a special second companion texture to it. This second texture encodes normal information in place of the RGB colors. So, instead of using floats that are 4 bytes each, it uses 1-byte values for the xyz of normal vectors that conveniently fit inside a single 4-byte pixel. Since the vectors usually don't have to be super-accurate, the 8-bit resolution is just fine and is very memory efficient. So, these normals are generated in a way to map directly to the vertical features you want highlighted.

Because normals can have negative values as well as positive (negative when pointing away from the sun), the xyz values are centered in the range of 0 to 1. That is, -127 to +127 must be mapped to anywhere between 0 and 1. So, the "red" component, which is typically the x part of the vector, would be calculated as follows:

$$red = (x+1)/2.0$$

And of course this is similar for the green and blue bits.

Now look at the formula expressed in the GL_DOT3_RGB entry of Table 6–3. This takes the RGB triplet as the vector and returns its length. N is the normal vector, and L is the light vector, so the length is solved as follows:

$$length = 4 \times ((R_n - .5) \times (R_l - .5) + (G_n - .5) \times (G_l - .5) + (B_n - .5) \times (B_l - .5))$$

So if the face is aimed directly toward the light along the x-axis, the normal's red would be 1.0, and the light's red or x value would also be 1.0. The green and blue bits would be .5, which is the encoded form of 0. Plugging that into the previous equation would look like this:

$$length = 4 \times ((1_n - .5) \times (1_l - .5) + (.5_n - .5) \times (.5_l - .5) + (.5_n - .5) \times (.5_l - .5))$$

$$length = 4 \times (.25 + 0 + 0) = 1.0$$

This is exactly what we'd expect. And if the normal is pointing up and away from the surface in the z direction, encoded in the blue byte, the answer should be 0 because the normals are largely aimed up away from the texture's X and Y planes. The image on the left in Figure 6–14 shows a bit of our earth map, while the image on the right shows its corresponding normal map.

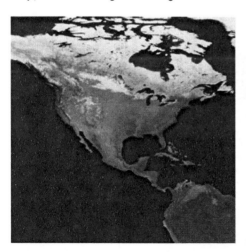 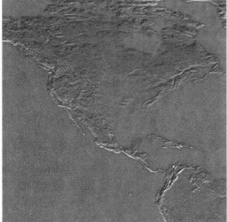

**Figure 6–14.** *The left side is our image; the right is the matching normal map.*

And why is the normal map primarily purple? The straight-up vector pointing away from the earth's surface is encoded such that the red=.5, green=.5, and blue=1.0. (Keep in mind that .5 is actually 0.)

When the texture combiner is set to the DOT3 mode, it uses the normal and a lighting vector to determine the intensity of each texel. That value is then used to modulate the color of the real image texture.

Now it's time to recycle the previous multitexture project. This time, the second texture needs to be composed of the bump map available from the Apress site. Following that, the combiners are set up to handle the normal map and any leftover animation from past exercises.

Load in the normal map for this example, and then add the new routine, `multiTextureBumpMap()`, as shown in Listing 6–5.

**Listing 6–5.** *Setting Up the Combiners for Bump Mapping*

```
static float lightAngle=0.0f;
      public void multiTextureBumpMap(GL10 gl, int mainTexture, int normalTexture)
   {
        float x,y,z;

        lightAngle+=.3f;                                                        //1

        if(lightAngle>180)
        lightAngle=0;

        // Set up the light vector.
        x = (float) Math.sin(lightAngle * (3.14159 / 180.0f));                  //2
        y = 0.0f;
        z = (float) Math.cos(lightAngle * (3.14159 / 180.0f));

        // Half shifting to have a value between 0.0f and 1.0f.
        x = x * 0.5f + 0.5f;                                                    //3
        y = y * 0.5f + 0.5f;
        z = z * 0.5f + 0.5f;

        gl.glColor4f(x, y, z, 1.0f);                                           //4

        //The color and normal map are combined.
        gl.glActiveTexture(GL10.GL_TEXTURE0);                                  //5
        gl.glBindTexture(GL10.GL_TEXTURE_2D, mainTexture);

        gl.glTexEnvf(GL10.GL_TEXTURE_ENV, GL10.GL_TEXTURE_ENV_MODE, GL11.GL_COMBINE);//6
        gl.glTexEnvf(GL10.GL_TEXTURE_ENV, GL11.GL_COMBINE_RGB, GL11.GL_DOT3_RGB); //7
        gl.glTexEnvf(GL10.GL_TEXTURE_ENV, GL11.GL_SRC0_RGB, GL11.GL_TEXTURE);    //8
        gl.glTexEnvf(GL10.GL_TEXTURE_ENV, GL11.GL_SRC1_RGB, GL11.GL_PREVIOUS);   //9
```

```
        // Set up the Second Texture, and combine it with the result of the Dot3
    combination.

        gl.glActiveTexture(GL10.GL_TEXTURE1);                                   //10
        gl.glBindTexture(GL10.GL_TEXTURE_2D, normalTexture);

        gl.glTexEnvf(GL10.GL_TEXTURE_ENV, GL10.GL_TEXTURE_ENV_MODE, GL10.GL_MODULATE);  //11
}
```

The preceding operation takes place using two *stages*. The first blends the bump, or normal map with
the primary color, which is established using the glColor4f() call. The second takes the results of
that and combines it with the color image using our old friend GL_MODULATE.

So let's examine it piece by piece:

- In line 1 we define lightAngle that will cycle between 0 and 180 degrees
  around the texture to show how the highlights look under varying lighting
  conditions.

- Calculate the xyz values of the light vector in line 2.

- In line 3, the xyz components need to be scaled to match those of the bump map.

- Now color the fragments using the light vector components in line 4.

- Set and bind the bump map first, which is *tex0* in line 5f.

- GL_COMBINE in line 6 tells the system to expect a combining type to follow.

- In line 7, we specify that we're going to combine just the RGB values using
  GL_DOT3_RGB operations (GL_DOT3_RGBA includes the alpha, but is not needed
  here).

- Here we set up "stage 0," the first of two stages.  The source of the first bit of
  data is specified in line 8. This says to use the texture from the current texture
  unit (GL_TEXTURE0) as the source for the bump map assigned in line 5.

- Then we have to tell it to blend with the previous color—in this case, that which
  was set via glColor() in line 4. For stage 0, GL_PREVIOUS is the same as
  GL_PRIMARY_COLOR, because there is no previous texture to use.

- Now set up stage 1 in line 10 and the following line. The argument, tex1, is the
  color image.

- Now all we want to do is combine the image with the bump map, which is what
  line 11 does.

My source texture is selected so that you can easily see the results. When started, the light should
move from left to right and illuminate the edges of the land masses, as shown in Figure 6–15.

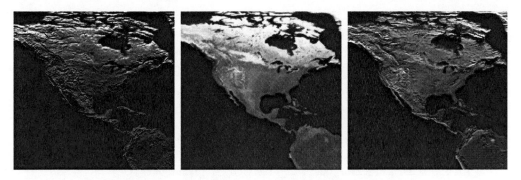

**Figure 6–15.** *Bumpmapped North America at morning, noon, and evening, respectively*

Looks pretty cool, eh? But can we apply this to a spinning sphere? Give it a shot and recycle the solar-system model from the end of the previous chapter. To make the fine detail of the bump map more easily seen, the sun is dropped in lieu of a somewhat larger image for the earth. So, we'll load the bump map, move the earth to the center of the scene, tweak the lighting, and add the combiner support.

Underneath where you allocate the main image, add the following:

```
    if(imageId == true)
{
    m_BumpmapID = createTexture(gl, context, imageId, resourceId);
}
```

And add this:

```
    int m_BumpmapID;
```

Now make sure this is called with the new parameter in `init()` located in the solar system's controller object.

Use Listing 6–6 as the new `draw()` method to be placed in `Planet.java` and called from the `bumpmappingController`'s `executePlanet()` routine. This mainly sets things up for the texture combiners and calls `multiTextureBumpMap` in Listing 6–6.

**Listing 6–6.** *The Modified Execute for Bump Mapping*

```
public void draw(GL10 gl)
{
        gl.glMatrixMode(GL10.GL_MODELVIEW);
        gl.glEnable(GL10.GL_CULL_FACE);
        gl.glCullFace(GL10.GL_BACK);
        gl.glEnable(GL10.GL_LIGHTING);

        gl.glFrontFace(GL10.GL_CW);
```

```
        gl.glEnable(GL10.GL_TEXTURE_2D);
        gl.glEnableClientState(GL10.GL_VERTEX_ARRAY);
        gl.glVertexPointer(3, GL10.GL_FLOAT, 0, m_VertexData);

        gl.glEnableClientState(GL10.GL_TEXTURE_COORD_ARRAY);
        gl.glClientActiveTexture(GL10.GL_TEXTURE0);

        gl.glBindTexture(GL10.GL_TEXTURE_2D, textures[0]);

        gl.glTexCoordPointer(2, GL10.GL_FLOAT, 0, m_textureData);

        gl.glClientActiveTexture(GL10.GL_TEXTURE1);
        gl.glTexCoordPointer(2, GL10.GL_FLOAT,0,m_textureData);

        gl.glMatrixMode(GL10.GL_MODELVIEW);

        gl.glEnableClientState(GL10.GL_NORMAL_ARRAY);
        gl.glNormalPointer(GL10.GL_FLOAT, 0, m_NormalData);

        gl.glColorPointer(4, GL10.GL_UNSIGNED_BYTE, 0, m_ColorData);
        multiTextureBumpMap(gl, m_BumpmapID, textures[0]);
        gl.glDrawArrays(GL10.GL_TRIANGLE_STRIP, 0, (m_Slices+1)*2*(m_Stacks-1)+2);


    }
```

The method `multiTextureBumpMap()` is identical to the previous one except for the light vector calculations that can be removed (up through line 4), so merely copy that over to your planet object.

Now go to where you initialize the lights in your solar-system controller, and comment out the call to create the specular material. Bump mapping and specular reflections don't get along too well.

Listing 6–7 is the new execute routine; likewise for the controller. This dumps the sun, moves the earth into the center of things, and places the main light off to the left.

**Listing 6–7.** *Replace the Old execute() Routine with This*

```
    private void execute(GL10 gl) {
        float posFill1[]={-8.0f, 0.0f, 7.0f, 1.0f};
        float cyan[]={0.0f, 1.0f, 1.0f, 1.0f};
        float orbitalIncrement=0.5f;
        float sunPos[]={0.0f, 0.0f, 0.0f, 1.0f};

        gl.glLightfv(SS_FILLLIGHT1, GL10.GL_POSITION, makeFloatBuffer(posFill1));

        gl.glEnable(GL10.GL_DEPTH_TEST);
        gl.glClearColor(0.0f, 0.25f, 0.35f, 1.0f);
        gl.glClear(GL10.GL_COLOR_BUFFER_BIT);
```

```
        gl.glPushMatrix();

        gl.glTranslatef(-m_Eyeposition[X_VALUE],-m_Eyeposition[Y_VALUE],-
            m_Eyeposition[Z_VALUE]);
        gl.glLightfv(SS_SUNLIGHT, GL10.GL_POSITION, makeFloatBuffer(sunPos));

        gl.glEnable(SS_FILLLIGHT1);
        gl.glEnable(SS_FILLLIGHT2);

        gl.glPushMatrix();

        angle+=orbitalIncrement;
        gl.glRotatef(angle, 0.0f, 1.0f, 0.0f);
        executePlanet(m_Earth, gl);
        gl.glPopMatrix();
        gl.glPopMatrix();
    }
```

If you now see something like Figure 6–16, you may officially pat yourself on the back.

**Figure 6–16.** *The bumpy earth*

OK, now for an experiment. Move the light's position so that it comes in from the right instead of the left. Figure 6–17 is the unexpected result. What's going on here? Now the mountains look like valleys.

**Figure 6–17**. *Huh?*

What's happening is that we are going where no combiner has gone before. By sticking in our own lighting, the effect of the simulated lighting as provided by the light vector is removed. With our light on the left, it just happens to look good mainly by luck. Bump mapping here works OK if the lighting of your scene is relatively static. It doesn't like multiple light sources. In fact, the pseudo-lighting effect specified via the light vector is ignored in lieu of the "real" light sources. Furthermore, if you turn off those sources, the light vector ignores any of the shading on the object altogether. In this case, you would see the entire planet lighten up and darken because that's what is happening to the texture itself, because it is merely a 2D surface. If part of it is lit, all is lit. So, what's a GL nerd to do? *Shaders my friend. Shaders.* And that is where OpenGL ES 2.0 and the Android extensions come in.

## Summary

In this chapter, you learned about the blending capabilities supplied by OpenGL ES 1. Blending has its own unique language as expressed through the blending functions and combiners. You've learned about translucency, including how and when to apply it. Also covered were some of the neat tricks available by using both blending and textures for animation and bump mapping. In the next chapter, I'll start to apply some of these tricks and show others that can make for a more interesting 3D universe.

**7**

# Well-Rendered Miscellany

*If we knew what it was we were doing, it would not be called research,
would it?*

—Albert Einstein

When starting this chapter, I tried to find a suitable quote about miscellany. Unfortunately, all I could find were collections of miscellaneous quotes. But the one by Albert Einstein is a real gem and can *almost* apply because you, dear reader, are conducting research—research in how to make richer, more involving, and fun software.

In books like this, sometimes it's hard to make clean classifications of a particular topic, and we just have to dump a lot things into a single chapter when they might not warrant a chapter of their own. So, here I'm going to cover some classic presentation and rendering tricks, whether they can be applied to the solar-system project or, so at the end you'll exclaim "So, that's how they do that!"

## Frame Buffer Objects

Usually referred to as FBOs, you can think of frame buffer objects as simply rendering surfaces. Up until now, you've been using one and probably didn't know it; the EGL context that your scene renders to via the GLSurfaceView object is an FBO. What you probably didn't know is that you can have multiple screens at the same time. As before, we'll start off with the old standard, our bouncing slab of rainbow-hued Jell-O, and then see where it can go from there.

# Hedley Buffer Objects

You know the drill by this time: find the exercise from Chapter 5, with the original 2D bouncing textured square (Figure 5-13), and use this as a reference. As most of the code is ultimately changed, I suggest creating a new project from scratch. The activity file will be the standard default one. We need to create a separate object just for the FBO support; call this FBOController.java. It will cover both initialization and execution of the FBO. It should look like Listing 7–1, minus a few utility functions that you should have elsewhere to save space. Those are noted in the description.

**Listing 7–1.** *The Frame Buffer Object Controller*

```
    public class FBOController
{
        public Context context;
        int[] m_FBO1 = new int[3];
        int[] m_FBOTexture = new int[1];
        public String TAG = "FBO Controller";
        int[] originalFBO = new int[1];
        int[] depthBuffer = new int[1];
        int m_ImageTexture;
        static float m_TransY = 0.0f;
        static float m_RotX = 0.0f;
        static float m_RotZ = 0.0f;
        static float m_Z = -1.5f;
        int[] m_DefaultFBO = new int[1];
        int m_Counter=0;
        boolean m_FullScreen = false;

    public int init(GL10 gl, Context contextRegf,int resource, int width,
        int height)
        {
                GL11ExtensionPack gl11ep = (GL11ExtensionPack) gl;             //1

                //Cache the original FBO, and restore it later.

                gl11ep.glGetIntegerv(GL11ExtensionPack.GL_FRAMEBUFFER_BINDING_OES,   //2
                        makeIntBuffer(originalFBO));

                gl11ep.glGenRenderbuffersOES(1, makeIntBuffer(depthBuffer));        //3
                gl11ep.glBindRenderbufferOES(GL11ExtensionPack.GL_RENDERBUFFER_OES,
                        depthBuffer[0]);

                gl11ep.glRenderbufferStorageOES(GL11ExtensionPack.GL_RENDERBUFFER_OES,
                GL11ExtensionPack.GL_DEPTH_COMPONENT16, width, height);

                //Make the texture to render to.
```

```java
gl.glGenTextures(1, m_FBOTexture, 0);                              //4
gl.glBindTexture(GL10.GL_TEXTURE_2D, m_FBOTexture[0]);

gl.glTexImage2D(GL10.GL_TEXTURE_2D, 0, GL10.GL_RGB, width, height, 0,
        GL10.GL_RGB, GL10.GL_UNSIGNED_SHORT_5_6_5,null);

gl.glTexParameterf(GL10.GL_TEXTURE_2D, GL10.GL_TEXTURE_MIN_FILTER,
        GL10.GL_LINEAR);
gl.glTexParameterf(GL10.GL_TEXTURE_2D, GL10.GL_TEXTURE_MAG_FILTER,
        GL10.GL_LINEAR);
gl.glTexParameterf(GL10.GL_TEXTURE_2D, GL10.GL_TEXTURE_WRAP_S,
        GL10.GL_CLAMP_TO_EDGE);
gl.glTexParameterf(GL10.GL_TEXTURE_2D, GL10.GL_TEXTURE_WRAP_T,
        GL10.GL_CLAMP_TO_EDGE);

//Now create the actual FBO.

gl11ep.glGenFramebuffersOES(1, m_FBO1,0);                          //5

gl11ep.glBindFramebufferOES(GL11ExtensionPack.GL_FRAMEBUFFER_OES,
        m_FBO1[0]);

// Attach the texture to the FBO.                                 //6
gl11ep.glFramebufferTexture2DOES(GL11ExtensionPack.GL_FRAMEBUFFER_OES,
        GL11ExtensionPack.GL_COLOR_ATTACHMENT0_OES,
        GL10.GL_TEXTURE_2D,
        m_FBOTexture[0], 0);

// Attach the depth buffer we created earlier to our FBO.         //7
gl11ep.glFramebufferRenderbufferOES
        (GL11ExtensionPack.GL_FRAMEBUFFER_OES,
        GL11ExtensionPack.GL_DEPTH_ATTACHMENT_OES,
        GL11ExtensionPack.GL_RENDERBUFFER_OES, depthBuffer[0]);

// Check that our FBO creation was successful.

gl11ep.glCheckFramebufferStatusOES
        (GL11ExtensionPack.GL_FRAMEBUFFER_OES);

        int uStatus =
gl11ep.glCheckFramebufferStatusOES(GL11ExtensionPack.GL_FRAMEBUFFER_OES);

if(uStatus != GL11ExtensionPack.GL_FRAMEBUFFER_COMPLETE_OES)
        return 0;

gl11ep.glBindFramebufferOES(GL11ExtensionPack.GL_FRAMEBUFFER_OES,  //8
        originalFBO[0]);
```

```
                m_ImageTexture = createTexture(gl,contextRegf,resource);        //9

                return 1;
    }

    public int getFBOName()
            return m_FBO1[0];

    public int getTextureName()
            return m_FBOTexture[0];

    public void draw(GL10 gl)
    {
            GL11ExtensionPack gl11 = (GL11ExtensionPack) gl;

        float squareVertices[] =                                          //10
        {
            -0.5f, -0.5f, 0.0f,
             0.5f, -0.5f, 0.0f,
            -0.5f,  0.5f, 0.0f,
             0.5f,  0.5f, 0.0f
        };

        float fboVertices[] =
        {
            -0.5f, -0.75f, 0.0f,
             0.5f, -0.75f, 0.0f,
            -0.5f,  0.75f, 0.0f,
             0.5f,  0.75f, 0.0f
        };

        float textureCoords1[] =
        {
            0.0f, 0.0f,
            1.0f, 0.0f,
            0.0f, 1.0f,
            1.0f, 1.0f
        };

        if((m_Counter%250)==0)                                            //11
        {
            if(m_FullScreen)
                m_FullScreen=false;
            else
                m_FullScreen=true;
        }
```

```
        gl.glDisable(GL10.GL_CULL_FACE);
        gl.glEnable(GL10.GL_DEPTH_TEST);

    if(m_DefaultFBO[0] == 0)                                           //12
{
        gl11.glGetIntegerv(GL11ExtensionPack.GL_FRAMEBUFFER_BINDING_OES,
            makeIntBuffer(m_DefaultFBO));
}

        gl.glDisableClientState(GL10.GL_COLOR_ARRAY | GL10.GL_DEPTH_BUFFER_BIT);

        gl.glEnable(GL10.GL_TEXTURE_2D);

    //Draw to the off-screen FBO first.

    if(!m_FullScreen)                                                  //13
        gl11.glBindFramebufferOES(GL11ExtensionPack.GL_FRAMEBUFFER_OES,
            m_FBO1[0]);

        gl.glClearColor(0.0f, 0.0f, 1.0f, 1.0f);
        gl.glClear(GL10.GL_COLOR_BUFFER_BIT|GL10.GL_DEPTH_BUFFER_BIT);

        gl.glPushMatrix();

        gl.glMatrixMode(GL10.GL_MODELVIEW);
        gl.glLoadIdentity();

        gl.glTranslatef(0.0f, (float)(Math.sin(m_TransY)/2.0f),m_Z);

        gl.glRotatef(m_RotZ, 0.0f, 0.0f, 1.0f);

        gl.glBindTexture(GL10.GL_TEXTURE_2D,m_ImageTexture);             //14

        gl.glTexCoordPointer(2, GL10.GL_FLOAT,0, makeFloatBuffer(textureCoords1));
        gl.glEnableClientState(GL10.GL_TEXTURE_COORD_ARRAY);

        gl.glVertexPointer(3, GL10.GL_FLOAT, 0, makeFloatBuffer(squareVertices));
        gl.glEnableClientState(GL10.GL_VERTEX_ARRAY);

        gl.glDrawArrays(GL10.GL_TRIANGLE_STRIP, 0, 4);

        gl.glPopMatrix();

    //Now draw the offscreen frame buffer into another framebuffer.

    if(!m_FullScreen)                                                  //15
{
        gl.glPushMatrix();
```

```
                    gl11.glBindFramebufferOES(GL11ExtensionPack.GL_FRAMEBUFFER_OES,
                        m_DefaultFBO[0]);

                    gl.glMatrixMode(GL10.GL_MODELVIEW);
                    gl.glLoadIdentity();

                    gl.glTranslatef(0.0f, (float)(Math.sin(m_TransY)/2.0f), m_Z);
                    gl.glRotatef(m_RotX, 1.0f, 0.0f, 0.0f);

                    gl.glBindTexture(GL10.GL_TEXTURE_2D, m_FBOTexture[0]);

                    gl.glClearColor(1.0f, 0.0f, 0.0f, 1.0f);
                    gl.glClear(GL10.GL_COLOR_BUFFER_BIT | GL10.GL_DEPTH_BUFFER_BIT);

                    gl.glTexCoordPointer(2, GL10.GL_FLOAT, 0,
                        makeFloatBuffer(textureCoords1));
                    gl.glEnableClientState(GL10.GL_TEXTURE_COORD_ARRAY);

                    gl.glVertexPointer(3, GL10.GL_FLOAT, 0,
                        makeFloatBuffer(fboVertices));
                    gl.glEnableClientState(GL10.GL_VERTEX_ARRAY);
                    gl.glDrawArrays(GL10.GL_TRIANGLE_STRIP, 0, 4);

                    gl.glPopMatrix();
            }

                    m_TransY += 0.025f;
                    m_RotX+=1.0f;
                    m_RotZ+=1.0f;
                    m_Counter++;
        }

        //createTexture(), makeFloatBuffer() and makeIntBuffer() removed for clarity.   //16

}
```

You should recognize the pattern here, because creating FBOs is a lot like many of the other OpenGL objects. You generate a "name," bind it, and then create and modify the object. In this case, there is an awful lot of creatin' and modifyin' going on. So, let's break it down:

▓ In line 1, we get something called GL11ExtensionPack. The extension pack is an officially recognized set of extra API calls that are not required for a particular version of OpenGL ES to be approved. These can be added at the discretion of the GPU vendors, but they still must follow specs for the various extra features. An example of this has to do with—*ta-da!*—frame buffer objects! Originally FBOs were part of OpenGL ES 2.0, but they were so darned useful, it was decided to open them up to 1.1 users as well. All API calls and definitions have the suffix of OES. Since FBOs are part of the normal 2.0 spec, those calls do not need OES.

▓ Line 2 gets the current FBO, which most likely will be the normal screen. It's cached so it can be restored later.

▓ Since we're creating out own private FBO, we need to handle all of the setup ourselves, which includes creating and adding a depth buffer to our target. Line 3 and the one following generate a new buffer name, bind it, and then allocate storage.

▓ At this point in lines 4ff, we need to allocate a texture image and have it linked up to our frame buffer. This is the interface required to camouflage our FBO so that it looks just like any other texture to OpenGL. Here we can also set up some of the normal texture settings for edge conditions and use bilinear filtering.

▓ Up until now we've merely created the depth buffer and image interface. In lines 5f, we actually create the frame buffer object and attach the previous bits to it.

▓ Line 6 attaches the texture first. Notice the use of GL_COLOR_ATTACHMENT0_OES. The texture bit actually holds the color information, so it is called the *color attachment.*

▓ In Line 7, we do the same for the depth buffer, using GL_DEPTH_ATTACHMENT_OES. And remember that in OpenGL ES we have only three types of buffer attachments: depth, color, and stencil. The latter does things such as blocking rendering in a certain part of the screen and will be covered later in this chapter. The adult version of OpenGL adds a fourth kind, GL_DEPTH_STENCIL_ATTACHMENT.

▓ Line 8 restores the previous FBO, and line 9 generates the actual texture of our Easter Island friend, Hedly, for use in the bouncy square.

The next step is to move on to the draw method, and we'll see how the FBOs are swapped in and out as needed.

▓ In lines 10ff, you'll immediately recognize the standard square data, with the addition of vertices for the FBO.

▓ Lines 11ff are needed to allow us to swap between the FBO as the full-screen texture and the normal original screen.

- Next we cache the main screen's FBO again in lines 12f, as was done in the create method.

- Line 13 is where we actually tell OpenGL to use our new FBO. Following that is the standard code to manage the transformations, and so on, that should make you feel at home.

- In line 14, we bind the Hedly image and then set up the vertices and texture coordinate, followed by `glDrawArray()`.

- Now the fun begins. In Lines 15ff, the FBO is the "new" texture that can now be bound into the main screen. First the original screen's FBO is bound, followed by another set of transformation calls, along with another `glClear()`. To make things really obvious, the main screen is cleared to red, while the FBO's background is cleared to blue.

So, that's merely creating an FBO. You'll see that it is a fairly no-frills piece of code, using the built-in functions available in both OpenGL ES 1 and 2. And yes, it does seem a little overly complicated, but it's easily wrapped with a helper function.

But we're still not quite done, because we now have to rejigger the driver to use both FBOs. The first part of the rejiggering process is to see whether your device can actually support frame buffer objects. For this we can harken back to the discussion in Chapter 5 about using the extension enumerator. For this case, the following code will work, with thanks to the OpenGL ES working group for standardizing these sorts of things.

```
private boolean checkIfContextSupportsExtension(GL10 gl, String extension)
{
    String extensions = " " + gl.glGetString(GL10.GL_EXTENSIONS) + " ";
    return extensions.indexOf(" " + extension + " ") >= 0;
}
```

Now make the follow calls to where your initialization code is located, such as onSurfaceChanged():

```
m_FBOSupported=checkIfContextSupportsExtension(gl,"GL_OES_framebuffer_object");

if(m_FBOSupported)
{
        int resid = book.BouncyCube1.R.drawable.hedly;

        m_FBOController = new FBOController();
        m_FBOController.init(gl, this.context, resid, width, height);
}
```

You should be able to run it and see it in all of its gaudy glory. If you intend to stare at it for an extended period of time, your doctor's permission may be necessary. The leftmost image in Figure 7–1 is where the new secondary FBO becomes the primary rendering surface, while the other surface is now nested within.

Feel free to try and do a third or fourth FBO with different images and colors.

**Figure 7–1.** *On the left, just Hedly is spinning. Both Hedly and his window are now spinning counterclockwise in the middle. And on the right, the frame is spinning end over end.*

## Sun Buffer Objects

You can do a lot of fun and bizarre things with buffer objects, equivalent to having 3D superpowers. For example, you could simulate some animations on a little model of a TV set. You could show multiple views of the same data in a reflection of a puddle on the ground or the rearview mirror in a car. Better yet, put one OpenGL frame animating a scene on the sun in our solar-system simulator. It's not particularly realistic, but it's pretty cool.

I'll leave this up to the student this time around, but I used Chapter 5's final project for starters. You can also just download it from the website.

I hope you get something like Figure 7–2, with Hedly bouncing up and down on the sun.

**Figure 7–2.** *Using an off-screen FBO to animate texture on another one*

# Lens Flare

We've all seen it. Those ghostly, glowing gossamer lights dancing around television scenes or invading an image whenever a camera is aimed toward the sun. This happens as the sun's light merrily bounces around to and fro in the camera's optics, causing numerous secondary images. These can be seen both as a bright broad haze and as many smaller artifacts. Figure 7–3 (left) illustrates this with an image from the Apollo 14 moon landing mission in 1971. The flare obscures most of the lunar module. Even the iPhone has the similar issues, as demonstrated with the image on the right in Figure 7–3. Even though the Hasselblad cameras that were used on the moon were the best in the world, we couldn't beat lens flare. Unfortunately, it has become one of the more common clichés in computer graphics, used as a tool that shouts "Hey! This is not a fake computer image, because it has *lens flare*!" However, lens flares do have their uses, especially in the arena of space simulations because the fake imagery frequently looks at the fake sun. In that case, both consciously and subconsciously, you'd expect some visual cue that you were looking at something very, very, very bright. It also helps give an extra sense of depth to the image. The flare is generated in the optics that are really near the user while the target is a bazillion miles away.

**Figure 7–3.** *On the left is a view on the moon from Apollo 14, and a Motorola Xoom image is on the right.*

Depending on the specific optics and their various internal coatings, the flares can take many different forms, but they usually end up being just of bunch of ghostly polygons of varying sizes and hues. In the next exercise, we'll create a simple lens flare project that will illustrate using 2D images in a 3D environment. Because there is a lot of code for the setup, I will highlight only the key bits here. You will need to go to www.apress.com to get the full project.

Geometrically, lens flares are generally pretty simple because of their symmetry. They exhibit two main characteristics: all lens flares require a very bright light source, and they'll lie along a diagonal line going through the center of the screen, as shown in Figure 7–4.

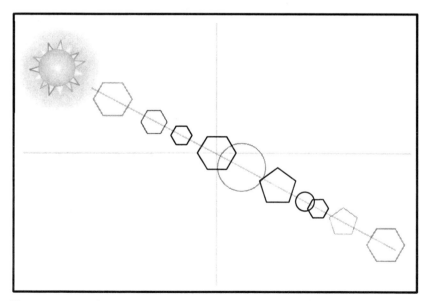

**Figure 7–4.** *Lens flares are caused by the inner reflections of a bright light source within a camera's lens.*

Since flare images are 2D, how do we put them in a 3D space? Going back to the original sample, the bouncy square was also 2D object. But displaying it relied on some defaults as to how the object was mapped to the screen. Here we get a little more specific.

Remember in Chapter 3 where I spoke of perspective vs. orthographic projections? The former is the way we perceive the dimensionality of objects; the latter is used when precise sizes and shapes are required, eliminating the distortion that perspective adds to the scene. So, when drawing 2D objects, you will generally want to ensure that their visual dimensions are untouched by any of the 3D-ness of the rest of your world.

When it comes to generating your lens flares, you will need a small collection of different shapes to represent some of the mechanics of the actual lens. The hexagonal or pentagonal images are those of the iris used to vary the intensity of the incoming light; see Figure 7–5. They will also exhibit different tints as a result of the various coatings used to protect the lenses or filter out unwanted wavelengths.

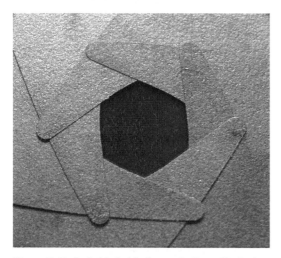

**Figure 7–5.** *A six-blade iris (image by Dave Fischer)*

The following steps are needed to generate the flare set:

1. Import the various images.

2. Detect where on the screen the source object is.

3. Create the imaginary vector that goes through the center of the screen so as to hold the individual pieces of art.

4. Add a dozen or more images, with random sizes, colors, and translucency, scattered up and down the vector.

5. Support touch dragging to test it in all different positions.

I started with the standard template and added support for touching and dragging the visuals. You will notice that there is no more 3D sun object. It is now a glowy 2D texture that is rendered at the current position of a user's finger, as demonstrated in Listing 7–2.

**Listing 7–2.** *The Top-Level onDrawFrame()*

```
    public void onDrawFrame(GL10 gl)
{
        CGPoint centerRelative = new CGPoint();
        CGPoint windowDefault = new CGPoint();
        CGSize        windowSize = new CGSize();
        float cx,cy;
        float aspectRatio

        gl.glClearColor(0.0f, 0.0f, 0.0f, 1.0f);
        gl.glClear(GL10.GL_COLOR_BUFFER_BIT);

        DisplayMetrics display = context.getResources().getDisplayMetrics();          //1
        windowSize.width = display.widthPixels;
        windowSize.height = display.heightPixels;

        cx=windowSize.width/2.0f;
        cy=windowSize.height/2.0f;

        aspectRatio=cx/cy;

        centerRelative.x = m_PointerLocation.x-cx;
        centerRelative.y =(cy-m_PointerLocation.y)/aspectRatio;

        CT.renderTextureAt(gl, centerRelative.x, centerRelative.y, windowSize,        //2
            m_FlareSource, 3.0f, 1.0f, 1.0f, 1.0f, 1.0f);

        m_LensFlare.execute(gl, windowSize, m_PointerLocation);                       //3
}
```

There are three lines to take note of here:

- Lines 1ff get the center of the screen and creates the information needed to track the flare source (the sun) with the pointer (your finger).

- In line 2, the flare's source object, usually the sun, is rendered.

- Line 3 calls the helper routine that draws the actual lens flare.

The next bit in Listing 7–3 draws a 2D texture to the screen. You will find this very handy and will use it frequently for displaying things like text or HUD-like graphics on your screen. In short, this draws a rectangular object, just like the bouncy square. To make it 2D, it uses a new call called glOrthof() when setting up the projection matrix.

**Listing 7–3.** *Rendering a 2D Texture*

```
public void renderTextureAt(GL10 gl, float postionX, float postionY,          //1
    CGSize windowsSize, int textureId, float size, float r, float g, float b,
        float a)
{
    float scaledX, scaledY;
    float zoomBias = .1f;

    float scaledSize;

    float squareVertices[] =
    {
        -1.0f, -1.0f, 0.0f,
         1.0f, -1.0f, 0.0f,
        -1.0f,  1.0f, 0.0f,
         1.0f,  1.0f, 0.0f
    };

    float textureCoords[] =
    {
        0.0f, 0.0f,
        1.0f, 0.0f,
        0.0f, 1.0f,
        1.0f, 1.0f
    };

    float aspectRatio = windowsSize.height / windowsSize.width;

    scaledX = (float) (2.0f * postionX / windowsSize.width);          // 2
    scaledY = (float) (2.0f * postionY / windowsSize.height);

    gl.glDisable(GL10.GL_DEPTH_TEST);                                 // 3
    gl.glDisable(GL10.GL_LIGHTING);

    gl.glMatrixMode(GL10.GL_PROJECTION);                             // 4
    gl.glPushMatrix();
    gl.glLoadIdentity();

    gl.glOrthof(-1.0f, 1.0f, -1.0f * aspectRatio, 1.0f * aspectRatio, -1.0f, 1.0f); // 5

    gl.glMatrixMode(GL10.GL_MODELVIEW);                             // 6
    gl.glLoadIdentity();

    gl.glTranslatef(scaledX, scaledY, 0);                           // 7

    scaledSize = zoomBias * size;                                   // 8
```

```
        gl.glScalef(scaledSize, scaledSize, 1);                          // 9

        gl.glVertexPointer(3, GL10.GL_FLOAT, 0, makeFloatBuffer(squareVertices));
        gl.glEnableClientState(GL10.GL_VERTEX_ARRAY);

        gl.glEnable(GL10.GL_TEXTURE_2D);                                 // 10
        gl.glEnable(GL10.GL_BLEND);
        gl.glBlendFunc(GL10.GL_ONE, GL10.GL_ONE_MINUS_SRC_COLOR);
        gl.glBindTexture(GL10.GL_TEXTURE_2D, textureId);                 // 11
        gl.glTexCoordPointer(2, GL10.GL_FLOAT, 0, makeFloatBuffer(textureCoords));
        gl.glEnableClientState(GL10.GL_TEXTURE_COORD_ARRAY);

        gl.glColor4f(r, g, b, a);

        gl.glDrawArrays(GL10.GL_TRIANGLE_STRIP, 0, 4);

        gl.glMatrixMode(GL10.GL_PROJECTION);                             // 12
        gl.glPopMatrix();

        gl.glMatrixMode(GL10.GL_MODELVIEW);
        gl.glPopMatrix();
        gl.glEnable(GL10.GL_DEPTH_TEST);
        gl.glEnable(GL10.GL_LIGHTING);
        gl.glDisable(GL10.GL_BLEND);
    }
```

So, here is what's going on:

- In line 1, the *position* is the origin of the texture in pixels relative to the center of the texture, which is converted to normalized values later. The size is relative and needs to be played with to find the most appropriate. The final parameters are the colors and alpha. If you don't want any coloring, pass 1.0 for all of the values. Following this line, you'll recognize our old friends, the vertices and texture coordinates.

- Line 2 converts the pixel locations to relative values based on the width and height of the frame. The values are scaled by 2 because our viewport will be 2 units wide and high, going from -1 to 1 in each direction. These are the values eventually passed on to glTranslatef().

- Next, line 3 turns off the any depth testing, just to be safe, along with the lighting, because the flares have to be calculated apart from the actual lighting in the scene.

▧ Since we're going to use orthographic projection, let's reset the GL_PROJECTION matrix to the identity (the default) in lines 4ff. Remember that any time you want to touch a specific matrix, you need to specify which one ahead of time. The glPushMatrix() lets us tinker with the projection matrix without messing up anything prior in the chain of events.

▧ Line 5 is the heart of this routine. glOrthof() is a new call and sets up the orthographic matrix. In effect, it specifies a box. In this case, the box's width and depth go all from -1 to 1, while the height is scaled a little extra using the aspect ratio to compensate for it being a nonsquare display. This is why the scaledX and scaledY values were multiplied by 2.

▧ Next, set the modelview matrix to its identity in lines 6f, followed by the call to glTranslatef() in line 7.

▧ Line 8 determines how to scale the collection of flares based on the field of view for our scene, followed by line 9 that performs the actual scaling. This is relative and depends on the magnification ranges you want to deal with. Right now, pinch to zoom is not implemented, so this stays constant. The zoomBias affects all the elements, which makes it easy to scale everything at once.

▧ Lines 10ff set up the blending function using the most common of the choices. This causes each of the reflections to blend in a very believable way, especially when they start stacking up in the center.

▧ Now in lines 11ff, the texture is tinted, bound, and finally drawn.

▧ And again, be a good neighbor and pop the matrices so they won't affect anything else. And reset a bunch of other junk.

Note that this is a very inefficient routine. Normally you would batch up the draw operations in a way that would avoid all of the state changes that have high overhead. (Performance issues like this are covered in Chapter 9.)

I created a Flare.java for the individual flares, and the LensFlare parent object to handle setting up the vector, contain each of the individual images, and place them when ready. The main loop from LensFlare.java in Listing 7–4 should need very little explanation at this point. It merely calculates the start of the flare vector and then enumerates through the flare array to execute each entity.

**Listing 7–4.** *The Execute Loop for the Entire Lens Flare Effect from* LensFlare.java

```
public void execute(GL10 gl,CGSize size, CGPoint source)
{
        int i;
        float cx,cy;
        float aspectRatio;

        cx=(float) (size.width/2.0f);
```

```
    cy=(float) (size.height/2.0f);

    aspectRatio=cx/cy;

    startingOffsetFromCenterX = cx-source.x;
    startingOffsetFromCenterY = (source.y-cy)/aspectRatio;

    offsetFromCenterX = startingOffsetFromCenterX;
    offsetFromCenterY = startingOffsetFromCenterY;

    deltaX = (float) (2.0f * startingOffsetFromCenterX);
    deltaY = (float) (2.0f * startingOffsetFromCenterY);

    for (i = 23; i >= 0; i--)
{
        offsetFromCenterX -= deltaX * myFlares[i].getVectorPosition();
        offsetFromCenterY -= deltaY * myFlares[i].getVectorPosition();

        myFlares[i].renderFlareAt(gl, m_Flares[i], offsetFromCenterX,
                offsetFromCenterY, size, this.context);
    }
        counter++;
}
```

Finally, each of the individual flare images must be loaded on initialization and added into an NSArray.
A couple of lines follow:

```
    resid = book.lensflare.R.drawable.hexagonblur;
    m_Flares[0] = myFlares[0].init(gl, context, resid, .5f, .05f-ff, 1.0f, .73f,
        .30f, .4f);

    resid = book.lensflare.R.drawable.glow;
    m_Flares[1] = myFlares[1].init(gl, context, resid, 0.5f, .05f-ff, 1.0f, .73f,
        .50f, .4f);
```

This demo has 24 such objects. Figure 7–6 shows the result.

**Figure 7–6.** *Simple lens flare*

Unfortunately, there is one big gotcha in the lens flare biz. What happens if your light source goes behind something else? If it is a regular and known entity such as a round sphere in the center of the scene, it is pretty easy to figure out. But if it is a random object at a random place, it becomes much more difficult. Then what happens if the source is only partially eclipsed? Reflections will then dim and flicker out only when the entire object is hidden. The solution is left for you for the time being.

# Reflective Surfaces

Another effect that is rapidly becoming a bit of a visual cliché, albeit still a cool one, is that of a mirrored surface underneath part of or the entire scene. Mac-heads see that every time they look at the Dock, for example, with the happy little icons dancing their jig-of-joy up and down, in effect saying "Look here! look here!" Underneath you will see a faint little reflection. It's the same for many third-party apps, of course, led by Apple's own designs and examples. See Figure 7–7.

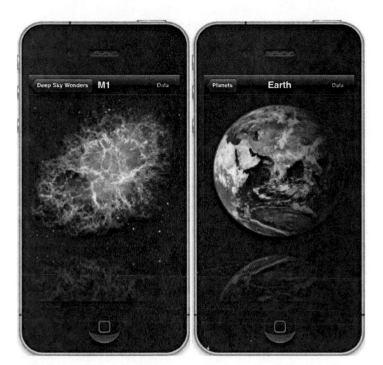

**Figure 7–7.** *Reflections in Distant Suns. (Yes, it is a gratuitous plug.)*

Google has just started to get into the act with its marketplace, displaying some of the books and movie images with a little reflection underneath as well. This will introduce the next topic, which is about both stencils and reflections, because the two are frequently tied together. In this case we'll be creating a reflecting surface, a (*stage*) beneath our object, do a mirror image of the object, and use the stencil to clip the reflection along the edges of the stage.

Besides the "color" buffer (that is, the image buffer) and the depth buffer, OpenGL also has something called a *stencil buffer.*

The stencil format can be either 8 bits or 1 bit and is typically the latter.

Adding a stencil is a snap in Android and takes us back to the onCreate() method of the activity file, where the GLSurfaceView is initialized. The default format of the OpenGL surface is RGB565, with a 16-bit depth buffer and no stencil buffer. The latter can be addressed by the following of code with setEGLConfigChooser() call, with the final parameter specifying a 1-bit stencil.

GLSurfaceView view = **new** GLSurfaceView(**this**);

```
        view.setEGLConfigChooser(8,8,8,8,16,1);
        view.setRenderer(new CubeRenderer(true));
```

Essentially, you render something to the stencil buffer as you would to any other, but in this case, any pixel and its value are used to determine how to render future images to the screen. The most common case is that any later image drawn to the stencil area will be rendered as it normally would, whereas anything outside of the stencil area is not rendered. These behaviors can be modified, of course, keeping with OpenGL's philosophy of making everything more flexible than the vast majority of engineers would use, let alone understand. Still, it can be very handy at times. We'll stay with the simple function for the time being (Listing 7–5).

**Listing 7–5.** *The Stencil Is Generated like a Normal Screen Object*

```
    public void renderToStencil(GL10 gl)
{

        gl.glEnable(GL10.GL_STENCIL_TEST);                           //1
        gl.glStencilFunc(GL10.GL_ALWAYS,1, 0xFFFFFFFF);             //2
        gl.glStencilOp(GL10.GL_REPLACE, GL10.GL_REPLACE, GL10.GL_REPLACE);  //3

        renderStage(gl);                                           //4

        gl.glStencilFunc(GL10.GL_EQUAL, 1, 0xFFFFFFFF);            //5
        gl.glStencilOp(GL10.GL_KEEP, GL10.GL_KEEP,GL10.GL_KEEP);   //6
}
```

So, you establish your stencil the following way:

- Enable the stencil as done in line 1.

- In line 2 we specify the comparison function used whenever something is writing to the stencil buffer. Since we clear it each time through, it will be all zeros. The function GL_ALWAYS says that every write will pass the stencil test, which is what we want when constructing the stencil itself. The value of 1 is called the *reference* value, which is used to perform additional tests for fine-tuning the behavior, but it is way out of the scope of this text. The final value is a mask for the bit planes to access. Since we're not concerned about it, let's just turn them all on.

- Line 3 specifies what to do when a stencil test succeeds or fails. The first parameter pertains if the stencil test fails, the second pertains if the stencil passes but the depth test fails, and the third pertains if both succeed. Since we are living in 3D space here, having the stencil tests coupled to depth testing recognizes that there may be situations in which one overrules the other. Some of the subtleties in the use of the stencil buffer can get quite complicated. In this case, set all three to GL_REPLACE. Table 7–1 shows all the other permissible values.

■ Line 4 calls our rendering function, pretty much as you would normally call it. In this case, it is writing both to the stencil buffer and to one of the color channels at the same time, so we can get a glint of sorts off of our new shiny stage or platform. Meanwhile, in the stencil buffer, the background will remain zeros, while the image will produce stencil pixels that are greater than 0, so it permits image data to write to it later.

■ Lines 5 and 6 prepare the buffer now for normal use. Line 5 says that if the value in the currently addressed stencil pixel is 1, keep it unchanged as given in line 6. Otherwise, pass the fragment through to be processed as if the stencil buffer wasn't there (although it may still be ignored if it fails the depth test). So, for any stencil pixel that is 0, the test will fail, and the incoming fragment will be locked out.

**Table 7–1.** *Possible Values for* glStencilOp()

| Op Type | Action |
| --- | --- |
| GL_KEEP | Keeps the current value. |
| GL_ZERO | Sets the stencil buffer value to 0. |
| GL_REPLACE | Sets the stencil buffer value to ref, as specified by glStencilFunc(). |
| GL_INCR | Increments the current stencil buffer value. Clamps to the maximum representable unsigned value. |
| GL_INCR_WRAP | Increments the current stencil buffer value. Wraps stencil buffer value to zero when incrementing the maximum representable unsigned value. |
| GL_DECR | Decrements the current stencil buffer value. Clamps to 0. |
| GL_DECR_WRAP | Decrements the current stencil buffer value. Wraps stencil buffer value to the maximum representable unsigned value when decrementing a stencil buffer value of zero. |
| GL_INVERT | Bitwise inverts the current stencil buffer value. |

As you can see, the stencil buffer is a very powerful instrument with a lot of subtlety. But any more extravagant use is reserved for future books as yet unnamed.

Now it's time for the renderStage() method, as shown in Listing 7–6.

**Listing 7–6.** Rendering the Reflective Area to the Stencil Buffer Only

```
public void renderStage(GL10 gl)
{
      float[] flatSquareVertices =
   {
         -1.0f,  0.0f, -1.0f,
          1.0f,  0.0f, -1.0f,
```

```
                    -1.0f,   0.0f,   1.0f,
                     1.0f,   0.0f,   1.0f
        };

            FloatBuffer vertexBuffer;

            float[] colors=
            {
                    1.0f,    0.0f,   0.0f, 0.5f,
                    1.0f,    0.0f,   0.0f, 1.0f,
                    0.0f,    0.0f,   0.0f, 0.0f,
                    0.5f,    0.0f,   0.0f, 0.5f
            };

            FloatBuffer colorBuffer;

                gl.glFrontFace(GL10.GL_CW);
                gl.glPushMatrix();
                gl.glTranslatef(0.0f,-2.0f,mOriginZ);
                gl.glScalef(2.5f,1.5f,2.0f);

                gl.glVertexPointer(3, GL11.GL_FLOAT,
                    0,makeFloatBuffer(flatSquareVertices));
                gl.glEnableClientState(GL10.GL_VERTEX_ARRAY);

                gl.glColorPointer(4, GL11.GL_FLOAT, 0,makeFloatBuffer(colors));

                gl.glEnableClientState(GL10.GL_COLOR_ARRAY);

                gl.glDepthMask(false);                               //1
                gl.glColorMask(true,false,false, true);             //2
                gl.glDrawArrays(GL10.GL_TRIANGLE_STRIP,0, 4);       //3
                gl.glColorMask(true,true,true,true);               //4
                gl.glDepthMask(true);                               //5

                gl.glPopMatrix();
        }
```

▨ In line 1, writing to the depth buffer is disabled, and line 2 disables the green and blue color channels, so only the red one will be used. That is how the reflected area gets its little red highlight.

▨ Now we can draw the image to the stencil buffer in line 3.

▨ Lines 4 and 5 reset the masks.

At this point, the onDrawFrame() routine has to be modified, yet again. And if you can keep your peepers open, check out Listing 7–7 for the cruel and unvarnished truth. Sorry for repeating so much of the previous code, but it's much easier than saying "…and after the bit about squirrel trebuchets add such-and-such a line…."

**Listing 7–7.** *The Reflection onDrawFrame() Method*

```java
    public void onDrawFrame(GL10 gl)
{
        gl.glClear(GL10.GL_COLOR_BUFFER_BIT | GL10.GL_DEPTH_BUFFER_BIT |        //1
        GL10.GL_STENCIL_BUFFER_BIT);
        gl.glClearColor(0.0f,0.0f,0.0f,1.0f);

        renderToStencil(gl);                                                   //2

        gl.glEnable(GL10.GL_CULL_FACE);
        gl.glCullFace(GL10.GL_BACK);

        gl.glMatrixMode(GL10.GL_MODELVIEW);
        gl.glLoadIdentity();

        gl.glPushMatrix();

        gl.glEnable(GL10.GL_STENCIL_TEST);                                     //3
        gl.glDisable(GL10.GL_DEPTH_TEST);

        //Flip the image.

        gl.glTranslatef(0.0f,((float)(Math.sin(-mTransY)/2.0f)-2.5f),mOriginZ); //4
        gl.glRotatef(mAngle, 0.0f, 1.0f, 0.0f);

        gl.glScalef(1.0f, -1.0f, 1.0f);                                        //5
        gl.glFrontFace(GL10.GL_CW);

        gl.glEnable(GL10.GL_BLEND);                                            //6
        gl.glBlendFunc(GL10.GL_ONE, GL10.GL_ONE_MINUS_SRC_COLOR);

        mCube.draw(gl);                                                        //7

        gl.glDisable(GL10.GL_BLEND);

        gl.glPopMatrix();

        gl.glEnable(GL10.GL_DEPTH_TEST);
        gl.glDisable(GL10.GL_STENCIL_TEST);

        //Now the main image.

        gl.glPushMatrix();
        gl.glScalef(1.0f, 1.0f, 1.0f);                                        //8
```

```
                    gl.glFrontFace(GL10.GL_CCW);

                    gl.glTranslatef(0.0f,(float)(1.5f*(Math.sin(mTransY)/2.0f)+2.0f),mOriginZ);

                    gl.glRotatef(mAngle, 0.0f, 1.0f, 0.0f);

                    mCube.draw(gl);

                    gl.glPopMatrix();

                    mTransY+=.075f;
                    mAngle+=.4f;
            }
```

And here's the breakdown:

- In line 1, GL_STENCIL_BUFFER_BIT is added to glClear(), which means it must be rebuilt each frame, as shown in line 2 of Listing 7–6. This will actually create the stenciled region, poking the hole that we'll draw through next.

- Enable the stencil test in line 3.

- Here in lines 4 and 5 the reflection is drawn. First translate it down a little, subtracting 1.5, to ensure that it is below the real object. And then it's a simple matter of "scaling" the y-axis to -1.0, which has the effect of flipping it upside-down. You will need to change the front face to clockwise at this point; otherwise, you'll see the back faces only.

- We want to make the lower image translucent instead of the full intensity, as we'd expect. In lines 6f, blend is enabled and uses the most common blending function of GL_ONE and GL_ONE_MINUS_SRC_COLOR covered in Chapter 6.

- In line 7 we can draw our object, the cube in this case.

- Since scale was touched to invert the image, in line 8 scale is reset to the default. The translation has been modified with a couple of other small values. This shifts it up a little bit just to get extra clearance for the inverted cube.

And now the test: Figure 7–8 is what you should see.

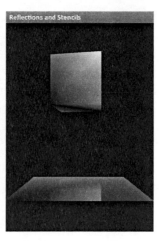

**Figure 7–8.** *Using stencils to create reflections*

# Coming of the Shadows

Shadow casting has always been a bit of a black art in OpenGL, and it still is to a certain extent. However, with faster CPUs and GPUs, many tricks of the trade that were previously the subject of a grad student's paper can finally step out of theory into the warm glow of real-world deployment. Rigorous solutions to shadow casting are still the domain of the non-real-time rendering that Hollywood employs, but basic shadows, under limited conditions, are available to full-motion rendering. With thanks to the various hardware manufacturers that have added both shadow and lighting support to their GPUs, our 3D universes look richer than ever before because few elements in computer graphics can add more realism than carefully managed shadows. (Ask any lighting director on a Hollywood movie.) And don't forget the per-pixel support via the use of shaders in OpenGL ES 2, which can let a programmer delicately shade every corner of every spooky castle in *Blow Up Everything 3*.

There are many ways to cast shadows, or at least shadow-looking things. Perhaps the simplest is to have a prerendered shadow blob: a bitmap that looks like a shadow on the ground, cast by your object. It's cheap, fast, but extremely limited. At the other extreme is the full-blown render-everything-you-can-ever-see software that eats GPUs by the handful for lunch. In between the two, you'll find *shadow mapping, shadow volumes,* and *projection shadows*.

## Shadow Mapping

At one time, one of the most popular forms of shadow casting was through the use of shadow mapping frequently employed in games. Although it is a bit of a bother to set up, not to mention describe, the theory is pretty simple...considering.

Shadow mapping requires two snapshots of the scene. One is from the light's point of view, and the other is from that of the camera's. When rendered from the light, the image will, by definition, see everything illuminated by itself. The color information is ignored, but the depth information is preserved, so we end up with a map of the visible fragments and their relative distances. Now take a shot from the camera's viewpoint. By comparing the two images, we can find out what bits the camera sees that the light cannot. Those bits are in shadow.

In practice, of course, it is a little more complicated than that.

## Shadow Volumes

Shadow volumes are used for determining what part of your scene is illuminated and what is not by making very clever use of certain properties of the stencil buffer. What makes this technique so powerful is that it permits shadows to be cast across arbitrary geometric shapes as opposed to *projection shadows* (discussed later), which really works only for the simplified case of the shadow being thrown against a flat surface.

When a scene is rendered using the shadow volume technique, the stencil buffer will be left in a state in which any part of the resulting image that is shaded will have a corresponding stencil pixel that is greater than zero, while any part that is illuminated will have a zero. See Figure 7–9.

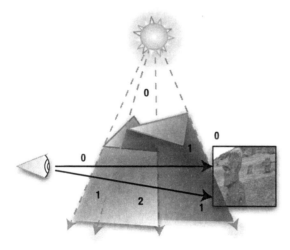

**Figure 7–9.** *Shadow volumes showing the corresponding values in the stencil buffer: 0 for any parts that are illuminated, >0 for regions in shadow*

This is done in three stages. The first pass is to render the image only with ambient light so that the shaded parts of the scene can still be visible. Next is the pass that writes only to the stencil buffer, and the final stage writes the normal image with full illumination. However, only the nonstenciled pixels can be written to the illuminated areas, while they're blocked from writing to the shaded parts, leaving just the original ambient pixels visible.

Going back to the mysterious glStencilOp() function used in the reflectance exercise earlier, we can now make use of those weird GL_INCR and GL_DECR operations. GL_INCR can increase the count in a stencil pixel by one, and GL_DECR will reduce the count by one, both operations triggered under certain conditions.

The term *shadow volume* comes from the following example: imagine it's a foggy night. You take a bright light such as one of your car's headlights and shine it into the mist. Now do some shadow puppetry in the beam. You'll still see part of the beam going around your poorly done shadow of the state of Iowa and wandering off into the distance. We're not interested in that part. What we want is the darkened part of the beam, which is the shadow that is cast by your hands. That is the shadow volume.

In your OpenGL scene, assume you have one light source and a few occluders. These cast shadows upon anything behind them, be it a sphere, cone, or bust of Woodrow Wilson. As you look from the side, you will see objects that are shaded and those that are illuminated. Now draw a vector from any fragment, illuminated or not, to your camera. If the fragment is illuminated, the vector must, by definition, travel through an even number of walls of your shadow volumes: one when it goes into the shaded volume and one when it comes out (of course, ignoring the special case for a vector on the edge of a scene that might not have to pass through any shaded regions). For a fragment inside one of the volumes, the vector will have to pass through an odd number of walls; the single extra wall that makes it odd comes from its own volume of residence.

Now back to stencils. The shadow volumes are generated to look like any other geometry but are drawn only to the stencil, making them invisible since the color buffers are all switched off. The depth buffer is used so that the volume's walls will be rendered in the stencil only *if it is closer* than the real geometry. This trick lets the shadow trace the profiles of arbitrary objects without having to do complicated and fussy calculations of intersecting planes against spheres or Easter Island statues. It merely uses the depth buffer to do pixel-by-pixel tests to decide where shadow ends. So, when the volume is rendered to the stencil, each side of each "cone" of the shadow will affect the stencil in a different way. The side facing us will increment the value in the stencil buffer by one, while the other side will decrement it. So, any regions on the other side of the volume that are illuminated will match part of the stencil mask in which all of the pixels are set to zero, because the vector must go through the same number of faces going in as going out. Any part that is in shade will have a corresponding stencil value of one.

That is why shadow volumes were never chosen for this exercise.

## Blob Shadows

Blob shadows are a total cheat. It simply assumes that there is no real direct light source, so the object's shadow is little more than a blob underneath, as shown in Figure 7–10. As you can see, this won't work too well if our occluder (the shadow casting thing) is a giant man-eating burrito.

**Figure 7–10.** *A blob shadow texture that is placed under all objects*

## Projection Shadows

Projection shadows are the "easiest" of the dynamic shadows algorithms to implement, but that also means they come with many restrictions—namely, that projection shadows work best when casting a shadow on a large flat surface, as shown in Figure 7–11. Also, shadows cannot be cast on arbitrary objects. As with the other approaches, the basic process is to take a snapshot of sorts from the light's point of view and one from the camera's. The light's view is squashed down flat on the plane, painted a suitable shadowy color (aka dark), followed by the occluder being rendered on top.

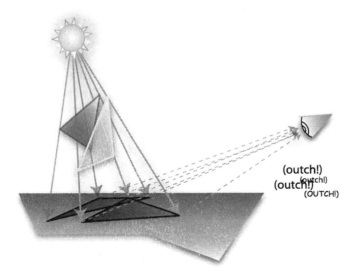

**Figure 7–11.** *Projection of a shadow on a flat plane that is then "reprojected" out to poke the viewer's eye*

The shaded area is calculated by using the intersection of the vectors and the plane, which travel from the light source by way of each of the vertices. Each point on the plane forms a "new" object that can then be transformed, as anything else on the plane would be. Listing 7–11 shows how this is coded.

Let's start again with the basic bouncy cube demo (even though much of it will be changed for the shadow code, it'll still serve as a working template), but we'll swap in different controller code. Listing 7–8 covers some of the initialization parameters you need to add first.

**Listing 7–8.** *The Initialization Stuff to Add to the Renderer*

```
float mSpinX=-1.0f;
float mSpinY=0.0f;
float mSpinZ=0.0f;

float mWorldY=-1.0f;
float mWorldZ=-20.0f;

float mWorldRotationX=35.0f;
float mWorldRotationY=0.0f;
float mLightRadius=2.5f;
```

These simply set up the lighting, lookangle, and animation of the scene.

Listing 7–9 covers the onDrawFrame() method.

**Listing 7–9.** *The onDrawFrame() Method for Projected Shadows*

```
    public void onDrawFrame(GL10 gl)
{
        gl.glClear(GL10.GL_COLOR_BUFFER_BIT | Gl10.GL_DEPTH_BUFFER_BIT);
        gl.glClearColor(0.0f,0.0f,0.0f,1.0f);

        gl.glEnable(GL10.GL_DEPTH_TEST);

        updateLightPosition(gl);                                          //1

        gl.glMatrixMode(GL10.GL_MODELVIEW);
        gl.glLoadIdentity();

        gl.glTranslatef(0.0f,mWorldY,mWorldZ);                            //2
        gl.glRotatef(mWorldRotationX, 1.0f, 0.0f, 0.0f);
        gl.glRotatef(mWorldRotationY, 0.0f, 1.0f, 0.0f);

        renderStage(gl);                                                  //3

        gl.glDisable(GL10.GL_DEPTH_TEST);                                 //4

        calculateShadowMatrix();                                         //5
```

```
        drawShadow(gl,true);                                              //6

        gl.glShadeModel(GL10.GL_SMOOTH);

        gl.glTranslatef(0.0f,(float)(Math.sin(mTransY)/2.0)+mMinY, 0.0f); //7

        gl.glRotatef( mSpinZ, 0.0f, 0.0f, 1.0f );
        gl.glRotatef( mSpinY, 0.0f, 1.0f, 0.0f );
        gl.glRotatef( mSpinX, 1.0f, 0.0f, 0.0f );

        gl.glEnable( GL10.GL_DEPTH_TEST);                                 //8
        gl.glFrontFace(GL10.GL_CCW);

        mCube.draw(gl);                                                   //9

        gl.glDisable(GL10.GL_BLEND);

        mFrameNumber++;

        mSpinX+=.4f;                                                      //10
        mSpinY+=.6f;
        mSpinZ+=.9f;

        mTransY+=.075f;
    }
```

So, what's going on here?

- Line 1 will cause the light to spin around the cube, dynamically changing the shadows.

- Lines 2ff aims your eyepoint.

- We recycle the stage from the previous exercise, in the third line.

- We need to disable the depth test when actually drawing the shadow (Line 4); otherwise, there will be all sorts of z contention that generates cool but useless flickering.

- Line 5 calls the routine to generate the shadow's matrix (detailed later), followed by line 6, which actually draws the shadow using the cleverly named method drawShadow().

- Lines 7ff positions and rotates the occluder, our cube.

- Line 8f safely turns on the depth testing again, after which we can safely draw the cube in line 9.

▓  And in the last bit, lines 10ff, the cube's position and attitude are updated for the next go around.

Before moving on to the next step, check out the following code snippet from renderStage() that describes the stage's geometry:

```
    float[] flatSquareVertices =
{
        -1.0f,  -0.01f, -1.0f,
         1.0f,  -0.01f, -1.0f,
        -1.0f,  -0.01f,  1.0f,
         1.0f,  -0.01f,  1.0f
};
```

Note the tiny negative y value. That is a quick hack to fix a problem called *z-fighting*, in which pixels from co-planer objects may or may not share the same depth value. The result is two faces flickering at one moment; face A is the frontmost, and the next, the pixels of face B, now think they are frontmost. *(Note that hardware may show it differently than the emulator. This is yet another reason to always test on hardware.)* If you look hard enough in almost any real-time 3D software, you will likely see some z's fighting in the background. See Figure 7–12.

**Figure 7–12.** *Z-fighting between the platform and the shadow*

Now we get to the real fun stuff, actually calculating and drawing the shadow. Listing 7–10 shows how the matrix is generated, while Listing 7–11 draws the squashed shadow.

**Listing 7–10.** *Calculating the Shadow Matrix*

```
public void calculateShadowMatrix()
{
        float[] shadowMat_local =
        {
            mLightPosY,   0.0f,   0.0f,      0.0f,
            -mLightPosX,  0.0f,   -mLightPosZ,           -1.0f,
                          0.0f,   0.0f,      mLightPosY, 0.0f,
                          0.0f,   0.0f,      0.0f,       mLightPosY
        };

        for (int i=0;i<16;i++)
        {
                mShadowMat[i] = shadowMat_local[i];
        }
}
```

This is actually a simplified version of the more generalized matrix given by the following:

$$\begin{bmatrix} dotp - l[0]p[0] & -l[1]p[0] & -l[2]p[0] & -l[3]p[0] \\ -l[0]p[1] & dotp - l[1]p[1] & -l[2]p[1] & -l[3]p[1] \\ -l[0]p[2] & -l[1]p[2] & dotp - l[2]p[2] & -l[3]p[2] \\ -l[0]p[3] & -l[1]p[3] & -l[2]p[3] & dotp - l[3]p[3] \end{bmatrix}$$

dotp is the dot product between the light vector and the normal to the plane, l is the position of the light, and p is the plane (the "stage" in my code). Since our platform is in the x/z plane, the plane equation looks like p=[0,1,0,0], or otherwise, p[0]=p[2]=p[3]=0. This means most of the terms in the matrix get zeroed out. Once the matrix is generated, multiplying it by the existing modelview matrix maps the points to your local space along with everything else. Got that? Neither did I, except it seems to work.

Listing 7–11 performs all of the needed transformations for the shadow and renders through the occluder itself, the cube.

**Listing 7–11.** *The drawShadow() Routine*

```
public void drawShadow(GL10 gl,boolean wireframe)
{
        FloatBuffer vertexBuffer;

        gl.glPushMatrix();

        gl.glEnable(GL10.GL_DEPTH_TEST);
        gl.glRotatef(mWorldRotationX, 1.0f, 0.0f, 0.0f);          //1
        gl.glRotatef(mWorldRotationY, 0.0f, 1.0f, 0.0f);
```

```
        gl.glMultMatrixf(makeFloatBuffer(mShadowMat));                      //2

        //Place the shadows.

        gl.glTranslatef(0.0f,(float)(Math.sin(mTransY)/2.0)+mMinY, 0.0f);   //3

        gl.glRotatef((float)mSpinZ,0.0f,0.0f,1.0f);
        gl.glRotatef((float)mSpinY,0.0f,1.0f,0.0f);
        gl.glRotatef((float)mSpinX,1.0f,0.0f,0.0f);

        //Draw them.

        if(mFrameNumber>150)                                                //4
                mCube.drawShadow(gl,true);
        else
                mCube.drawShadow(gl,false);

        gl.glDisable(GL10.GL_BLEND);

        gl.glPopMatrix();
}
```

▨   First rotate everything to world space, just as we have done before, in line 1.

▨   Line 2 multiplies the shadow matrix with the current Modelview matrix.

▨   Lines 3ff perform the same transformations and rotations on the shadow as on
    the actual cube.

▨   And in lines 4ff, the cube renders its own shadow. The two calls there will cause
    the shadow to flip between solid and wireframe, as shown in Figure 7–13.

Listing 7–12 covers the drawShadow() method in Cube.java.

**Listing 7–12.** *Drawing the Shadow*

```
    public void drawShadow(GL10 gl,boolean wireframe)
{
        gl.glDisableClientState(GL10.GL_COLOR_ARRAY);                       //1
        gl.glDisableClientState(GL10.GL_NORMAL_ARRAY);

        gl.glEnable(GL10.GL_BLEND);                                         //2
        gl.glBlendFunc(GL10.GL_ZERO,GL10.GL_ONE_MINUS_SRC_ALPHA);

        gl.glColor4f(0.0f,0.0f,0.0f,0.3f);

        gl.glEnableClientState(GL10.GL_VERTEX_ARRAY);
        gl.glVertexPointer(3, GL10.GL_FLOAT, 0,makeFloatBuffer(mVertices)); //3
```

```
        if(wireframe)
    {
            gl.glLineWidth(3.0f);                                                    //4
            gl.glDrawElements(GL10.GL_LINES, 6 * 3,GL10.GL_UNSIGNED_BYTE, mTfan1);
            gl.glDrawElements(GL10.GL_LINES, 6 * 3,GL10.GL_UNSIGNED_BYTE, mTfan2);
    }
        else
    {
            gl.glDrawElements(GL10.GL_TRIANGLE_FAN,6*3,GL10.GL_UNSIGNED_BYTE,mTfan1);
            gl.glDrawElements(GL10.GL_TRIANGLE_FAN,6*3,GL10.GL_UNSIGNED_BYTE,mTfan2);
    }
    }
```

This will draw either a wireframe shadow, to show how it is composed, or the more traditonal solid model.

■ We first turn off the color and normal arrays in the first line, because they are not needed here.

■ Blending is activated in lines 2ff, so the 0.3 alpha value will keep the shadow from being pure black.

■ Here in the third line, the cube's own vertices are reused, so there is no need to have special geometry for the shadow. That means that you can get a very accurate representation of even the most complex models.

■ Line 4 shows the wireframe code, The line is set to be 3 pixels wide, and glDrawElements() is called with using the GL_LINES type instead of GL_TRIANGLE_FAN.

Now it's time to update the light's position, as in Listing 7–13.

**Listing 7–13.** *Updating the Light's Position*

```
        private void updateLightPosition(GL10 gl)
    {
            mLightAngle +=1.0f;                    //in degrees

            mLightPosX    = (float) (mLightRadius * Math.cos(mLightAngle/57.29f));
            mLightPosY    = mLightHight;
            mLightPosZ    = (float) (mLightRadius * Math.sin(mLightAngle/57.29f));

            mLightPos[1] = mLightPosY;

            mLightPos[0]=mLightPosX;
            mLightPos[2]=mLightPosZ;

            gl.glLightfv(GL10.GL_LIGHT0, GL10.GL_POSITION, makeFloatBuffer(mLightPos));
```

}

This updates the light's position one degree each refresh. The y-value is fixed, so the light traces its little orbit in the x/z plane.

After it's compiled, do you see something like Figure 7–13?

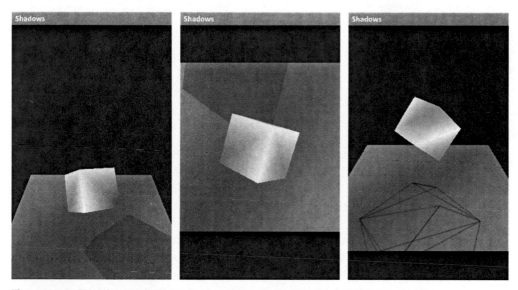

**Figure 7–13**. *The left and middle images have the solid shadow; the right has the wireframe.*

And what's to stop you from having multiple lights? See Figure 7–14, with two lights side by side.

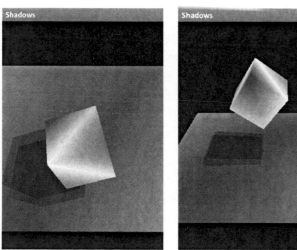

**Figure 7–14.** *The cube with multiple lights*

In all of these images, the background is black. Change the coloring of the background and run. What's going on in Figure 7–15?

**Figure 7–15.** *Surprise! The shadow is not clipped to the platform.*

What's happening here is that we were cheating when it came to clipping the shadow against the platform. With the background black, the part of the shadow that rendered off the platform was invisible. But now as the background is brightened, you can see the full shadow. What happens if you need a light background in the first place? Easy—just use stencils to clip around the platform.

# Summary

In this chapter, we covered a number of extra tricks to add more realism to an OpenGL ES scene. First were frame buffer objects that let you draw to multiple OpenGL frames and merge them together. Next came lens flares that can add visual drama to outdoor scenes, followed by reflections that are heavily used by Apple in a lot of its UI design including CoverFlow. We ended with one of the many ways shadows can be cast against a background using shadow projection. Next, some of these tricks will be applied to our little solar-system project.

# Putting It All Together

*A single lifetime, even though entirely devoted to the sky, would not be enough for the investigation of so vast a subject.*

—Seneca, Roman philosopher

Well, now we've made it all the way up to Chapter 8. This is when we can take what was learned from the exercises up to this point and slap it together into a more complete solar-system model (although it's still missing things like comets, killer asteroids, neutrinos, and trans-Neptunian objects). And afterward, I hope you will say, "Wow! That's kinda cool!"

This chapter will be very code heavy, because the model requires both a number of new routines and modifications to existing projects. And as with some of the listings in Chapter 7, I will not present entire code files because of their length and to avoid repetition, or just to get to sleep earlier (gosh, it's 2:45 a.m. right now); therefore, you are encouraged to fetch the full projects, as well as any necessary data files, from the Apress site to ensure that you have fully functional examples. Complete the set, I always say.

A few new tricks will also be tossed in for good measure, such as how to integrate the standard Android widgets and the use of quaternions. Note that although a lot of the following code is based on previous exercises, there are likely some small tweaks needed to integrate it into the larger package, so unfortunately this won't simply be a cut-and-paste situation.

## Revisiting the Solar System

If you want to fill in the code yourself, I recommend fetching the Chapter 5 variant of the solar-system model, and not the Chapter 7 one, which was used merely as a surface for displaying dynamic textures on 3D objects and won't be used here in that way.

This first exercise will be to add some navigational elements to the show so that you can move your eyepoint around the earth.

But first we need to resize our models to make a slightly more realistic presentation. As of right now, it looks like the earth is about a third the size of the sun and only a few thousand miles away. Considering that it is a pleasant summer day here in Northern California and the earth is anything but a burnt cinder, I bet the model is wrong. Well, let's make it right. This will be done in the `initGeometry()` method in your solar-system controller. And while we're at it, the type of `m_Eyeposition` will be changed to upgrade it to a slightly more objectified object customized for 3D operations. The new routine is in Listing 8–1. Make sure to add a texture for the sun's surface while you are at it; otherwise, nasty things may happen.

**Listing 8–1.** *Resizing the Objects for the Solar System*

```
private void initGeometry(GL10 gl)
{
        // Let 1.0=1 million miles.
        // The sun's radius=.4.
        // The earth's radius=.04 (10x larger to make it easier to see).

        m_Eyeposition[X_VALUE] = 0.0f;
        m_Eyeposition[Y_VALUE] = 0.0f;
        m_Eyeposition[Z_VALUE] = 93.25f;

        m_Earth = new Planet(48, 48, .04f, 1.0f, gl, myAppcontext, true,
                        book.SolarSystem.R.drawable.earth);
        m_Earth.setPosition(0.0f, 0.0f, 93.0f);

        m_Sun = new Planet(48, 48, 0.4f, 1.0f, gl, myAppcontext, false, 0);
        m_Sun.setPosition(0.0f, 0.0f, 0.0f);
}
```

The scale of our model is set at 1 unit=1 million miles (1.7m kilometers or 8.3m furlongs, or 3.52e+9 cubits). The sun has a radius of 400,000 miles, or .4 in these units. That means the earth's radius would be .004, but I've increased it by 10 times, to .04, to make it a little easier to deal with. Because the earth's default position is along the +z-axis, let's put the eye position right behind the earth, only a quarter million miles away, at "93.25." And in the `execute` method for the solar-system object, remove `glRotatef()` so that the earth will now stay fixed. That makes things a lot simpler for the time being. Change the field of view from 50 degrees to 30; also, set `zFar` in `setClipping` to be 2000 (to handle future objects). You should ultimately get something that looks like Figure 8–1. Since the sun is actually behind the earth from our viewpoint, I cranked up the specular lighting for `SS_FILLLIGHT1`.

Solar System

**Figure 8–1.** *Our home on a tiny screen*

"All well and good, code-boy!" you must be muttering under your breath. "But now we're stuck in space!" True enough, so that means the next step is to add a navigational element. And that means (cue dramatic music) we'll be adding *quaternions*.

## What Are These Quaternion Things Anyway?

On October 16, 1843, in Dublin, Irish mathematician Sir William Hamilton was taking a stroll by the Royal Canal when he had a sudden flash of mathematical inspiration. He'd been working on ways to meaningfully multiply and divide two points in space and suddenly saw the formula for quaternions in his mind: $i^2 = j^2 = k^2 = ijk = -1$. Impressive, huh?

He was so excited that he couldn't resist the temptation to carve it into the stonework of the Brougham Bridge he had just come to (no doubt nestled in between lesser graffiti like "Eamon loves Fiona, 1839" or "Patrick O'Callahan rulz!"). Radically new ways to look at physics and geometry descended directly from this insight. The classic Maxwell's equations in electromagnetic theory were described entirely through the use of quaternions, for example. As newer methods of dealing with similar situations came about, quaternions were shunted aside until the late 20th century, when they found a significant role in 3D computer graphics, in navigation of the Apollo spacecraft to the moon, and in other areas that rely heavily on rotations in space. Because of their compact nature, they could describe a direction vector, and hence a 3D rotation, more efficiently than the standard 3x3 matrix. Not only that, but they provided a much superior means of concatenating a series of rotations on top of each other. So, what does this mean?

In Chapter 2, we covered the traditional 3D transformation math using matrices. If you wanted to rotate an object 32° around the z-axis, you would instruct OpenGL ES to perform a rotation via the command glRotatef(32,0,0,1). Similar commands would be executed for the x- and y-axes as well. But what if you wanted a funky sort of rotation that an airplane might make when banking to the left? How would that be described in the glRotatef() format? Using the more traditional way, you would generate separate matrices for the three rotations and then multiply them in order of *yaw* (rotation around the y-axis), *pitch* (rotation around the x-axis), and *roll* around the z-axis. That's a lot of math merely to aim toward one direction. But if this is for a flight simulator, your banking motion will constantly update to new rolls and headings, incrementally. That would mean you'd have to calculate the three matrices each time for the deltas of your trajectory since the last frame and not absolute values from some starting point.

In the early days of computers, when floating-point calculations were expensive and shortcuts were regularly invoked for performance reasons, round-off errors were common and would likely build up over time, causing the current matrices to be "out of square." However, quaternions were brought to the rescue because they had a couple of very compelling properties.

The first is that a quaternion can represent a rotation of an object in space roughly equivalent to how glRotate() works but by using fractional axis values. It's not a direct one-to-one correlation, because you still need to go about some of that math stuff to convert attitudes to and from a quaternion.

The second and more important property derives from the fact that an arc on a sphere can be described by two quaternions, one at each endpoint. And any point between them on the arc can also be described by a quaternion simply by interpolating the distance from one endpoint to the other by using spherical geometry, as shown in Figure 8–2. That is, if you were going through an arc of 60°, you could find an intermediate quaternion, say, 20° from the starting point, by tracing a third of the way along the arc. In the next frame, if you were to jump to 20.1°, you merely add a teeny-tiny more of that arc to your *current* quaternion instead of having to go through the tedious process of generating the three matrices each time and multiplying them together. This process is called *slerping,* where *slerp* stands for *spherical linear interpolation*. Because an axis/angle pair does not rely on a cumulative summation of all previous ones like when using matrices but on an instantaneous value, there is no error buildup as a result of the former.

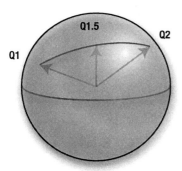

**Figure 8–2.** *An intermediate quaternion; Q1.5 on a sphere can be interpolated from two others, Q1 and Q2*

Slerp is used to provide those smooth animations of a viewpoint's "camera" when going from one point to another. It can be part of a flight simulator, a space simulator, or the view from a chase car for a racing game. And naturally they are used in real flight guidance systems as well.

So, now with that bit of background, we're going to use quaternions to help move the earth around.

## Moving Things in 3D

Since we are not animating the earth currently, we need a way to move it around so that we can investigate it from all ends. With that in mind, since the earth is our target of interest, we'll set up a situation in which the eye point will effectively hover over the earth directed by pinch and move gestures.

The first step is to add gesture recognizers, which come through Android's onTouchEvent() call. You'll need to support both pinch and drag functions. Pinch is to zoom in and out, while pan lets you drag the planet around underneath you, always keeping it centered. More sophisticated motions such as momentum-swipe, or "flings," are left up to you to implement, which unfortunately can get a little messy.

The code is structured a little differently. The core module that has traditionally been an implementation of GLSurfaceView.Renderer is now a GLSurfaceView subclass called SolarSystemView. The renderer is now the new SolarSystem object. The former primarily serves as an event sink for the pinch and drag events, while the latter handles the main update loop and serves as a container for any solar-systemy type of objects.

Here in the new SolarSystemView, we'll need only the pinch and pan gestures. You use the onTouchEvent() to handle all touch events, initialize some values, and decide whether you are doing a pinch or drag function. To your view controller's onTouchEvent() method, add Listing 8–2.

**Listing 8–2.** *Handling Pinch and Drag Events*

```
    public boolean onTouchEvent(MotionEvent ev)
{
    boolean retval = true;

    switch (ev.getAction() & MotionEvent.ACTION_MASK)
    {
        case MotionEvent.ACTION_DOWN:
            m_Gesture = DRAG;                                        //1
            break;

        case MotionEvent.ACTION_UP:
        case MotionEvent.ACTION_POINTER_UP:
            m_Gesture = NONE;                                       //2
            m_LastTouchPoint.x = ev.getX();
            m_LastTouchPoint.y = ev.getY();
            break;

        case MotionEvent.ACTION_POINTER_DOWN:
            m_OldDist = spacing(ev);                                //3

            midPoint(m_MidPoint, ev);
            m_Gesture = ZOOM;
            m_LastTouchPoint.x = m_MidPoint.x;
            m_LastTouchPoint.y = m_MidPoint.y;
            m_CurrentTouchPoint.x=m_MidPoint.x;
            m_CurrentTouchPoint.y=m_MidPoint.y;

            break;

        case MotionEvent.ACTION_MOVE:
            if (m_Gesture == DRAG)                                  //4
        {
                retval = handleDragGesture(ev);
        }
            else if (m_Gesture == ZOOM)
        {
                retval = handlePinchGesture(ev);
        }
            break;
    }

    return retval;
}
```

Here's the breakdown:

- Section 1 handles the your finger touching the display, or the first finger for a multitouch event. Initialize the motion type, m_Gesture, to DRAG.

- Section 2 handles when a motion is done.

- Section 3 takes care of pinch-to-zoom functions. m_MidPoint is used to determine what point on the screen to zoom in to. This is not needed here because we'll only zoom into the earth in the center of the screen, but it's nice reference code nonetheless.

- Finally in section 4, the proper gesture actions are called.

Next we need to add the two handlers, handleDragGesture() and handlePinchGesture(), as shown in Listing 8–3.

**Listing 8–3.** *The Two Handlers for the Gesture Recognizers*

```
final PointF m_CurrentTouchPoint = new PointF();
PointF m_MidPoint = new PointF();
PointF m_LastTouchPoint = new PointF();
static int m_GestureMode = 0;
static int DRAG_GESTURE = 1;
static int PINCH_GESTURE = 2;

public boolean handleDragGesture(MotionEvent ev)
{
    m_LastTouchPoint.x = m_CurrentTouchPoint.x;
    m_LastTouchPoint.y = m_CurrentTouchPoint.y;

    m_CurrentTouchPoint.x = ev.getX();
    m_CurrentTouchPoint.y = ev.getY();

    m_GestureMode = DRAG_GESTURE;
    m_DragFlag = 1;

    return true;
}


public boolean handlePinchGesture(MotionEvent ev)
{
    float minFOV = 5.0f;
    float maxFOV = 100.0f;
    float newDist = spacing(ev);

    m_Scale = m_OldDist/newDist;

    if (m_Scale > m_LastScale)
    {
        m_LastScale = m_Scale;
    }
    else if (m_Scale <= m_LastScale)
```

```
        {
               m_LastScale = m_Scale;
        }

        m_CurrentFOV = m_StartFOV * m_Scale;
        m_LastTouchPoint = m_MidPoint;
        m_GestureMode = PINCH_GESTURE;

        if (m_CurrentFOV >= minFOV && m_CurrentFOV <= maxFOV)
        {
               mRenderer.setFieldOfView(m_CurrentFOV);
               return true;
        }
        else
               return false;
    }
```

Both of these are pretty basic. handleDragGesture() sets keeps track of the current and previous touch points, used when determining the speed of a drag operation. The larger the deltas between the two, the faster the screen's animation should be. handlePinchGesture() does the same for the pinch-to-zoom operations. m_OldDist and newDist are the previous and new distances between the two pinch-fingers. The difference determines how much to change the field of view. Compressing the figures zooms in, while spreading them out zooms out to a maximum of 100 degrees.

The gestures are then processed in the onDrawFrame() method, as shown in Listing 8–4.

**Listing 8–4.** *Processing the New Pinch and Drag States*

```
    public void onDrawFrame(GL10 gl)
{
        gl.glClear(GL10.GL_COLOR_BUFFER_BIT | GL10.GL_DEPTH_BUFFER_BIT);
        gl.glClearColor(0.0f, 0.0f, 0.0f, 1.0f);

        if (m_GestureMode == PINCH_GESTURE && m_PinchFlag == 1)                 //1
        {
            setClipping(gl, origwidth, origheight);
            m_PinchFlag = 0;
        }
        else if (m_GestureMode == DRAG_GESTURE && m_DragFlag == 1)              //2
        {
            setHoverPosition(gl, 0, m_CurrentTouchPoint, m_LastTouchPoint, m_Earth);

            m_DragFlag = 0;
        }

        execute(gl);
    }
```

In section 1, the pinch is processed only if a new gesture was detected and flagged via m_PinchFlag, which is reset after processing. Without this, the zoom would continue for each successive call to onDrawFrame(). The view frustum is updated each time via setClipping() using the m_FieldOfView value, because that mechanism actually determines the magnification of the view. Section 2 is the same for drag gestures. In this case, setHoverPosition() is called with the current and previous touch points. This also has a toggle in it via m_DragFlag, which turns off any further drag processing until a new event is detected. Otherwise, you'll get a drift in your viewpoint even if your finger isn't moving.

And if you want to see the pinch-zoom in action right now, comment out the line setHoverPosition() in the previous listing, and then compile and run.

You should be able to zoom in and out from the earth model, as shown in Figure 8–3.

**Figure 8–3.** *Zooming in and out using pinch gestures*

Now we're going to do the rotation support, which includes those quaternion things. This perhaps the most involved of any of the exercises up to this point. We'll need a number of helper routines to aim your viewpoint and to move it in "orbit" around the earth. So, let's start at the top and work down. Listing 8–5 is the heart of the "hover mode."

**Listing 8–5.** *Sets a New Hover Position Around the Earth*

```
        public void setHoverPosition(GL10 gl, int nFlags, PointF location,
                PointF prevLocation, Planet m_Planet)
    {
            double dx;
```

```
            double dy;
            Quaternion orientation = new Quaternion(0, 0, 0, 1.0);
            Quaternion tempQ;
            Vector3 offset = new Vector3(0.0f, 0.0f, 0.0f);
            Vector3 objectLoc = new Vector3(0.0f, 0.0f, 0.0f);
            Vector3 vpLoc = new Vector3(0.0f, 0.0f, 0.0f);
            Vector3 offsetv = new Vector3(0.0f, 0.0f, 0.0f);
            Vector3 temp = new Vector3(0.0f, 0.0f, 0.0f);
            float reference = 300.0f;
            float scale = 2.0f;
            float matrix3[][] = new float[3][3];
            boolean debug = false;

            gl.glMatrixMode(GL10.GL_MODELVIEW);
            gl.glLoadIdentity();

            orientation = Miniglu.gluGetOrientation(); //1

            vpLoc.x = m_Eyeposition[0];                                         //2
            vpLoc.y = m_Eyeposition[1];
            vpLoc.z = m_Eyeposition[2];

            objectLoc.x = m_Planet.m_Pos[0];                                    //3
            objectLoc.y = m_Planet.m_Pos[1];
            objectLoc.z = m_Planet.m_Pos[2];

            offset.x = (objectLoc.x - vpLoc.x);                                 //4
            offset.y = (objectLoc.y - vpLoc.y);
            offset.z = (objectLoc.z - vpLoc.z);

            offsetv.z = temp.Vector3Distance(objectLoc, vpLoc);                 //5

            dx = (double) (location.x - prevLocation.x);
            dy = (double) (location.y - prevLocation.y);

            float multiplier;

            multiplier = origwidth / reference;

            gl.glMatrixMode(GL10.GL_MODELVIEW);

            // Rotate around the X-axis.

            float c, s;                                                         //6
            float rad = (float) (scale * multiplier * dy / reference)/2.0;

            s = (float) Math.sin(rad * .5);
            c = (float) Math.cos(rad * .5);
```

```
        temp.x = s;
        temp.y = 0.0f;
        temp.z = 0.0f;

        Quaternion tempQ1 = new Quaternion(temp.x, temp.y, temp.z, c);

        tempQ1 = tempQ1.mulThis(orientation);

        // Rotate around the Y-axis.

        rad = (float) (scale * multiplier * dx / reference);          //7

        s = (float) Math.sin(rad * .5);
        c = (float) Math.cos(rad * .5);

        temp.x = 0.0f;
        temp.y = s;
        temp.z = 0.0f;

        Quaternion tempQ2 = new Quaternion(temp.x, temp.y, temp.z, c);

        tempQ2 = tempQ2.mulThis(tempQ1);

        orientation=tempQ2;

        matrix3 = orientation.toMatrix();          //8

        matrix3 = orientation.tranposeMatrix(matrix3);               //9
        offsetv = orientation.Matrix3MultiplyVector3(matrix3, offsetv);

        m_Eyeposition[0] = (float)(objectLoc.x + offsetv.x);          //10
        m_Eyeposition[1] =  (float)(objectLoc.y + offsetv.y);
        m_Eyeposition[2] =  (float)(objectLoc.z + offsetv.z);

        lookAtTarget(gl, m_Planet);                                   //11
    }
```

I bet you're wondering just what's going on here?

■ First we get the cached quaternion from a new helper class that we'll create a little later. The quaternion is the current orientation of our eyepoint in line 1, which we'll need along with the viewpoint's xyz location from the solar-system object in Line 2.

■ Lines 3ff get the target's location. In this case, the target is merely the earth. With that in hand, we need to find the offset of our eye point from the earth's center and then calculate that distance, as in lines 4ff.

- Line 5 takes the screen coordinates of the previous and current drags, so we know just how much we moved since the last time.

- Lines 6ff create a fractional rotation in radians for each new position of the drag operation around the X-axis. This is then multiplied by the actual orientation quaternion (recovered in line 1) to ensure that the new orientation from each touch position is preserved. The 2.0 divisor scales back the vertical motions; otherwise, they'd be much to fast. This represents the cumulative rotations of the eye point. The three values of scale, multiplier, and reference are all arbitrary. Scale is fixed and was used for some fine-tuning to ensure things moved at just the right speed that ideally will match that of your finger. The multiplier is handy for orientation changes because it is a scaling factor that is based on the screen's current width and a reference value that is also arbitrary.

  Another quaternion encapsulating rotation around the Y-axis is generated in much the same way in lines 7ff. That is multiplied with the previous one for the final rotation. Line 8 then converts that to a traditional matrix.

- Lines 9f use the transpose of the matrix against the offset value to arrive at the new location in space and is stored in m_Eyeposition. Since we're going from the local coordinates of the earth to world coordinates we take the transpose to, in effect, reverse the operation.

- Even though our eyepoint is moved to a new position, we still need to actually aim it back at the hover target, the earth, as done in line 11 via lookAtTarget().

Now we need to create a few of the aforementioned helper routines that will help cinch everything together.

In normal OpenGL, I've mentioned the existence of a utility library called GLUT. Unfortunately, there is no complete GLUT library for Android as of this writing, although there are a few incomplete versions out there. I have put them into a file called Miniglu.java, available from the Apress site with this project.

> **NOTE:** Android has a very small but official suite of GLU routines located in android.opengl.GLU, but it didn't have all that I needed.

Listing 8–6 contains the Miniglu version of gluLookAt(), a hyper-useful utility that does just what it says: aims your lookangle. You pass it the location of your eyepoint, the thing you want to look at, and an up vector to specify roll angles. Naturally, straight up would be equal to no roll whatsoever. But you still need to supply it.

**Listing 8–6.** *Looking at Anything Using* gluLookAt

```
static Quaternion m_Quaternion = new Quaternion(0, 0, 0, 1);

public static void gluLookAt(GL10 gl, float eyex, float eyey, float eyez,
        float centerx, float centery, float centerz, float upx,
```

```
          float upy, float upz)
{
    Vector3 up = new Vector3(0.0f, 0.0f, 0.0f);                    //1
    Vector3 from = new Vector3(0.0f, 0.0f, 0.0f);
    Vector3 to = new Vector3(0.0f, 0.0f, 0.0f);
    Vector3 lookat = new Vector3(0.0f, 0.0f, 0.0f);
    Vector3 axis = new Vector3(0.0f, 0.0f, 0.0f);
        float angle;

    lookat.x = centerx;                                           //2
    lookat.y = centery;
    lookat.z = centerz;

    from.x = eyex;
    from.y = eyey;
    from.z = eyez;

    to.x = lookat.x;
    to.y = lookat.y;
    to.z = lookat.z;

    up.x = upx;
    up.y = upy;
    up.z = upz;

    Vector3 temp = new Vector3(0, 0, 0);                          //3
    temp = temp.Vector3Sub(to, from);
    Vector3 n = temp.normalise(temp);

    temp = temp.Vector3CrossProduct(n, up);
    Vector3 v = temp.normalise(temp);

    Vector3 u = temp.Vector3CrossProduct(v, n);

    float[][] matrix;

    matrix = temp.Matrix3MakeWithRows(v, u, temp.Vector3Negate(n));

    m_Quaternion = m_Quaternion.QuaternionMakeWithMatrix3(matrix);    //4

    m_Quaternion.printThis("GluLookat:");

    axis = m_Quaternion.QuaternionAxis();
    angle = m_Quaternion.QuaternionAngle();

    gl.glRotatef((float) angle * DEGREES_PER_RADIAN, (float) axis.x,
        (float) axis.y, (float) axis.z);                          //5
```

```
    }
```

Here's what's going on:

- As referenced earlier, we need to grab points or vectors to fully describe our position in space and that of the target, as in lines 1ff. The up vector is local to your eye point, and it is typically just a unit vector pointing up the y-axis. You could modify this if you wanted to do banking rolls. The Vector3 objects are part of a small math library associated with this project. Many such libraries exist, however.

- In lines 2ff, the terms passed through in discrete values are mapped to Vector3 objects that can then be used with the vector math libraries. Why instead of vectors in? The official GLUT libraries don't use vector objects, so this matches the existing standard.

- Lines 3ff generate three new vectors, two using cross products. This ensures everything is both normalized and the axis squared.

- Some examples of gluLookAt() generate a matrix. Here, quaternions are used instead. In line 4, the quaternion is created by our new vectors and is used to get the axis/angle parameters that glRotatef() likes to use, as in line 5. Note that the resulting quaternion is cached via a global that can be picked up later if the instantaneous attitude is needed via gluGetOrientation(). It's clumsy, but it works. In real life, you probably wouldn't want to do this, because it assumes only a single viewpoint in your entire world. In reality, you might want to have more than one—if, for example, you wanted two simultaneous displays showing your object from two different vantage points.

Finally, we can take a look at the resulting image. You should now be able to spin our fair little world to your heart's content (see Figure 8–4). The little yellow blotch that sometimes shows is the sun.

**Figure 8–4.** *The hover mode lets you rotate the earth at will.*

So, that's part one of today's exercise. Remember those lens flare things from Chapter 7? Now we can put them to use.

# Adding Some Flare

From Chapter 7, grab the three source files from the lens flare exercise, and add them to your project along with the artwork. These will be the `CreateTexture.java` helper library, `Flare.java` for each of the reflections, and `LensFlare.java`. This will also require some substantial tweaks to the renderer object, mainly in the execute routine.

Something like a lens flare effect has all sorts of small side issues that will be addressed. Namely, if the flare's source object, in the case the sun, goes behind the earth, the flare itself should vanish. Also, note that it won't vanish immediately but will actually fade out. There are a couple of new utility routines that need to be added before the flare itself can be rendered.

First make sure to initialize the LensFlare object in your `onSurfaceCreated()` handler:

```
int resid;
resid = book.SolarSystem.R.drawable.gimpsun3;
m_FlareSource = CT.createTexture(gl, myAppcontext, true, resid);
m_LensFlare.createFlares(gl, myAppcontext);
```

Now is time to just dump any image utilities over into their own routine. It is called `CreateTexture.java`. This will help support the preceding call. The `.png` file can be whatever you want that will replace the current 3D sun model. We want this so that we can draw a flat bitmap of the sun where the spherical model would normally render as it has in the past. The reason is that we can finely control the look of our star to make it more closely resemble how the eye might perceive this. The stark yellow ball, while technically more accurate, just doesn't look right because any optical receptor to this would add all sorts of various distortions, reflections, and highlights (lens flares, for example). Shaders could be employed that mathematically model the optics of the eye, but that's a lot of work for a fuzzy ball-like-thing for the time being. You can download my own artwork from the Apress site if you choose. Or just copy something to suit your own tastes. Figure 8–5 is what I am using. Interesting enough, this image fools my own eyes enough to make my brain think that I am actually looking at something too bright, because it causes all sorts of eyestrain when I stare at it.

This uses a technique called *billboarding*, which takes a flat 2D texture and keeps it aimed toward the viewer no matter where they are. It permits complex and fairly random organic objects (things called *trees* I think) to be easily depicted while using only simple textures. As your viewpoint changes, the billboard objects rotate to compensate.

**Figure 8–5.** *The sun image used to give a more authentic-looking glow*

Both the lens flare manager, which I call LensFlare.java, and the individual Flare.java objects need to be modified. To the execute method of LensFlare.java I've added two new parameters. execute() should now look like this:

```
public void execute(GL10 gl,CGSize size, CGPoint source, float scale, float alpha)
```

The new scale parameter is a single value that will increase or decrease the size of the entire flare chain, needed when you zoom in or out of the scene, and alpha is used to dim the entire flare as the sun starts sliding behind the earth. Both parameters will likewise need to be added to the individual flare object's execute method and then used to twiddle with the size and alpha parameters passed to CreateTexture's renderTextureAt() method, as follows:

```
public void renderFlareAt(GL10 gl, int textureID, float x, float y, CGSize size,
    Context context, float scale, float alpha)
{
    CreateTexture ct = new CreateTexture();
    ct.renderTextureAt(gl, x, y, 0f, size, textureID, m_Size*scale,
        m_Red*alpha, m_Green*alpha, m_Blue*alpha, m_Alpha);
}
```

The next listing, Listing 8–7, covers two other Miniglu calls. First there is gluGetScreenLocation(), which returns the 2D coordinates on your screen of a 3D object. It's little more than a front end to gluProject(), which maps, or projects, 3D points against its viewport. Even though these might be "canned" routines, it is still instructive to see how they work. They are used here to get the position of the sun to place the 2D bill boarded artwork. Later they can be used to place other 2D items in the sky, such as the constellation names.

**Listing 8–7.** *gluProject() and gluGetScreenCoords()*

```
public static boolean gluProject(float objx, float objy, float objz,
        float[] modelMatrix, float[] projMatrix, int[] viewport,float[] win)
{
    float[] in = new float[4];
    float[] out = new float[4];

    in[0] = objx;                                                    //1
```

```
    in[1] = objy;
    in[2] = objz;
    in[3] = 1.0f;

    gluMultMatrixVector3f (modelMatrix, in, out);                    //2

    gluMultMatrixVector3f (projMatrix, out, in);

                    if (in[3] == 0.0f)
    in[3] = 1.0f;

    in[0] /= in[3];
    in[1] /= in[3];
    in[2] /= in[3];

            /* Map x, y and z to range 0-1 */

    in[0] = in[0] * 0.5f + 0.5f;                                     //3
    in[1] = in[1] * 0.5f + 0.5f;
    in[2] = in[2] * 0.5f + 0.5f;

            /* Map x,y to viewport */

    win[0] = in[0] * viewport[2] + viewport[0];
    win[1] = in[1] * viewport[3] + viewport[1];
    win[2] = in[3];

    return (true);
}

public static void gluGetScreenLocation(GL10 gl, float xa, float ya, float za,
    float screenRadius, boolean render, float[] screenLoc)
{
    float[] mvmatrix = new float[16];
    float[] projmatrix = new float[16];
    int[] viewport = new int[4];
    float[] xyz = new float[3];

    GL11 gl11 = (GL11) gl;

    gl11.glGetIntegerv(GL11.GL_VIEWPORT, viewport, 0);              // 4
    gl11.glGetFloatv(GL11.GL_MODELVIEW_MATRIX, mvmatrix, 0);
    gl11.glGetFloatv(GL11.GL_PROJECTION_MATRIX, projmatrix, 0);

    gluProject(xa, ya, za, mvmatrix, projmatrix, viewport,xyz);

    xyz[1]=viewport[3]-xyz[1];                                      //5
```

```
                    screenLoc[0] = xyz[0];
                    screenLoc[1] = xyz[1];
                    screenLoc[2] = xyz[2];
            }
```

Let's examine the code a bit closer:

▨ Lines 1ff map the object coordinates to an array that will then be multiplied by the
   modelMatrix (supplied as one of the arguments).

▨ At lines 2ff, the multiplication is done via another GLUT helper routine that I added
   because it was quicker to write than to track down. First the modelview matrix
   and then the projection matrix operate on our object's xyz coordinates.
   (Remember, the first transform in the list is the last to be executed.) Note that the
   first call to gluMultMatrixVector3f() passes the "in" array, followed by the
   "out," while the second one passes the two arrays in reverse order. There's
   nothing clever here—the second instance reverses the use of the two just to
   recycle the existing arrays.

▨ In lines 3ff, the resulting values of the earlier calculations are normalized and then
   mapped against the screen's dimensions, giving us the final values.

▨ We'd likely never to have to call gluProject() directly; instead, the caller is
   gluGetScreenLocation(), which merely gets the needed matrices in lines 4ff,
   passes them on to gluProject(), and retrieves the screen coordinates. Because
   of the inversion of the y-axis that OpenGL ES does, we need to uninvert it in line 5.

The execute() routine in the SolarSystem renderer must be modified quite a bit to manage the
calling and placement of the lens flare, while along with an enhanced executePlanet() adds some
new parameters to actually identify where the flare should be located on the screen. Both are provided
in Listing 8–8.

Listing 8–8. *Execute with Lens Flare Support*

```
public void execute(GL10 gl)
{
    float[] paleYellow = { 1.0f, 1.0f, 0.3f, 1.0f };
    float[] white = { 1.0f, 1.0f, 1.0f, 1.0f };
    float[] black = { 0.0f, 0.0f, 0.0f, 0.0f };
    float[] sunPos = { 0.0f, 0.0f, 0.0f, 1.0f };
    float sunWidth=0.0f;
    float sunScreenLoc[]=new float[4];          //xyz and radius
    float earthScreenLoc[]=new float[4];        //xyz and radius

    gl.glMatrixMode(GL10.GL_MODELVIEW);
    gl.glShadeModel(GL10.GL_SMOOTH);

    gl.glEnable(GL10.GL_LIGHTING);
    gl.glEnable(GL10.GL_BLEND);
    gl.glBlendFunc(GL10.GL_SRC_ALPHA, GL10.GL_ONE_MINUS_SRC_ALPHA);
```

```java
gl.glPushMatrix();

gl.glTranslatef(-m_Eyeposition[X_VALUE], -m_Eyeposition[Y_VALUE],          //1
            -m_Eyeposition[Z_VALUE]);

gl.glLightfv(SS_SUNLIGHT, GL10.GL_POSITION, makeFloatBuffer(sunPos));
gl.glEnable(SS_SUNLIGHT);

gl.glMaterialfv(GL10.GL_FRONT_AND_BACK, GL10.GL_EMISSION,
            makeFloatBuffer(paleYellow));

executePlanet(m_Sun, gl, false,sunScreenLoc);                              //2

gl.glMaterialfv(GL10.GL_FRONT_AND_BACK, GL10.GL_EMISSION,makeFloatBuffer(black));

gl.glPopMatrix();

if ((m_LensFlare != null) && (sunScreenLoc[Z_INDEX] > 0.0f))              //3
{
      CGPoint centerRelative = new CGPoint();
      CGSize     windowSize = new CGSize();
      float sunsBodyWidth=44.0f;                    //About the width of the sun's body
                                                    // within the glare in the bitmap,
                                                                in pixels.
       float cx,cy;
       float aspectRatio;
       float scale=0f;

       DisplayMetrics display =
           myAppcontext.getResources().getDisplayMetrics();
       windowSize.width = display.widthPixels;
       windowSize.height = display.heightPixels;

          cx=windowSize.width/2.0f;
          cy=windowSize.height/2.0f;

       aspectRatio=cx/cy;                                                 //4

       centerRelative.x = sunScreenLoc[X_INDEX]-cx;
       centerRelative.y =(cy-sunScreenLoc[Y_INDEX])/aspectRatio;

       scale=CT.renderTextureAt(gl, centerRelative.x, centerRelative.y, 0f,
           windowSize,
       m_FlareSource,sunScreenLoc[RADIUS_INDEX], 1.0f,1.0f, 1.0f, 1.0f); //5

       sunWidth=scale*windowSize.width*sunsBodyWidth/256.0f;             //6
}
```

```
gl.glEnable(SS_FILLLIGHT2);

gl.glMatrixMode(GL10.GL_MODELVIEW);
gl.glPushMatrix();

gl.glTranslatef(-m_Eyeposition[X_VALUE], -m_Eyeposition[Y_VALUE],        //7
-m_Eyeposition[Z_VALUE]);

gl.glMaterialfv(GL10.GL_FRONT_AND_BACK, GL10.GL_DIFFUSE,
makeFloatBuffer(white));

gl.glMaterialfv(GL10.GL_FRONT_AND_BACK, GL10.GL_SPECULAR,
    makeFloatBuffer(white));

executePlanet(m_Earth, gl, true,earthScreenLoc);                        //8

gl.glPopMatrix();

if ((m_LensFlare != null) && (sunScreenLoc[Z_INDEX] > 0))              //9
{
float scale = 1.0f;
float delX = origwidth / 2.0f - sunScreenLoc[X_INDEX];
float delY = origheight / 2.0f - sunScreenLoc[Y_INDEX];
float grazeDist = earthScreenLoc[RADIUS_INDEX] + sunWidth;
float percentVisible = 1.0f;
float vanishDist = earthScreenLoc[RADIUS_INDEX] - sunWidth;

float distanceBetweenBodies = (float) Math.sqrt(delX * delX + delY * delY);

if ((distanceBetweenBodies > vanishDist)&& (distanceBetweenBodies
    < grazeDist))                                                      //10
{
    percentVisible=(float) ((distanceBetweenBodies - vanishDist) /sunWidth);

        if (percentVisible > 1.0)                                      //11
        percentVisible = 1.0f;
        else if (percentVisible < 0.3)
        percentVisible = .5f;
    }
    else if (distanceBetweenBodies > grazeDist)
    {
        percentVisible = 1.0f;
    }
    else
    {
        percentVisible = 0.0f;
    }
```

```
        scale = STANDARD_FOV / m_FieldOfView;                          //12
        CGPoint source = new CGPoint();
        source.x = sunScreenLoc[X_INDEX];
        source.y = sunScreenLoc[Y_INDEX];
        CGSize winsize = new CGSize();
        winsize.width = origwidth;
        winsize.height = origheight;

        if (percentVisible > 0.0)
        {
            m_LensFlare.execute(gl, winsize, source, scale,    percentVisible);
        }
    }
}
```

OK, now for the chalk talk:

- You'll notice that two identical glTranslatef() calls are made. The first one in line 1 sets things up for line 2 results. But we need to pop it off the stack when our custom sun image is rendered in line 5. It needs to be called again in line 7, when the earth is drawn to the screen.

- In line 2 it looks like we're rendering the sun. But not really. This is to extract the location on the main screen that the sun would actually draw to. The third parameter, render, if false, will have the routine just return the screen location and expected radius but not actually draw the sun.

- Line 3 decides whether we should draw both the new sun and lens flare object if the sun is likely to be visible based on its z-coordinate. If z is negative, it is behind us, so we can skip it altogether.

- The aspectRatio in line 4 handles nonsquare viewports, which means almost all of them. Afterward we calculate the location of the sun's expected billboard image based on the center of the screen.

- The new renderToTextureAt() call now puts the sun's billboard up on the screen, as shown in m_FlareSource in line 5. sunScreenLoc{RADIUS_INDEX] is one of the values fetched from executePlanet() and corresponds to what the size of the actual 3D image would likely be. The returned value of scale hints at what the final bitmap was sized at, as a percent of the screen. This is used in line 6 to calculate the actual width of the "hot spot" in the sun's bitmap, since the center image of the sun's body will naturally be far smaller than the bitmap's dimensions.

- Again in line 7 we perform the translation, since the previous one was lost when the matrix was popped. Followed by line 8 that renders the earth, but in this case, passes a render flag of true. However, it still gets the screen location info, in this case, merely to get the dimensions of the image so we know when to start blanking out the lens flare.

▪ Then we come down to where the flare is actually rendered starting with lines 9ff. Most of the code here largely handles one basic effect: what happens when the sun goes behind the earth? Naturally, the flare will vanish, but it won't pop in or out instantly because the sun has a finite diameter. So, values such as the *grazeDist* and *vanishDist* tell us when the sun first intersects the earth, starting the dimming process, and when it is finally covered completely, blanking out the flare altogether. Using the earth's screen x and y values as well as those for the sun, it becomes an easy matter to specify a fade function.

▪ Any value that falls between the vanishDist and grazeDist values specifies what percentage of dimming should be done, as in line 10, while lines 11ff actually calculate the value. Notice the line:

```
else if(percentVisible<0.3)
    percentVisible=0.5f
```

Extra credit: what does this do and why?

▪ Lines 12ff calculate the size of the flare and its corresponding elements. As you zoom in with a decreasing field of view—that is, a higher-power lens—the sun's image will increase and the flare should as well.

The last bit to this exercise is to take a look at executePlanet(), as in Listing 8–9.

*Listing 8–9.* ExecutePlanet() Modified to Get the Screen Coordinates

```
public void executePlanet(Planet planet, GL10 gl, Boolean render,float[] screenLoc)
{
    Vector3 planetPos = new Vector3(0, 0, 0);
    float temp;
    float distance;
    float screenRadius;

    gl.glPushMatrix();

    planetPos.x = planet.m_Pos[0];
    planetPos.y = planet.m_Pos[1];
    planetPos.z = planet.m_Pos[2];

    gl.glTranslatef((float) planetPos.x, (float) planetPos.y,(float) planetPos.z);

    if (render)
    {
        planet.draw(gl);                                                    //1
    }

    Vector3 eyePosition = new Vector3(0, 0, 0);

    eyePosition.x = m_Eyeposition[X_VALUE];
    eyePosition.y = m_Eyeposition[Y_VALUE];
```

```
eyePosition.z = m_Eyeposition[Z_VALUE];

distance = (float) planetPos.Vector3Distance(eyePosition, planetPos);

float fieldWidthRadians = (m_FieldOfView /DEGREES_PER_RADIAN) / 2.0f;
temp = (float) ((0.5f * origwidth) / Math.tan(fieldWidthRadians));

screenRadius = temp * getRadius(planet) / distance;

if(screenLoc!=null)                                              //2
{
    Miniglu.gluGetScreenLocation(gl, (float) planetPos.x, (float) -planetPos.y,
        (float) planetPos.z, (float) screenRadius, render,screenLoc);
}

screenLoc[RADIUS_INDEX]=screenRadius;

gl.glPopMatrix();
angle += .5f;
}
```

In this final bit, line 1 draws the planet as normal, if and only if the render flag is true. Otherwise, it just fetches the screen location and dimension, as in line 2, so that we can draw it ourselves.

That should do it. I am sure you'll be able to compile with no errors or warnings, because you're just that good. And because you are just that good, you will likely be rewarded with the images in Figure 8–6. And feel free to play with ambient light and specular lighting as I have done. The effect might not be very realistic, but it looks very nice.

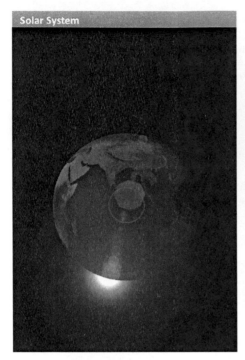

**Figure 8–6.** *Look, Ma! Lens flare!*

## Seeing Stars

Most of the new code needed for the next exercise is mainly for loading and managing all of the new data. Because this is a book on OpenGL and not XML or data structures or how to effectively type in code from a book, I'll dispense with still more tedious listings of stuff you might already know.

Of course, no solar-system model would be complete without some nice stars in the background. Up to this point, all of the examples have been small enough to print their entirety here in the text, but now that will change just a bit as we add a simple star field in the background. The difference is largely in the database required that you will need to fetch from the Apress web site, because it will contain just over 500 stars down to a magnitude of 4.0 as well as an additional database containing constellation outlines and names for a number of the more prominent groupings.

Besides the triangular faces that OpenGL ES uses for creating solid models, you can also specify that each vertex of your model be rendered as a point image of a given magnitude and size, providing your Android device can support multipixel point representations. At this point, part of the uglier side of Android's business model starts showing through.

What Google is doing with Android is simple: trying to establish it as the preeminent mobile operating system in the world. And to do so, Google makes it free and permits manufacturers to modify it to their heart's content. As a result, dreaded fragmentation quickly sneaks in. Superficially, consumers shouldn't have to worry about this because they have a huge selection of phones to choose from. But from a developer's side, it makes writing software to work on hundreds if not thousands of devices a nightmare because each device can have its own little quirks. And in the long run, this does affect consumers because developers may opt not to support a specific family of devices, or if they do, they might suffer release delays and cost increases to ensure their latest title will work on everything. And nowhere are such differences felt more than in graphics support.

There are many different manufactures of graphics processing units. Vivante, maker of the GC860, supplies chips to Marvell; AMD sends its GPUs to Toshiba, and PowerVR sells to Apple and Samsung. What makes it worse is that each specific model of GPU will likely have more capabilities than previous generations from the same manufacturer. This means you will likely have to code to the lowest common denominator by leaving out cool features that more recent devices might support, or you might have to roll your own if you really need a specific feature to work across all platforms. Or, as a third approach, you might have to code only to specific devices, leaving others out of the equation. For the most part, Apple has managed to navigate around these waters with their iOS devices, while Microsoft (which used the "Android" method for older Windows Mobile phones) now shies away from fragmentation by ensuring their Windows Mobile 7 licensees adhere to very strict set of specifications. As a result, selection of your target machines is critical.

Now back to the stars. So, what makes this so special? Simple. Not all devices can support OpenGL's GL_POINTS rendering greater than a single pixel in size. Or those that do may not support rounded anti-aliased points. The former could almost work, but for only the previous generation of low-resolution screens, say, 75 DPI or so. But now with the newer high-resolution displays (such as Apple's Retina display), a single pixel is so small as to be nearly invisible, making it imperative to show stars made up as a collection of pixels. Such was the case with the development of this exercise, as you will soon see. But first, to the stars.

> **NOTE:** Price or manufacturer of a device seem to have little bearing on the 3D capabilities they support. For example, the first-generation Motorola Xoom could do fat points, but only square ones. The Kindle Fire does wide lines, but only single-pixel points, while a cheap no-name device does both fat lines and points.

The stellar database for this first bit was compiled from my Distant Suns data into Apple's plist XML file format. That was then tweaked a little to make parsing it easer for demo purposes. The same approach was used for the constellation data. When loaded, it was drawn very much as previous objects, such as the sphere, but instead of specifying GL_TRANGLE_STRIPS, GL_POINTS were used. Listing 8–10 shows the execute() method for the stars.

**Listing 8–10.** *Rendering the Stars*

```
public void execute(GL10 gl)
{
    int len;
    float[] pointSize = new float[2];
    GL11 gl11 = (GL11) gl;

    gl.glDisable(GL10.GL_LIGHTING); `                          //1
    gl.glDisable(GL10.GL_TEXTURE_2D);
    gl.glDisable(GL10.GL_DEPTH_TEST);

    gl.glEnableClientState(GL10.GL_VERTEX_ARRAY);
    gl.glEnableClientState(GL10.GL_COLOR_ARRAY);               //2

    gl.glMatrixMode(GL10.GL_MODELVIEW);
    gl.glBlendFunc(GL10.GL_ONE, GL10.GL_ONE_MINUS_DST_ALPHA);
    gl.glEnable(GL10.GL_BLEND);

    gl.glColorPointer(4, GL10.GL_FLOAT, 0, m_ColorData);
    gl.glVertexPointer(3,GL10.GL_FLOAT, 0, m_VertexData);

    gl.glEnable(GL10.GL_POINT_SMOOTH);                         //3
    gl.glPointSize(5.0f);

    gl.glDrawArrays(GL10.GL_POINTS,0,totalElems/4); `          //4

    gl.glDisableClientState(GL10.GL_VERTEX_ARRAY);
    gl.glDisableClientState(GL10.GL_COLOR_ARRAY);
    gl.glEnable(GL10.GL_DEPTH_TEST);
    gl.glEnable(GL10.GL_LIGHTING);
}
```

And now for the rest of the story:

- Line 1 is essential to rendering any object that is self-illuminating or that you just want visible all of the time. In this case, the stars are in the former category, while various identifiers such as constellation names and outlines are in the latter. Turning off the lights ensures that they will be visible no matter what. (In earlier exercises, the sun was rendered as an emissive object but was still left as an illuminated one just to get a slight gradient across the surface that looked very nice.)

- Colors in line 2 are being used to specify the intensity of a star's magnitude. A more sophisticated system would encode both the star's real color and luminosity, but here we're just doing the simple stuff.

> **NOTE:** A star's magnitude is its apparent brightness; the larger the value, the dimmer the star is. The brightest star in the sky next to the sun, of course, is Sirius, at a visual magnitude of -1.46. The dimmest stars visible to the naked eye are about magnitude 6.5. Binoculars top out at about 10th magnitude, while the Hubble Space Telescope reaches way out to magnitude 31.5. Each whole number is a difference of about 2.5 times in actual brightness, so a star of magnitude 3 is about 2.5 times brighter than one that is magnitude 4.

- Hard edged stars are not that interesting to look at, so lines 3f turn on anti-aliasing for points and ensure that the points are big enough to be visible.
- Line 4 draws the arrays as usual but makes use of the GL_POINT rendering style instead of GL_TRIANGLES used for solid bodies.

Let's go back to line 3. Remember the discussion about different devices and GPUs having different features available or not? Here is one such case. In the development of this exercise, the hardware used was a first generation of a Motorola Droid. As it turned out, it did *not* support multipixel points, so each star was but a single pixel on a very high-resolution screen. The solution would be to use "point sprites," a way to assign small bitmaps to each point drawn. OpenGL ES can support this also but, as said before, only on certain devices. Sigh. Or as the official OpenGL documentation states:

*Only size 1 is guaranteed to be supported; others depend on the implementation.*

If larger points are supported, without any further modifications they will be drawn as squares. Here is where you want to turn on GL_POINT_SMOOTHING. If implemented, it will attempt to create rounded points. However, the sizes allowed for point smoothing is implementation dependent. You can check

that out by the following call:

```
float[] pointSize = new float[2];

gl11.glGetFloatv(GL10.GL_SMOOTH_POINT_SIZE_RANGE, makeFloatBuffer(pointSize));
```

If point smoothing is not available, pointSize will show 0.0f, 0.0f. However, smoothed points are not necessarily nice-looking points. For better points yet, turn on blending. Then the system will anti-alias the images. However, this "depends on the implementation." Sigh.

Figure 8–7 shows the differences between the three possibilities.

**Figure 8–7.** *From left to right, a close-up on an 8–pixel-wide unsmoothed point, with smoothing, and with smoothing and blending*

Ultimately you will have to handle your own point rendering if you want to reach the largest possible audience.

## Seeing Lines

Of course, there is much more to the sky then stars and planets. There are the constellations. As with the stars earlier, you will have to fetch the constellation database from the Apress site. This contains data for 17 different constellations. The data includes the common name and line data to form the constellation outlines. In this case, the setup is virtually identical to the stars, as described earlier, but instead of drawing a point array, we draw a line array:

```
gl.glDrawArrays(GL10.GL_LINE_STRIP,0,numVertices);
```

As with points (depending on implementation), lines may also be drawn larger than single-pixel widths. The following call will do the trick:

```
gl.glLineWidth(lineWidth);
```

However, line widths greater than 1, all in unison now, *depend on the implementation*.

You should be able to check for available line widths by calling this:

```
int[] pointSize = new int[2];
gl11.glGetIntegerv(GL10.GL_ALIASED_LINE_WIDTH_RANGE, makeIntBuffer(pointSize));
```

Lines of widths greater than 1 depend on the implementation, although it seems like more devices permit wide lines than wide pixels.

One problem in the OpenGL ES implementations of lines is that anti-aliased lines (smooth) are not supported as opposed to the desktop version. This means that any lines you draw using the standard technique will look most unpleasant on older, lower-resolution displays. But as higher DPIs become available, anti-aliasing is less necessary. But if you still want to consider it, one trick commonly used is to draw the lines as really thin polygons and use texture mapping, which can be anti-aliased and can add things such as dotted lines to the picture. Cumbersome? You bet. Works? Pretty well. Another way in the OpenGL ES universe is use something called multitexture anti-aliasing. However, this will depend on the implementation!

MSAA creates two OpenGL rendering surfaces. One is what we see, and the other is twice the size and hidden from view. The blending of the two smooths out all images in the entire screen and can look quite good, although at the expense of performance and memory usage. Figure 8–8 shows a comparison of the two.

**Figure 8–8.** *Without MSAA on the left; with it enabled on the right*

# Seeing Text

For all of the capabilities of OpenGL, text support is not one of them. A long-standing nuisance, the only way to really do text right is to use textures with the text on them. After all, that is what any text is to begin with: just a bunch of little textures.

The easiest way to do things if you have very small text needs is to prerender the text blocks and import them just as other textures. If you have a lot of text, you can generate them on the fly as each string is needed. This is a nice approach if you want to use a wide variety of fonts. Overall, the best way is to use something called a texture atlas (also called a sprite sheet).

When used in conjunction with text rendering, a texture atlas will take all of the characters associated with your desired font and store them on a single bitmap, as shown in Figure 8–9. To draw the text, we use techniques previously employed in the lens flare to render 2D bitmaps.

```
! " # $ % & ' ( ) * + , - . / 0
1 2 3 4 5 6 7 8 9 : ; < = > ? @ A
B C D E F G H I J K L M N O P Q R
S T U V W X Y Z [ \ ] ^ _ ` a b c
d e f g h i j k l m n o p q r s t
u v w x y z { | } ~ ⬛ €   , ƒ „ …
† ‡ ^ ‰ Š ‹ Œ Ž   ' ' " " • —
```

**Figure 8–9.** *Times New Roman, the texture atlas edition*

Taking the texture atlas and using fractional texture mapping (see Chapter 5's Figure 5-6), the letters can be combined into any string needed on the fly. Since OpenGL doesn't natively support any sort of font handling, we either have to roll out own font manager or look to third parties. Fortunately, since this problem is so pervasive, a number of kind souls have created tools and libraries to and make them freely available. Figure 8–9 was generated with a very nice PC-based tool called CBFG and may be downloaded from `www.codehead.co.uk/cbfg/`.

This includes the tool along with drop-in C++ and Java readers, the latter being used in this example. To create and initialize for font usage, use the following code:

```
m_TexFont = new TexFont(context, gl);
m_TexFont.LoadFont("TimesNewRoman.bff", gl);
```

Listing 8–11 shows how to use this. The excerpt comes from `Outline.java` in the example code.

**Listing 8–11.** *Writing Text to an OpenGL View*

```
public void renderConstName(GL10 gl, String name, int x, int y, float r, float g,
    float b)
{
    gl.glDisable(GL10.GL_LIGHTING);
    gl.glBlendFunc(GL10.GL_SRC_ALPHA, GL10.GL_ONE_MINUS_SRC_ALPHA);
    gl.glEnable(GL10.GL_BLEND);

    if(name!=null)
    {
        m_TexFont.SetPolyColor(r, g, b);
        m_TexFont.PrintAt(gl, name.toUpperCase(), x, y);
    }
}
```

Now that we have the lines, points, and text up, what should we see? Ah, the question is what *will* we see (Figure 8–10). After all, it *will depend on the implementation*.

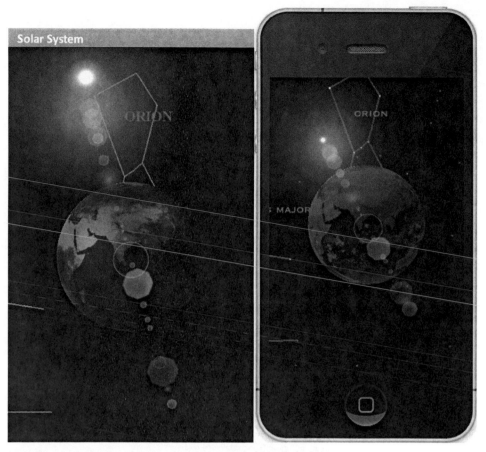

**Figure 8–10.** *Invisible one-pixel stars on the left; the way to do things on the right*

# Seeing Buttons

Of course, any app that doesn't have a means to interact with it is usually called a demo. But here our little demo will in fact gain both a simple user-interface and HUD graphics.

When it comes to adding UI elements to your Android app, I have some very good news: the phrase "depends on implementation" will not be found. Adding simple control elements is very easy. Of course, you'd normally not use an OpenGL display as mere background for an app, and UI elements should still be isolated in their own space in general; it all depends on your goals. With that in mind, a simple UI panel can be added as demonstrated with Listing 8–12 in SolarSystemActivity and should look something like Figure 8–11.

**Listing 8–12.** *Adding UI to the Sky*

```
public void onCreate(Bundle savedInstanceState)
{
        super.onCreate(savedInstanceState);
        getWindow().setFlags(WindowManager.LayoutParams.FLAG_FULLSCREEN,
            WindowManager.LayoutParams.FLAG_FULLSCREEN);
        mGLSurfaceView = new SolarSystemView(this);
        setContentView(mGLSurfaceView);
        mGLSurfaceView.requestFocus();
        mGLSurfaceView.setFocusableInTouchMode(true);

        ll = new LinearLayout(this);
        ll.setOrientation(VERTICAL_ORIENTATION);
        b_name = new Button(this);
        b_name.setText("names");
        b_name.setBackgroundDrawable(getResources().getDrawable(
            book.SolarSystem.R.drawable.bluebuttonbig));
        ll.addView(b_name);

        b_line = new Button(this);
        b_line.setText("lines");
        b_line.setBackgroundDrawable(getResources().getDrawable
            (book.SolarSystem.R.drawable.greenbuttonbig));
        ll.addView(b_line, 1);

        b_lens_flare = new Button(this);
        b_lens_flare.setText("lens flare");
          b_lens_flare.setBackgroundDrawable(getResources().getDrawable
              (book.SolarSystem.R.drawable.redbuttonbig));
        ll.addView(b_lens_flare);

    this.addContentView(ll, new LayoutParams(LayoutParams.WRAP_CONTENT,
        LayoutParams.WRAP_CONTENT));

        b_name.setOnClickListener(new Button.OnClickListener() {

            @Override
            public void onClick(View v) {
                if (name_flag == false)
                    name_flag = true;
                else if (name_flag == true)
                    name_flag = false;
                Log.d(TAG, "b_name clicked");
            }
        });

            b_line.setOnClickListener(new Button.OnClickListener() {
```

```
                @Override
                public void onClick(View v) {
                if (line_flag == false)
                    line_flag = true;
                else if (line_flag == true)
                    line_flag = false;
                Log.d(TAG, "b_line clicked");
            }
        });


        b_lens_flare.setOnClickListener(new Button.OnClickListener() {

            @Override
            public void onClick(View v) {
                if (lens_flare_flag == false)
                    lens_flare_flag = true;
                else if (lens_flare_flag == true)
                    lens_flare_flag = false;
                Log.d(TAG, "b_lensflare clicked");
            }
        });
```

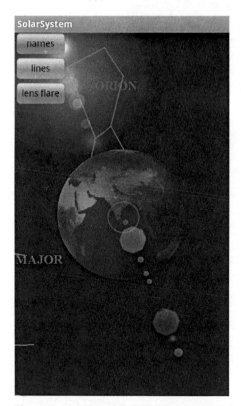

**Figure 8–11.** *Putting UI components on top of an OpenGL screen*

If you do expect to have a lot of UI elements, you might want to consider creating all of them in OpenGL. This is particularly helpful if you plan on supporting multiple platforms, because OpenGL skips all of the platform specific toolkits, although it makes the initial job somewhat more tedious. Games are the applications that can benefit most from such an approach, particularly since they usually have highly customized UIs. A well-written OpenGL-only application might take only a few days to port from one platform to another as compared to a few months. Distant Suns on the iPhone uses a mix of the two, mainly to see how they can complement each other. I used all OpenGL for the little time-setting widget in Figure 8–12, while using standard UI components for everything else.

**Figure 8–12.**  *Distant Suns with custom date wheel on the left side yet with a standard UIKit toolbar at the same time*

# Summary

In this chapter, we took many of the tricks learned in previous chapters and combined them into a more complete and more attractive (read: less lame) solar-system model, depending on implementation. A one-planet solar system is not that impressive as it stands. So, I'll leave it up to you, dear reader, to add the moon, add some other planets, and get the earth to revolve around the sun.

We added lens flare from Chapter 7 and point and line objects for the stars and constellation outlines, inserted text into an OpenGL environment, and mixed both OpenGL views and standard Android controls on the same screen.

I also pointed out how the graphics subsystem is the one that can vary most from device to device, causing much pain, anguish, gnashing of teeth, and rending of garments. In the next chapter, we'll look into optimization tricks, and following that, OpenGL ES 2.0 and how that might be applied to enhancing our earth model.

# Chapter 9

# Performance 'n' Stuff

*An ounce of performance is worth pounds of promises.*

—Mae West

*I'm so fast that last night I turned off the light switch in my hotel room and was in bed before the room was dark.*

—Muhammad Ali

When dealing with 3D worlds, performance is nearly always an issue because of the intensive mathematics required for even simple scenes. If all you want to render is an animated spinning triangle with adorable robots festooned upon its visage, then not to worry, but if you want to display the universe, then you'll always be concerned about performance.

Up until now, the exercises have been presented in a way to be reasonably clear (I hope) but not necessarily efficient. And unfortunately, efficient code is rarely the clearest and easily understood. So now, we're going to start looking at the slightly messier stuff and see how it can be integrated into your applications.

In the trade, these tips are called *best practices*. Some may be obvious, but others are not.

## Vertex Buffer Objects

The two main arenas of performance enhancements are minimizing the data transfer to and from the graphics hardware and minimizing data itself. Vertex buffer objects (VBOs) are part of the former process. When you generated your geometry and sent it merrily along to be displayed, the usual process was to tell the system where to find each of the needed blocks of data, enabling which data to use (vertex, normals, colors, and texture coordinates), and then drawing it. Each time `glDrawArrays()` or `glDrawElements()` is called, all of the data must be packed up and shipped over to the graphics processing unit (GPU). Each data transfer takes a finite amount of time, and obviously performance could be increased if, say, some of the data could be cached on the GPU itself. VBOs are a means of allocating commonly used data on the GPU that can then be called for display without having to resubmit the data each time.

The process of creating and using VBOs should be familiar to you because it mimics that used for textures. First generate a "name," then allocate space for the data, then load the data, and then use `glBindBuffer()` whenever you want to use said data. Another practice I'll cover at the same time is that of interleaving the data, illustrated in Figure 9–1, which I'll do first before submitting it to the VBO. This may or may not make much difference, but if the drivers and GPU are optimized for data locality, interleaved arrays could help.

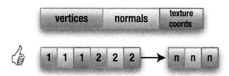

**Figure 9–1.** *Data ordering. The VBO example uses the top format, while the bottom illustrates data interleaving.*

In my own tests I found the difference to be negligible. But still, keep interleaving in mind for your projects; it can't hurt to design for it because future hardware might make better use of it. Refer to Listing 9–1 to see how the planet's geometry can interleaved.

**Listing 9–1.** *Creating an Interleaved Array*

```java
private void createInterleavedData()
{
    int i;
    int j;
    float[] interleavedArray;
    int size;

    size=NUM_XYZ_ELS+NUM_NXYZ_ELS+NUM_RGBA_ELS+NUM_ST_ELS;

    interleavedArray=new float[size*m_NumVertices];

    for(i=0;i<m_NumVertices;i++)
    {
        j=i*size;

        //Vertex data

        interleavedArray[j+0]=m_VertexData.get();
        interleavedArray[j+1]=m_VertexData.get();
```

```
            interleavedArray[j+2]=m_VertexData.get();

            //Normal data

            interleavedArray[j+3]=m_NormalData.get();
            interleavedArray[j+4]=m_NormalData.get();
            interleavedArray[j+5]=m_NormalData.get();

            //cColor data

            interleavedArray[j+6]=m_ColorData.get();
            interleavedArray[j+7]=m_ColorData.get();
            interleavedArray[j+8]=m_ColorData.get();
            interleavedArray[j+9]=m_ColorData.get();

            //Texture coordinates

            interleavedArray[j+10]=m_TextureData.get();
            interleavedArray[j+11]=m_TextureData.get();
        }

        m_InterleavedData=makeFloatBuffer(interleavedArray);

        m_VertexData.position(0);
        m_NormalData.position(0);
        m_ColorData.position(0);
        m_TextureData.position(0);
    }
```

This is all pretty self-explanatory, but note the final four lines. They reset the internal counters for the FloatBuffer objects, needed if you want to use any of the individual arrays of data elsewhere.

Listing 9–2 shows how I created a VBO out of the planetary data. Since most planets are generally the same shape, roundish, it is possible to cache one model of the sphere on the CPU and use it for any planet or moon, short of Demos or Hyperion or Nix or Miranda…or any of the smaller moons that look more like moldy potatoes. Hear that, Phobos? I'm talkin' to *you*!

**Listing 9–2.** *Creating a VBO for the Planet Model*

```
    public void createVBO(GL10 gl)
    {
        int size=NUM_XYZ_ELS+NUM_NXYZ_ELS+NUM_RGBA_ELS+NUM_ST_ELS;

        createInterleavedData();

        GLES11.glGenBuffers(1,m_VertexVBO,0);                            //1
        GLES11.glBindBuffer(GL11.GL_ARRAY_BUFFER, m_VertexVBO[0]);       //2
```

```
        GLES11.glBufferData(GLES11.GL_ARRAY_BUFFER,size*FLOAT_SIZE*m_NumVertices,  //3
                m_InterleavedData,GLES11.GL_STATIC_DRAW);
}
```

Simple, eh? Note that VBOs didn't come along until OpenGL ES 1.1, which is why the GLES11 modifier is needed.

- Line 1 generates the name for the buffer. Since we are dealing with just a single dataset, we need only one.

- Next we bind it in line 2, making this the current VBO. To unbind it, you can bind a 0.

- The data from the interleaved array can now be sent over to the GPU in line 3. The first parameter is the time of data, which can be either a GL_ARRAY_BUFFER or a GL_ELEMENT_ARRAY_BUFFER. The former is used to pass the vertex data (which includes color and normal information), and the latter is used for passing an index connectivity array. But since we are using triangle strips, the index data is not needed.

So, how do we use VBOs? Very easily. Take a look at Listing 9–3.

**Listing 9–3.** *Rendering the Planet Using VBOs*

```
public void draw(GL10 gl)
{
    int startingOffset;
    int i;
    int maxDuplicates=10;                                              //1
    boolean useVBO=true;                                               //2


    int stride=(NUM_XYZ_ELS+NUM_NXYZ_ELS+NUM_RGBA_ELS                  //3
            +NUM_ST_ELS)*FLOAT_SIZE;

    GLES11.glEnable(GLES11.GL_CULL_FACE);
    GLES11.glCullFace(GLES11.GL_BACK);
    GLES11. glDisable ( GLES11.GL_BLEND);
    GLES11.glDisable(GLES11.GL_TEXTURE_2D);

    if(useVBO)                                                         //4
    {
        GLES11.glBindBuffer(GL11.GL_ARRAY_BUFFER, m_VertexVBO[0]);  //5

        GLES11.glEnableClientState(GL10.GL_VERTEX_ARRAY);            //6

        GLES11.glVertexPointer(NUM_XYZ_ELS,GL11.GL_FLOAT,stride,0);
```

```
        GLES11.glEnableClientState(GL11.GL_NORMAL_ARRAY);
        GLES11.glNormalPointer(GL11.GL_FLOAT,stride,NUM_XYZ_ELS*FLOAT_SIZE);

        GLES11.glEnableClientState(GL11.GL_TEXTURE_COORD_ARRAY);

        GLES11.glTexCoordPointer(2,GL11.GL_FLOAT,stride,
            (NUM_XYZ_ELS+NUM_NXYZ_ELS+NUM_RGBA_ELS)*FLOAT_SIZE);

        GLES11.glEnable(GL11.GL_TEXTURE_2D);
        GLES11.glBindTexture(GL11.GL_TEXTURE_2D, m_TextureIDs[0]);
    }
    else
    {
        GLES11.glBindBuffer(GL11.GL_ARRAY_BUFFER,0);                         //7

        m_InterleavedData.position(0);

        GLES11.glEnableClientState(GL10.GL_VERTEX_ARRAY);
        GLES11.glVertexPointer(NUM_XYZ_ELS,GL11.GL_FLOAT,stride,m_InterleavedData);

        m_InterleavedData.position(NUM_XYZ_ELS);

        GLES11.glEnableClientState(GL11.GL_NORMAL_ARRAY);
        GLES11.glNormalPointer(GL11.GL_FLOAT,stride,m_InterleavedData);

        m_InterleavedData.position(NUM_XYZ_ELS+NUM_NXYZ_ELS+NUM_RGBA_ELS);

        GLES11.glEnableClientState(GL11.GL_TEXTURE_COORD_ARRAY);
        GLES11.glTexCoordPointer(2,GL11.GL_FLOAT,stride,m_InterleavedData);
        GLES11.glEnable(GL11.GL_TEXTURE_2D);
        GLES11.glBindTexture(GL11.GL_TEXTURE_2D, m_TextureIDs[0]);
    }

    for(i=0;i<maxDuplicates;i++)                                            //8
    {
            GLES11.glTranslatef(0.0f,0.2f,0.0f);
            GLES11.glDrawArrays(GL11.GL_TRIANGLE_STRIP, 0,
                (m_Slices+1)*2*(m_Stacks-1)+2);
    }

    GLES11.glDisable(GL11.GL_BLEND);
    GLES11.glDisable(GL11.GL_TEXTURE_2D);
    GLES11.glDisableClientState(GL11.GL_TEXTURE_COORD_ARRAY);
    GLES11.glBindBuffer(GL11.GL_ARRAY_BUFFER,0);

    m_VerticesPerUpdate=maxDuplicates*m_NumVertices;
}
```

Rendering the VBOs is pretty straightforward, with only a single "huh?" in the process. I've decided to prepend all of the calls with the GLES11 prefix just for looks. Not all routines need it.

- Lines 1 and 2 let you configure the routine for testing purposes. maxDuplicates is the number of times the planet will be rendered. useVBO can turn off the VBO processing and use just the interleaved data for performance comparisons.

- Remember that the stride value, in line 3, indicates the number of bytes from vertex to vertex in an arbitrary array. This is essential for doing interleaved data, so the same array can be used for both vertex location and colors, for example. The stride just tells the system how many bytes to skip over before it finds the next vertex.

- Line 4 will turn on the actual VBO setup code. Line 5 binds it in the same way a texture is bound, making it the current object to use, until another is bound or this one is unbound with glBindBuffer(GL_ARRAY_BUFFER, 0);.

- Lines 6ff enable the various data buffers as has been done in previous draw() methods. The one major difference can be seen in the final argument to the various glEnable*Pointer() calls. Under normal use, you pass a pointer or reference to them. However, when using VBOs, the various "pointers" to the data blocks are the offset from the first element, which always starts at an "address" of zero instead of one in the app's own address space. This means that in our case, the vertex pointer starts at an address of 0, while the normals are right after the vertices, and the colors are texture coordinates follow the normals. These values are expressed in bytes from the start of data.

- Line 7 highlights the other section. Here we use just the interleaved data and pass it to the pointer routines in the more traditional way. This permits you to see what, if any, performance enhancement you get from the interleaved data.

- The section following line 8 loops through maxDuplicates calls to glDrawArrays(). The value of 10 works pretty well.

When it comes to optimizing code, I am one who needs to be convinced that a specific trick will work. Otherwise, I might spend a lot of time doing something that increases the frame rate by .23 percent. A game programmer might find that a badge of honor, but I feel that it steals either an optional new feature or a bug fix away from my users by diverting attention to something that probably won't make much difference. So, I developed a simple test program given by the previous listings.

The program simply draws ten planet Earths and rotates them, as shown in Figure 9–2. The spheres are created with 100 stacks and 100 slices, giving them 20,200 vertices each. I use the same instance, so I have to load the GPU only once at program startup. Without VBOs, the same model would be loaded ten times.

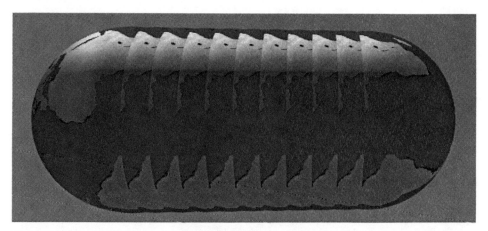

**Figure 9–2.** *Giant computer-generated sow bug. Or ten planet Earths stacked on top of each other.*

You can now add a frame-rate calculator to your onDrawFrame() handler and see what happens. My own setup uses a first-gen Motorola Xoom, and what follows are some basic tests that should give me a decent idea as to how the Xoom/Java platform performs when compared to others of a similar price range.

> **NOTE:** My own setup uses the first-gen Motorola Xoom that harbors an NVIDIA Tegra 2 GPU. As of this writing, all of Apple's iOS devices use the PowerVR family of chips made by Imagination Technologies; it's the same for Samsung's Galaxy Tab and Blackberry's Playbook. It might be worth your while to go to the developer's section of the manufacturer of your GPU. Both Imagination Tech and NVIDIA have excellent notes, SDKs, and demos that can take full advantage of their respective hardware.

The baseline configuration had texturing turned on, three lights, 32-bit color with depth buffer, blending on with the eyepoint at 5 units away, and the field of view set to 30 degrees. The results were quite surprising, as shown in Table 9–1.

**Table 9–1.** *Frame-Rate Comparison on a Motorola Xoom*

| Configuration | Frames/Second |
|---|---|
| Baseline | 6.15 |
| No VBO or interleaved data | 5.45 |

| | |
|---|---|
| Interleaved data only | 4.75 |
| Noninterleaved data | 5.45 |
| No texturing | 6.30 |
| Only a single light | 13.25 |
| No depth-buffering | 6.15 |
| 16-bit colors | 6.40 |
| Wireframe | 7.40 |
| Points | 6.70 |
| Eyepoint twice as far | 6.25 |
| Xoom loaded down with graphic apps | 6.15 |

In this case, the single largest CPU sink is the lighting, because the frame rate doubled by merely turning off two of the three lights. In Chapter 10, you'll see what really goes into managing lighting under the hood, and this will make a little more sense. Turning off depth buffering and texturing had virtually no effect as did dropping down to 16-bit color from 32 bits.

Another really surprising result is that the interleave data format seems to actually *reduce* performance! Opting to use the separate discrete buffers for each datatype, the "old way" speeds things up a little. Moving the eyepoint away reduced the number of pixels to process but barely added anything to the frame rate. This suggests that the GPU is nowhere near being pixel-bound and that the main performance culprit is the actual vertex calculations. Chances are that Java might certainly be playing a big role in this. As a partial solution to language-related issues, Android also comes with a native development kit (NDK).

The NDK was designed to let developers put their performance-critical code below the Java layer, into C or C++, using JNI to move back and forth between the two worlds. (*Performance-critical* might include image processing or large system modeling.) OpenGL will be optimized for whatever level you use, so chances are in a pure OpenGL comparison you'll see little improvement. Outside of that, even a quick search on the Web shows many developers creating tests comparing the two environments, and nearly all show dramatic increases in performance of 30 times or more for mathematically intensive tasks. But of course, you mileage may vary because of driver, OS, GPU, or compiler issues.

# Batching

Batch as much as possible operations that rely on the same state, because changing the system state (by using the `glEnable()` and `glDisable()` calls) is costly. OpenGL does not check internally to see whether a specific feature is already in the state you want. In the exercises in this book, I would frequently set states more often than I likely needed to, so as to ensure the behavior is easily predictable. But for commercial, performance-intensive apps, try to remove any redundant calls in the release build.

Also, batch your drawing calls as much as possible.

# Textures

A few of the texture optimization tricks have already been addressed, such as mipmapping. Others are just plain common sense: textures take a whopping lot of memory. Make them as small as possible and reuse them if needed. Also, set any image parameters ahead of loading them, because they act as a hint to tell OpenGL how to optimize the information before shipping up to the hardware.

Draw the opaque textures first, and avoid having a translucent OpenGL ES screen.

# Sprite Sheets

Sprite sheets (or texture atlases) were briefly referenced in Chapter 8 when covering displaying text in an OpenGL environment. Figure 9–3 illustrates what a sprite sheet looks like when used for rendering text to the screen.

**Figure 9–3.** *Sprite sheet for 24-point Copperplate*

This particular image was created using a free tool called LabelAtlasCreator for the Mac, as opposed to the CBFG tool used in Chapter 8. Besides the image file, it will generate a handy XML file in Apple's plist format that contains all of the placement details that are easy to convert to texture space.

But don't stop at fonts, because sprite sheets can also be applied any time you have a family of likeminded images. Switching from one texture to another can cause a lot of unneeded overhead, whereas a sprite sheet acts as a form of texture batching, saving a lot of GPU time. Check out the OS X–compatible Zwoptex tool or TexturePacker, which is used for general-purpose images.

## Texture Uploads

Copying textures to the GPU can be very expensive, because they must reformatted by the chip before they can be used. This can cause stuttering in the display for larger textures. Therefore, make sure to load them at the very start with `glTexImage2D`. Some GPU manufacturers, such as Imagination Technologies, maker of the chips used in Apple's products, have their own proprietary image formats fine-tuned for their own hardware. Of course, in the increasingly fragmented Android marketplace, you will have to sniff out what chips your users have at runtime and handle any special needs at that time.

## Mipmaps

Always make sure to use mipmaps for anything other than 2D unscaled images. Yes, they do use a little more memory, but the smaller mipmaps can save a lot of cycles for your objects when far away. It is recommended that you use `GL_LINEAR_MIPMAP_NEAREST` because it is faster than `GL_LINEAR_MIPMAP_LINEAR` (reference Table 5-3), albeit with a little less image fidelity.

## Fewer Colors

Other recommendations might include lower-resolution color formats. A lot of imagery would look almost as good at only 16 bits vs. 32, especially if there is no alpha mask. Android's default format is the ever-popular RGB565, which means it has 5 bits red, 6 bits for green, and 5 bits for blue. (The green color is given a boost because our eyes are most sensitive to it.) Other 16-bit formats include RGBA5551 or RBGA4444. On Distant Suns, my grayscale constellation artwork is only 8 bits, cutting memory usage by 75 percent. Should I want it tinted to match a specific theme, I let OpenGL do the work. With the proper tool and careful tweaking, some 16-bit textures are almost indistinguishable from the 32-bitters.

Figure 9–4 illustrates four of these formats created by TexturePacker, with the highest to lowest quality going from left to right. Image 1 shows the true-color texture we've been using, sometimes called RGBA8888. Image 2 uses the default RGB565 format that still looks quite good, considering. Image 3 in Figure 9–4 uses RGBA5551, allocating a 1-bit alpha channel (notice how much a difference the extra bit for green makes when compared to the previous texture), and image 4 is the lowest quality, using RGBA4444. TexturePacker also supports the PVRTC file types referenced in Chapter 5.

> **NOTE:** An alternate (and free) tool is available from Imagination Technologies Ltd., the maker of the PowerVR chips. It does the same texture modes as TexturePacker but doesn't create sprite sheets, like TexturePacker does. Note that it uses X11 as the UI that is skinned to look like Windows NT. Go to www.imgtec.com and look for PowerVR Insider Utilities under the developer's section. Look for PVRTexTool.

The images that work best when compressed are those with color palettes that rely heavily on one or two parts of the spectrum. The more varied your colors, the harder it will be minimize the artifacting. The image of Hedly works better than the Earth's texture map, because the former is largely grays and greens, while the latter is composed of greens, browns, grays (for the polar regions), and blue.

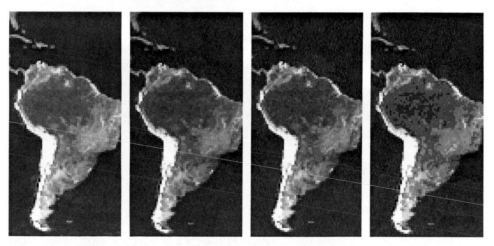

**Figure 9–4.** *Texture 1, 32 bit; texture 2, RGB565; texture 3, RGBA555; texture 4, RGBA:4444*

# Other Tips to Remember

The following are some useful tips to keep in mind:

- Even though multisample anti-aliasing can be very useful in smoothing out your images, it means sudden death in the performance department, cutting frame rates by 30 percent or more. So, you must really need to use it.

- Avoid using GL_ALPHA_TEST. This was never covered, but it can also kill performance as much as MSAA.

- When going to background, make sure to stop the animation and delete any easily re-created resources.

- Any calls that return information from the system (mainly the glGet* family of calls) query the state of the system, including the easily overlooked glGetError(). Many of these will force any previous commands to execute before state information can be retrieved.

- Use as few lights as possible, going down to only a single light (the sun) by turning off the fill and the ambient lights.

  Do not access the frame buffer from the CPU. Calls such as glReadPixels() should be avoided because they will force the frame buffer to flush all queued commands.

The preceding tips represent only the most basic recommended practices. There are many more arcane tricks the real graphics gurus have in their utility belts that a simple Google search will likely reveal.

# Summary

This chapter described the basic tricks and best practices you can use to make your OpenGL app really perform. VBOs will cut down on the saturation of the bus by keeping commonly used geometry on the GPU. Reducing the state changing and glGet* calls to a minimum can also yield a substantial improvement in rendering speed.

In Chapter 10, you'll learn a little about OpenGL ES 2.0 and those mysterious shader things that are all the rage these days with the kids.

# OpenGL ES 2, Shaders, and…

*Her angel's face, As the great eye of heaven shined bright, And made a sunshine in the shady place.*

—Edmund Spenser

There are two different versions of the OpenGL ES graphics library on your Android devices. This book has largely dealt with the higher-level one, known as OpenGL ES 1, sometimes referred to as 1.1, or 1.*x*. The second version is a rather confusingly named OpenGL ES 2. The first one is by far the easier of the two; it comes with all sorts of helper libraries doing much of the 3D mathematics and all of the lighting, coloring, and shading on your behalf. Version 2 eschews all of those niceties and is sometimes referred to as the "programmable function" version vs. the other's "fixed function" design. This is generally sneered at by the true pixel-jockeys who prefer more control over their imagery, usually reserved for immersive 3D game environments where every little visual footnote is emphasized. For that, OpenGL ES 2 was released.

Version 1 is relatively close to the desktop variety of OpenGL, making porting applications, particularly vintage ones, a little less painful than having a badger gnaw your face off. The things that were left out were done so to keep the footprint small on limited-resource devices and to ensure performance was as good as could be.

Version 2 defenestrated compatibility altogether and concentrated on performance-oriented features aimed primarily at entertainment software. Among the things left out were glRotate(), glTranslate(), matrix stack operations, and so on. But what we got in return are some delightful little morsels such as a programmable-pipeline via the use of *shaders*. Fortunately, Android comes with its own matrix and vector libraries (android.opengl.Matrix), which should make any code migration a little easier.

This topic is much too large to cover in a single chapter (it's usually relegated to entire books), but what follows is a general overview that should give you a good feel about shaders and their use and whether they're something you'd want to tackle at some point.

# Shaded Pipelines

If you have had a passing familiarity with OpenGL or Direct3D, the mere mention of the term *shaders* might give you the shivers. They seem like a mysterious talisman belonging to the most secretive circles of graphics priesthood.

Not so.

The "fixed function" pipeline of version 1 refers to the lighting and coloring of the vertices and fragments. For example, you are permitted to have up to eight lights, and each light has various properties. The lights illuminate surfaces, each with their own properties called *materials*. Combining the two, we get a fairly nice, but constrained, general-purpose lighting model. But what if you wanted to do something different? What if you wanted to have a surface fade to transparency depending on its relative illumination? What if you wanted to accurately model shadows of, say, the rings of Saturn, thrown upon its cloud decks, or the pale luminescent light you get right before sunrise? All of those would be next to impossible given the limitations of the fixed-function model, especially the final one because the lighting equations are quite complicated once you start taking into consideration the effect of moisture in the atmosphere, backscattering, and so on. Well, a programmable pipeline that lets you model those precise equations without using any tricks such as texture combiners is exactly what version 2 gives us.

# Shady Triangles

I'm going to start with the Android example projects that should have been installed when you installed Eclipse and the Android SDK. You should find them in a directory such as `samples/android-10`. Look for the massive ApiDemo. When compiled, it will give you a lengthy menu demonstrating everything from NFC to notification. Scroll down to the graphics section, and navigate to the OpenGL ES/OpenGL ES2.0 demo. This displays a simple spinning and textured triangle, as shown in Figure 10–1.

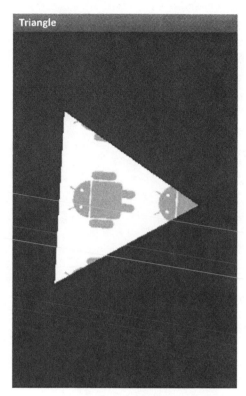

**Figure 10–1.** *The Android SDK example of shaders in action*

So, how is this done?

The pipeline architecture of ES 2 permits you to have two different access points in the geometric processing, as shown in Figure 10–2. The first hands over to your control each vertex along with the various attributes (for example, xyz coordinates, colors, opacity) information. This is called the *vertex shader*. At this point it is up to you to determine what this vertex should look like and how it should be rendered along with the supplied attributes. When done, the vertex is handed back to the hardware, rasterized with the data you calculated, and passed on as 2D bits to your *fragment* (or pixel) shader. It is here where you can combine the textures as needed, do any final processing, and pass it back to the system to eventually be rendered in the frame buffer.

If this sounds to you like a lot of work for each fragment of each object in your scene roaring along at 60 fps, you are right. But fundamentally, shaders are small programs that are actually loaded and run on the graphics hardware itself and, as a result, are very fast.

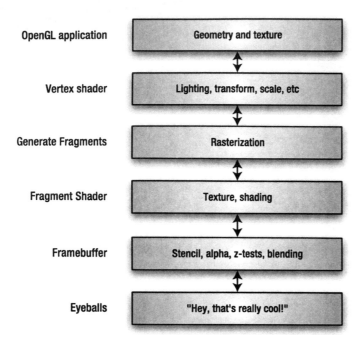

**Figure 10–2.** *Overview of OpenGL ES 2 architecture*

## Shader Structure

Both vertex and fragment shaders are similar in structure and look a little like a small C program. The entry point is always called main() as in C, while the syntax is likewise very C-ish as well.

The shader language, called GLSL (not to be confused with its Direct3d counterpart, HLSL), contains a rich set of built-in functions that belong to one of three main categories:

- Math operations oriented toward graphics processing such as matrix, vector, trig, derivative, and logic functions

- Texture sampling

- Small helper utilities such as modulo, comparisons, and valuators

Values are passed to and from shaders in the following types:

- *Uniforms*, which are values passed from the calling program. These might include the matrices for transformations, or projection. They are available in both the vertex and fragment shaders and must be declared as the same type in each place.

- *Varying variables* (yes, it is a dumb-sounding name), which are variables defined in the vertex shader that are passed on to the fragment shader.

Variables may be defined both as the usual numeric primitives or as graphics-oriented types based on vectors and matrices, as shown in Table 10–1.

**Table 10–1.** *Variable Types Allowed by GLSL*

| Class | Type | Description |
|---|---|---|
| Primitives | float, int, bool | Standard definitions apply. |
| Vectors | int, ivec2, ivec3, ivec4, float, vec2, vec3, vec4 bool, bvec2, bvec3, bvec4 | Float, int, and bools are "one-dimensional vectors." Boolean vectors hold only bool values in their components. |
| Matrices | mat2, mat3, mat4 | No Boolean matrices here. |

In addition to these, you can supply modifiers to define the precision of int-based and float-based types. These can be highp (24 bit), mediump (16 bit), or lowp (10 bit), with highp being the default. All transformations must all be done in highp, while colors need only mediump. (It beats me why there is no precision qualifier for bools, though.)

Any basic types can be declared as constant variables, such as const float x=1.0.

Structures are also allowed and look just like their C counterparts.

## Restrictions

Since shaders reside on the GPU, they naturally have a number of restrictions to them limiting their complexity. They may be limited by "instruction count," number of uniforms permitted (typically 128), number of temporary variables, and depth of loop nesting. Unfortunately, on OpenGL ES, there is no real way to fetch these limits from the hardware, so you can only be aware that they exist and keep your shaders as small as possible.

There are also differences between the vertex and fragment shaders. For example, highp support is optional on the fragment shader, whereas it is mandatory on the vertex shader. Bah.

## Back to the Spinning Triangle

So, now let's jump back to the triangle example and break down how a basic OpenGL ES 2 program is structured. As you'll see, the process of generating a shader is not unlike generating most any other application. You have your basic compile, link, and load sequence. Listing 10–1 demonstrates the first part of that process, compiling the thing.

> **NOTE:** The code in Listing 10-1 comes from the Android example called
> GLES20TriangleRenderer.java in the ApiDemo package.

**Listing 10–1.** *Compiling a Shader*

```java
private int createProgram(String vertexSource, String fragmentSource) {      //1
    int vertexShader = loadShader(GLES20.GL_VERTEX_SHADER, vertexSource);    //2
    if (vertexShader == 0) {
        return 0;
    }

    int pixelShader = loadShader(GLES20.GL_FRAGMENT_SHADER, fragmentSource);
    if (pixelShader == 0) {
        return 0;
    }

    int program = GLES20.glCreateProgram();                                  //3
    if (program != 0) {
        GLES20.glAttachShader(program, vertexShader);                        //4
        GLES20.glAttachShader(program, pixelShader);
        GLES20.glLinkProgram(program);                                       //5
        int[] linkStatus = new int[1];
        GLES20.glGetProgramiv(program, GLES20.GL_LINK_STATUS, linkStatus, 0); //6
        if (linkStatus[0] != GLES20.GL_TRUE) {
            Log.e(TAG, "Could not link program: ");
            Log.e(TAG, GLES20.glGetProgramInfoLog(program));
            GLES20.glDeleteProgram(program);
            program = 0;
        }
    }
    return program;                                                          //7
}

private int loadShader(int shaderType, String source) {
    int shader = GLES20.glCreateShader(shaderType);                          //8
    if (shader != 0) {
        GLES20.glShaderSource(shader, source);                              //9
        GLES20.glCompileShader(shader);                                     //10
        int[] compiled = new int[1];
        GLES20.glGetShaderiv(shader, GLES20.GL_COMPILE_STATUS, compiled, 0);//11
        if (compiled[0] == 0) {
            Log.e(TAG, "Could not compile shader " + shaderType + ":");
            Log.e(TAG, GLES20.glGetShaderInfoLog(shader));
            GLES20.glDeleteShader(shader);
            shader = 0;
        }
    }
    return shader;                                                          //12
}
```

In the preceding example, createProgram() is called from your onSurfaceCreated() method, where much of a given application's initialization is done. So, let's trace what's going on:

- In the argument list of createProgram(), as shown in line 1, strings of the actual executable code from both shaders are passed. You can do it this way or have them read in as a text file. Listing 10–2 has both shaders and will be discussed a little later.

- Lines 2ff call `loadShader()` for both programs and return their respective handles.

- Line 3 creates an empty program object. This hosts the two shaders and performs compatibility checking.

- Lines 4f attach both shaders to the program.

- Linking occurs in line 5. It is advised to check for any possible errors as done in the lines following. More than just an error code, the GLSL returns very good messages as to what uniform might be missing or unused, for example:

  `ERROR: 0:19: Use of undeclared identifier 'normalX'`

- If all works, we can return the program in line 7.

- `loadShader()`, defined in Lines 8ff, performs the actual compile. It first takes the raw source text and creates a shader of the specified type, (either vertex or fragment) using `glCreateShader()`. This returns an empty object that is then bound to the source text via `glShaderSource()` in Line 9.

- Line 10 compiles the actual shader, lines 11ff do error checking just as before, while line 12 returns the validated and compiled object.

If you want any further checks of your shader code, you can "validate" it with `glValidateProgram()`. Validation is a way for the OpenGL implementers to return information about any aspects of your code, such as recommended improvements. You would use this primarily during the development process.

The shaders are now ready for use. You can specify which one to use at any time while passing values back and forth between them and your calling code. This will be covered a little later. For now, let's take a close-up look at the two demo shaders. The author of this example elected to actually define the shader text as a large static strings. Others opt for reading them from a file. But in this case I have reformatted them from the original strings to make them more readable. Listing 10–2 covers the first half of the shader pair.

**Listing 10–2.** *The Vertex Shader*

```
uniform mat4 uMVPMatrix;                              //1
attribute vec4 aPosition;                             //2
attribute vec2 aTextureCoord;
varying vec2 vTextureCoord                            //3
void main                                             //4
{
    gl_Position = uMVPMatrix * aPosition;             //5
    vTextureCoord = aTextureCoord;                    //6
}
```

Now for a closer look:

- Line 1 defines a 4x4 model/view/perspective matrix *uniform* passed in from the calling program. It is really a matter of style if you want to perform the actual transformations in a shader or up at a higher level. And note that uniforms must be actually used within the shader, not just declared; otherwise, your calling program will fail if it tries to reference it.

- Lines 2f declare the attributes that we also specify in the calling code. Remember that attributes are arrays of data mapping directly to each vertex and are available only in the vertex shader. In this case, they are the vertex (referred by to the term *position*) and its corresponding texture coordinates. The shader is called once for each vertex.

- Line 3 declares a *varying variable* of the texture coordinates.

- As with good ol' C, the entry point is a main(), as shown in line 4.

- In line 5, the position (vertex) is multiplied by the matrix. You can do this either in the shaders or up in the calling software, which is the more traditional route.

- And finally, line 6 merely copies the texture coordinate to its varying counterpart so it can be picked up by the fragment shader.

Now the real magic happens in the fragment shader, as shown in Listing 10–3.

**Listing 10–3.** *The Fragment Shader*

```
precision mediump float;                                          //1
varying vec2 vTextureCoord;                                       //2

uniform sampler2D sTexture;                                       //3

void main()
{
    gl_FragColor = texture2D(sTexture, vTextureCoord);           //4
}
```

- You can specify the precision of the shader via line 1, as referenced earlier.

- The varying vTextureCoord is declared in line 2. All varyings must be declared in both shaders; otherwise, it will generate an error. Furthermore, varyings in the fragment shader are read-only, while they are read/write in the vertex shader.

- Line 3 declares a sampler2D object. Samplers are built-in uniforms used to pass the texture information into the fragment shader. Other samplers include sampler1D and sampler3D.

- gl_FragColor in line 4 is a built-in variable and is used to pass the final color of the fragment back to the system for display. In this case, we're just passing back the color of the texture at the specific point as defined by vTextureCoord. If you wanted to do any fancier stuff, you'd do it here. For example, you could strip out the blue and green components, leaving only the red layer to display, add motion blur, or demonstrate atmospheric backscattering.

Before we can use the shaders, we need to get the "position," or handles of the uniforms and attributes inside shaders right after we create the program as described previously. These are used to hand off any data from the calling methods to the GPU. Listing 10–4 shows the process as used in onSurfaceCreated() for the spinning triangle.

**Listing 10–4.** *Getting the Handles to the Uniforms and Attributes*

```
public void onSurfaceCreated(GL10 glUnused, EGLConfig config)
{
    mProgram = createProgram(mVertexShader, mFragmentShader);              //1
    if (mProgram == 0) {
        return;
    }
    maPositionHandle = GLES20.glGetAttribLocation(mProgram, "aPosition");   //2
    if (maPositionHandle == -1) {
        throw new RuntimeException("Could not get attrib location for aPosition");
    }
    maTextureHandle = GLES20.glGetAttribLocation(mProgram, "aTextureCoord");   //3
    if (maTextureHandle == -1) {
        throw new RuntimeException("Could not get attrib location for
            aTextureCoord");
    }

    muMVPMatrixHandle = GLES20.glGetUniformLocation(mProgram, "uMVPMatrix");   //4
    if (muMVPMatrixHandle == -1) {
        throw new RuntimeException("Could not get attrib location for uMVPMatrix");
    }
}
```

Lines 1, 2, and 3 get the handles for the attributes using their actual names from inside the shader. Line 4 gets the handle of the matrix's uniform. All four handles are saved for use in the main processing loop of our calling program. The GL10 interface that is passed in is ignored in lieu of the GLES20 class's static methods instead.

> **NOTE:** You can either get the locations of the objects as defined by OpenGL or set them yourself before linking. The latter method lets you ensure that similar uniforms or attributes all leverage the same handle across the entire family of shaders in your code.

The only thing left now is to execute a shader program and pass any data through to it. Listing 10–5 shows the triangle's entire `onDrawFrame()` method to demonstrate this.

**Listing 10–5.** *Calling and Using the Shaders*

```
public void onDrawFrame(GL10 glUnused)                                      //1
{
    GLES20.glClearColor(0.0f, 0.0f, 1.0f, 1.0f);                           //2
    GLES20.glClear( GLES20.GL_DEPTH_BUFFER_BIT | GLES20.GL_COLOR_BUFFER_BIT);
    GLES20.glUseProgram(mProgram);                                         //3

    GLES20.glActiveTexture(GLES20.GL_TEXTURE0);                            //4
    GLES20.glBindTexture(GLES20.GL_TEXTURE_2D, mTextureID);                //5

    mTriangleVertices.position(TRIANGLE_VERTICES_DATA_POS_OFFSET);         //6
    GLES20.glVertexAttribPointer(maPositionHandle, 3, GLES20.GL_FLOAT, false, //7
            TRIANGLE_VERTICES_DATA_STRIDE_BYTES, mTriangleVertices);
    GLES20.glEnableVertexAttribArray(maPositionHandle);                    //8

    mTriangleVertices.position(TRIANGLE_VERTICES_DATA_UV_OFFSET);          //9
    GLES20.glVertexAttribPointer(maTextureHandle, 2, GLES20.GL_FLOAT, false,//10
            TRIANGLE_VERTICES_DATA_STRIDE_BYTES, mTriangleVertices);
    GLES20.glEnableVertexAttribArray(maTextureHandle);                     //11

    long time = SystemClock.uptimeMillis() % 4000L;
    float angle = 0.090f * ((int) time);
    Matrix.setRotateM(mMMatrix, 0, angle, 0, 0, 1.0f);                     //12
    Matrix.multiplyMM(mMVPMatrix, 0, mVMatrix, 0, mMMatrix, 0);
    Matrix.multiplyMM(mMVPMatrix, 0, mProjMatrix, 0, mMVPMatrix, 0);

    GLES20.glUniformMatrix4fv(muMVPMatrixHandle, 1, false, mMVPMatrix, 0); //13
    GLES20.glDrawArrays(GLES20.GL_TRIANGLES, 0, 3);                        //14
}
```

Now, let's break this down:

- The argument to `onDrawFrame()` is the GL10 object. But since this is an OpenGL ES2 application, the GL10 handle is ignored in lieu of the static functions.

- Lines 2f are just the standard stuff to clear the screen.

- In Line 3 is where the fun begins. `glUseProgram()` switches on whatever shader you might want at the time. You can have as many as you need and freely jump between them.

- The texture we want to pass to the fragment shader is specified in line 4 and picked up by the `sampler2D` object. This code represents the actual texture unit used on the GPU.

- Line 5 binds your local texture handle to this unit.

- Line 6 prepares the actual triangle vertex array object for use by setting its internal position index to the point at which the actual vertex xyz values start.

- Now we can finally hand off something to the shader, as illustrated in line 7. In this case, the vertex data is sent down to the shader via `glVertexAtttribPointer()`, which takes the handle of the position attribute, `maPosition`; the type of data, `stride`; and a pointer to said data. Line 8 then enables the use of the array.

- Lines 9, 10, and 11 do the same to the texture coordinates.

- Lines 12ff perform the rotations and projection, using the Android's own Matrix libraries (`android.opengl.Matrix`) since OpenGL ES 2 does not have the `glRotate`/`glTranslate`/`glScale` functions. Otherwise, you'd need to write your own math libs.

- We can now take the results of the previous matrix operations and pass them onto the vertex shader using `glUniformMatrix4fv()` and the matrix handle we picked up earlier.

- And now in the last line, we call our old friend `glDrawArrays()`.

So, there you have it. A "simple" shader-based program. That wasn't so bad, was it? Now we can revisit our lame solar-system model and show how shaders might be used to make it a little less lame.

# Earth at Night

You're familiar with the daylight image used for the earth's surface (Figure 10–3, left), but you may have also seen a similar image of the earth at night (Figure 10–3, right). What would be neat is if we could show the night texture on the dark side of the earth, instead of just a dark version of the regular texture map.

**Figure 10–3**. *The daytime earth vs. the nighttime earth*

Under OpenGL 1.1 this would be very tricky if not impossible to accomplish. The algorithm should be relatively simple: render the earth twice, once with the day image and once with the night. Then vary the daylight-side alpha channel of the texture of the day-side earth based on the illumination. When illumination reaches 0, it is completely transparent, and the night portion shows through. However, under OpenGL ES 2, you can code the shaders very easily to match the algorithm almost exactly. (You could also render the earth once and supply the two textures at the same time. This technique is covered in the next exercise).

The program is structured like any one of the previous ones, with an "activity" file, a renderer, and in this case the Planet object.

The first example is all well and good, you're probably thinking, "But how do we actually command OpenGL to use the 2.*x* stuff vs. the 1.*x*?" Listing 10–6 has the answer.

First we need to detect whether the device actually has support for OpenGL ES 2. The new ones most assuredly will, but older ones perhaps not. The iPhone never got it until iOS 3.0. That is done via the getSystemService() method that retrieves a configuration info packet. If that passes, a simple call to GLSurfaceView().setEGLContextClientVersion(2) does the trick.

**Listing 10–6.** *Invoking OpenGL ES 2*

```
private boolean detectOpenGLES20()
{
    ActivityManager am =
        (ActivityManager) getSystemService(Context.ACTIVITY_SERVICE);

    ConfigurationInfo info = am.getDeviceConfigurationInfo();
    return (info.reqGlEsVersion >= 0x20000);
}

protected void onCreate(Bundle savedInstanceState)
{
    super.onCreate(savedInstanceState);
    GLSurfaceView view = new GLSurfaceView(this);

    if (detectOpenGLES20())
    {
            view.setEGLContextClientVersion(2);
    view.setEGLConfigChooser(8,8,8,8,16,1);
            view.setRenderer(new SolarSystemRendererES2(this));

            setContentView(view);
    }
}
```

Next the earth needs to be generated the usual way. This instance will use 50 slices and 50 stacks, along with fetching the two textures, as shown in Listing 10–7.

**Listing 10–7.** *Initializing the Earth*

```
private void initGeometry(GL10 glUnused)
{
    String extensions = GLES20.glGetString(GL10.GL_EXTENSIONS);

    m_DayTexture=createTexture(glUnused, m_Context,
            book.SolarSystem.R.drawable.earth_light);
    m_NightTexture=createTexture(glUnused, m_Context,
            book.SolarSystem.R.drawable.earth_night);

    m_Earth = new Planet(50, 50, 1.0f, 1.0f, glUnused, myAppcontext,true,-1);
}
```

The onSurfaceCreated() method loads and initializes two sets of shaders while calling initGeometry(), as shown in Listing 10–8.

**Listing 10–8.** *Loading the Shaders*

```
public void onSurfaceCreated(GL10 glUnused, EGLConfig config)
{
    int program;

    m_DaysideProgram=createProgram(m_DaySideVertexShader,m_DaySideFragmentShader);
    m_NightsideProgram=createProgram
        (m_NightSideVertexShader,m_NightSideFragmentShader);

    initGeometry(glUnused);
```

```
        Matrix.setLookAtM(m_WorldMatrix, 0, 0, 5f, -2, 0f, 0f, 0f, 0.0f, 1.0f, 0.0f);
    }
```

createProgram() is not much different from the previous example, but it has more uniforms and attributes to handle. Below, a new attribute for the normals is supplied so that we can handle lighting. In this example, we're binding a specific identifier to each attribute so that we can be assured that both sets of shaders use the same value. It can make things just a bit easier at times. And this *must* be done before linking.

```
GLES20. glBindAttribLocation(*program, ATTRIB_VERTEX, "aPosition");
GLES20. glBindAttribLocation(*program, ATTRIB_NORMAL, "aNormal");
GLES20. glBindAttribLocation(*program, ATTRIB_TEXTURE0_COORDS, "aTextureCoord");
```

And there are two new uniforms to handle in addition to the one for the model/view/projection matrix. Unlike the previous example, we still must get the locations after linking, so there is no assurance that their locations will be in the same places in other instances of the programs unless the programs have identical sets of variables. Here I cache all uniform handles into a single array that should work with both sets of shaders. The new uniforms are for the normal matrix and the light position. (For very simple models, you could actually hard-code the light's position in the vertex shader itself.)

```
m_UniformIDs[UNIFORM_MVP_MATRIX]=GLES20.glGetUniformLocation(program,
                          "uMVPMatrix") ;
m_UniformIDs[UNIFORM_NORMAL_MATRIX]=GLES20.glGetUniformLocation(program,
                          "uNormalMatrix");
m_UniformIDs[UNIFORM_LIGHT_POSITION]=GLES20.glGetUniformLocation(program,
                          "uLightPosition");;
```

So, the process to adding a new uniform is as follows:

1.  Declare it in the shader (i.e., uniform vec3 lightPosition;).

2.  Fetch its "location" using glGetUniformLocation(). That merely returns a unique ID for this session that is then used when setting or getting data from the shader. (Or use glBindAttribLocation to assign specific location values.)

3.  Use one of the many glUniform*() calls to dynamically set the values.

Naturally, the sphere generator will have to be modified a little as well. Leveraging off of the interleaved data example in the previous chapter, the new draw() method will look something like Listing 10–9.

**Listing 10–9.** *OpenGL ES 2 Compatible Draw Method in* Planet.java

```
public void draw(GL10 gl,int vertexLocation,int normalLocation,          //1
    int colorLocation, int textureLocation,int textureID)
{
    //Overrides any default texture that may have been supplied at creation time.

    if(textureID>=0)                                                     //2
    {
        GLES20.glActiveTexture(GLES20.GL_TEXTURE0);
        GLES20.glBindTexture(GLES20.GL_TEXTURE_2D, textureID);
    }
    else if(m_Texture0>=0)
    {
```

```
        GLES20.glActiveTexture(GLES20.GL_TEXTURE0);
        GLES20.glBindTexture(GLES20.GL_TEXTURE_2D, m_Texture0);
    }

    GLES20.glEnable(GLES20.GL_CULL_FACE);
    GLES20.glCullFace(GLES20.GL_BACK);

    m_InterleavedData.position(0);                                          //3

    GLES20.glVertexAttribPointer(vertexLocation, 3, GLES20.GL_FLOAT,
    false,m_Stride, m_InterleavedData);
    GLES20.glEnableVertexAttribArray(vertexLocation);

    m_InterleavedData.position(NUM_XYZ_ELS);

    if(normalLocation>=0)
    {
        GLES20.glVertexAttribPointer(normalLocation, 3, GLES20.GL_FLOAT,
        false,m_Stride, m_InterleavedData);
        GLES20.glEnableVertexAttribArray(normalLocation);
    }

    m_InterleavedData.position(NUM_XYZ_ELS+NUM_NXYZ_ELS);

    if(colorLocation>=0)
    {
        GLES20.glVertexAttribPointer(colorLocation, 4, GLES20.GL_FLOAT,
        false,m_Stride, m_InterleavedData);
        GLES20.glEnableVertexAttribArray(colorLocation);
    }

        m_InterleavedData.position(NUM_XYZ_ELS+NUM_NXYZ_ELS+NUM_RGBA_ELS);

    GLES20.glVertexAttribPointer(textureLocation, 2, GLES20.GL_FLOAT,
    false,m_Stride, m_InterleavedData);
    GLES20.glEnableVertexAttribArray(textureLocation);

    GLES20.glDrawArrays(GLES20.GL_TRIANGLE_STRIP, 0, (m_Slices+1)*2*(m_Stacks-1)+2);
}
```

As with other routines, we ignore the GL10 object passed to this and use the GLES20 static calls instead.

- In line 1, notice all of the additional arguments. These allow the handles, or locations, of the various attributes to be passed through and used here.

- Lines 2ff permit us to use a texture defined at object creation or swap in another at runtime.

- Lines 3ff set the attribute pointers the standard way as demonstrated earlier. After each pointer is set for a specific kind of data, the interleaved index is advanced to the start of the next data block.

Next we can look at the actual shaders, specifically, the vertex first in Listing 10–10. As with the previous ones, these shaders have been reformatted for readability. Note that for this and the next example, the day and night-side vertex shaders are identical.

**Listing 10–10.** *Vertex Shader for the Day and Night Sides*

```
attribute vec4 aPosition;
attribute vec3 aNormal;                                              //1
attribute vec2 aTextureCoord;
varying vec2 vTextureCoord;
varying lowp vec4 colorVarying;
uniform vec3 uLightPosition;                                         //2
uniform mat4 uMVPMatrix;
uniform mat3 uNormalMatrix;                                          //3

void main()
{
    vTextureCoord = aTextureCoord;
    vec3 normalDirection = normalize(uNormalMatrix * aNormal);//4
    float nDotVP = max(0.0, dot(normalDirection, normalize(uLightPosition)));
    vec4 diffuseColor = vec4(1.0, 1.0, 1.0, 1.0);
    colorVarying = diffuseColor * nDotVP;
    gl_Position = uMVPMatrix * aPosition;                           //5
}
```

We have three new parameters to worry about here, not to mention the lighting.

- Line 1 is the normal attribute for this vertex, needed of course for the lighting solutions.

- Line 2 supplies the light's position via a uniform.

- And line 3 supports a matrix for the normals. Why is there a separate matrix for normals when they should be just like the vertices? Under most cases, they are, but the normals will break down under certain conditions, such as when scaling your geometry unevenly in just a single direction. So, to isolate it from those situations, a separate matrix is needed.

- Lines 4ff do the lighting calculations. First the normal is normalized (I always get a kick out of saying that) and when multiplied by the normal's matrix produces the normalized normal direction. Normally.

  After that we take the dot product of the normal's direction and the normalized light position. That gives us the intensity of the light on a given vertex.

  After that a diffuse color is defined. It is set to all ones, since the sunlight is defined as white. (Hint, setting it to red really looks cool.) The diffused color is multiplied by the intensity, and the final result is then passed on to the fragment shader.

- Line 5 handles the final position of the vertex by multiplying the original vertex by the model/view/projection matrix. `gl_Position` is a built-in varying just for this purpose and needs not be declared.

The fragment shaders for both sides are different since the dark side will be handling the illumination differently than the daylight side. Listing 10–11 is the fragment shader for the day side.

**Listing 10–11.** *Fragment Shader for the Daylight Side of Earth*

```
varying lowp vec4 colorVarying;
precision mediump float;
varying vec2 vTextureCoord;
uniform sampler2D sTexture;
void main()
{
    gl_FragColor = texture2D(sTexture, vTextureCoord)*colorVarying;
}
```

This should look identical to the triangle's shader, except with the addition of `colorVarying`. Here the output derived from the `sTexture` is multiplied by the color for the final result.

However, things are a little more interesting on the night side, as shown in Listing 10–12.

**Listing 10–12.** *Fragment Shader for the Night Side of the Earth*

```
varying lowp vec4 colorVarying;
precision mediump float;
varying vec2 vTextureCoord;
uniform sampler2D sTexture;
void main()
{
    vec4 newColor;
    newColor=1.0-colorVarying;
    gl_FragColor = texture2D(sTexture, vTextureCoord)*newColor;
}
```

You'll notice that the parameters are the same as the other shader, but we get a couple of extra lines of code to calculate the coloring for the night side. Since we can do a dissolve from one texture to another based on illumination, it stands to reason that the coloring of the night side would be 1.0-daylight coloring. The nice vector libraries of the GLSL make math operations like these very simple to do.

Listing 10–13 shows the `onDrawFrame()` to finalize all of the operations.

**Listing 10–13.** *Putting It All Together*

```
public void onDrawFrame(GL10 glUnused)
{

    GLES20.glClearColor(0.0f, 0.0f, 0.0f, 1.0f);
    GLES20.glClear( GLES20.GL_DEPTH_BUFFER_BIT | GLES20.GL_COLOR_BUFFER_BIT);

    m_Angle+=0.20;


    Matrix.setRotateM(m_MMatrix, 0,m_Angle, 0, 1.0f, 0.0f);            //1
    Matrix.multiplyMM(m_MVMatrix, 0, m_WorldMatrix, 0, m_MMatrix, 0);
    Matrix.multiplyMM(m_MVPMatrix, 0, m_ProjMatrix, 0, m_MVMatrix, 0);

    m_NormalMatrix[0]=m_MVMatrix[0];                                   //2
```

```
            m_NormalMatrix[1]=m_MVMatrix[1];
            m_NormalMatrix[2]=m_MVMatrix[2];
            m_NormalMatrix[3]=m_MVMatrix[4];
            m_NormalMatrix[4]=m_MVMatrix[5];
            m_NormalMatrix[5]=m_MVMatrix[6];
            m_NormalMatrix[6]=m_MVMatrix[8];
            m_NormalMatrix[7]=m_MVMatrix[9];
            m_NormalMatrix[8]=m_MVMatrix[10];


            GLES20.glUseProgram(m_NightsideProgram);                            //3
            checkGlError("glUseProgram:nightside");

            GLES20.glUniformMatrix4fv(m_UniformIDs[UNIFORM_MVP_MATRIX], 1, false,
                m_MVPMatrix, 0);
            GLES20.glUniformMatrix3fv(m_UniformIDs[UNIFORM_NORMAL_MATRIX], 1, false,
                m_NormalMatrix,0);
            GLES20.glUniform3fv(m_UniformIDs[UNIFORM_LIGHT_POSITION], 1, m_LightPosition,0);

            m_Earth.setBlendMode(m_Earth.PLANET_BLEND_MODE_FADE);              //4
            m_Earth.draw(glUnused,ATTRIB_VERTEX,ATTRIB_NORMAL,-1,
                              ATTRIB_TEXTURE0_COORDS,m_NightTexture);
            checkGlError("glDrawArrays");


            GLES20.glUseProgram(m_DaysideProgram);                             //5
            checkGlError("glUseProgram:dayside");

            GLES20.glUniformMatrix4fv(m_UniformIDs[UNIFORM_MVP_MATRIX], 1, false,
                m_MVPMatrix, 0);
            GLES20.glUniformMatrix3fv(m_UniformIDs[UNIFORM_NORMAL_MATRIX], 1, false,
                m_NormalMatrix,0);
            GLES20.glUniform3fv(m_UniformIDs[UNIFORM_LIGHT_POSITION], 1, m_LightPosition,0);

            m_Earth.draw(glUnused,ATTRIB_VERTEX,ATTRIB_NORMAL,-1,
                ATTRIB_TEXTURE0_COORDS,m_DayTexture);
            checkGlError("glDrawArrays");
        }
```

Here's what's going on:

- Lines 1ff perform the expected rotations, first on the Y-axis, multiplied by the world matrix and then the projection matrix.

- Lines 2ff are a bit of a cheat. Remember what I said a little earlier about needing a normal matrix? In the reduced case, we can just use the modelview matrix, or at least part of it. Since the normal matrix is only 9x9 (eschewing translation components), we slice it out the rotational part of the larger 4x4 modelview matrix.

- Now the night-side part of the program is switched in, as shown in line 3. Afterward, the uniforms are populated.

- Line 4 sets a blend mode similar to the ones from OpenGL ES 1.1. In this case we nudge the system to actually recognize that alpha is to be used to actually manage translucency. The lower the alpha, the more translucent this one fragment. Right after that, the dark side is drawn.

- Line 5 now switches us over to the daylight program and does much of the same stuff.

Figure 10–4 should be the result. You can see now how easy it is to do very subtle effects, such as illumination from a full moon or reflection of the sun in the ocean.

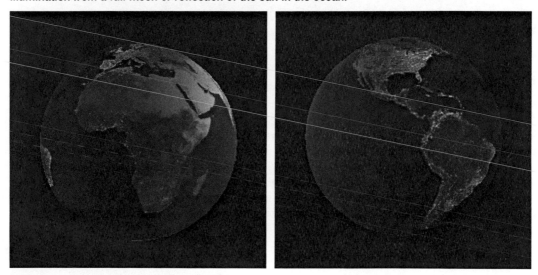

**Figure 10–4.** *Illuminating the darkness one fragment at a time*

## Bring in the Clouds

So, it certainly seems as if something else is missing. Oh, yeah. Those cloud things. Well, we're in luck because shaders can very easily manage that as well. Available in the downloadable project files, I've added a cloud map of the entire earth, as shown in Figure 10–5. The land masses are a little hard to see, but in the lower right is Australia, while in the left half you should be able to make out South America. So, our job is to overlay it on top of the color landscape map and drop out all of the dark bits.

**Figure 10–5.** *Full-earth cloud patterns*

Not only are we going to add clouds to our model, we'll also see how to handle multitexturing using shaders, as in, how does one tell a single shader to use more than one texture? Remember the lesson about texture units in Chapter 6? They come in really handy right now, because that is where the textures are stored, ready for the fragment shader to pick them up. Normally, for a single texture, the system defaults in a way that no additional setup is needed, save for the normal call to glBindTexture(). However, if you want to use more than one, there is some setup required. The steps are as follows:

1.    Load the new texture in your main program.

2.    Add a second uniform sampler2D to your fragment shader to support a second texture and pick it up via glGetUniformLocation().

3.    Tell the system which texture unit to use with which sampler.

4.    Activate and bind the desired textures to the specified TUs while in the main loop.

Now to a few specifics: you already know how to load textures; that is, of course, a no-brainer. So for step 2, you will want to add something like the following to the fragment shader, the same one used for the previous couple of exercises:

    uniform sampler2D sCloudTexture;

And to createProgram():

m_UniformIDs[*UNIFORM_SAMPLER0*] = GLES20.*glGetUniformLocation*(program, "sTexture");

m_UniformIDs[*UNIFORM_SAMPLER1*] = GLES20.*glGetUniformLocation*(program, "sCloudTexture");

Step 3 is added to onSurfaceCreated(). The glUniform1i() call takes the location of the uniform in the fragment shader for the first argument and takes the actual texture-unit ID in the second. So in this case, sampler0 is bound to texture unit 0, while sampler1 goes to texture unit 1. Since a single texture always defaults to TU0 as well as the first sampler, the setup code is not universally needed.

    GLES20.*glUseProgram*(m_DaysideProgram);

```
GLES20.glUniform1i(m_UniformIDs[UNIFORM_SAMPLER0],0);
GLES20.glUniform1i(m_UniformIDs[UNIFORM_SAMPLER1],1);

GLES20.glUseProgram(m_NightsideProgram);
GLES20.glUniform1i(m_UniformIDs[UNIFORM_SAMPLER0],0);
GLES20.glUniform1i(m_UniformIDs[UNIFORM_SAMPLER1],1);
```

When running the main loop in onDrawFrame(), in step 4, you can do the following to turn on both textures:

```
GLES20.glActiveTexture(GLES20.GL_TEXTURE0);
GLES20.glBindTexture(GLES20.GL_TEXTURE_2D,m_NightTexture);

GLES20.glActiveTexture(GLES20.GL_TEXTURE1);
GLES20.glBindTexture(GLES20.GL_TEXTURE_2D,m_CloudTexture);

GLES20.glUseProgram(m_NightsideProgram);
```

glActiveTexture() specifies what TU to use followed by a call to bind the texture. Afterward, the program can be used to the desired effect.

The cloud-lovin' fragment should now look something like Listing 10–14 to perform the actual blending.

**Listing 10–14.** *Blending a Second Texture with Clouds on Top of the Others*

```
varying lowp vec4 colorVarying;
precision mediump float;
varying vec2 vTextureCoord;
uniform sampler2D sTexture;
uniform sampler2D sCloudTexture;                                    //1

void main()
{
    vec4 cloudColor;
    vec4 surfaceColor;
    cloudColor=texture2D(sCloudTexture, vTextureCoord );            //2
    surfaceColor=texture2D(sTexture, vTextureCoord );

        if(cloudColor[0]>0.2)                                       //3
            {
                cloudColor[3]=1.0;
                gl_FragColor=(cloudColor*1.3+surfaceColor*.4)*colorVarying;
            }
        else
        gl_FragColor = texture2D(sTexture, vTextureCoord)*colorVarying;
}
```

Here's what is happening:

- Line 1 merely declares the new cloud texture.

- In line 2, we pick up the cloud color from the cloud sampler object.

- The new color is filtered and merged with the earth's surface image in lines 3ff. Since the clouds are neutral in color, all we need to do is to analyze one color component, red in this case. If it is brighter than a given value, then blend it with the earth's surface texture. The numbers used are quite arbitrary and can be tweaked based on your taste. Naturally, much of the finer detail will have to be cut out to ensure the colored landmasses show through.

The `cloudColor` is given a slight boost with the 1.3 multiplier while the underlying surface is uses only .4 so as to emphasize the clouds a little more, while still making them relatively opaque.

Below threshold of .2, just send back the surface coloring.

Since the clouds are grayscale objects, I need to pick up only a single color to test, because the normal RGB values are identical. So, I opted to handle all texels brighter than .2. Then I ensure that the alpha channel is 1.0 and combine all three components together.

Ideally you'll see something like Figure 10–6. Now that's what I call a planet!

**Figure 10–6.** *Adding cloud cover to the earth*

# But What About Specular Reflections?

Just as any other shiny thing (and the earth is shiny in the blue parts), you might expect to see reflections of the sun in the water. Well, you'd be right. Figure 10–7 shows a real image of earth, and right in the middle is the reflection of the sun. Let's try it on our own earth.

**Figure 10–7.** *Earth seen from space as it reflects the sun*

Naturally we are going to have to write our own specular reflection shader, or, in this case, add it to the existing daylight shader.

Listing 10–15 is for the daylight vertex shader. We'll just do the one side, but a full moon would likely have a similar effect on the night side. Here I precalculate the specular information along with normal diffuse coloring, but the two are kept separate until the fragment shader because not all parts of the earth are reflective, so the landmasses shouldn't get the specular treatment.

**Listing 10–15.** *Daylight Vertex Shader for the Specular Reflection*

```
attribute vec4 aPosition;
attribute vec3 aNormal;
attribute vec2 aTextureCoord;
varying vec2 vTextureCoord;
varying lowp vec4 colorVarying;
varying lowp vec4 specularColorVarying;                           //1
uniform vec3 uLightPosition;
uniform vec3 uEyePosition;
uniform mat4 uMVPMatrix;
uniform mat3 uNormalMatrix;

void main()
{
        float shininess=25.0;
        float balance=.75;
        float specular=0.0;
        vTextureCoord = aTextureCoord;
        vec3 normalDirection = normalize(uNormalMatrix * aNormal);
        vec3 lightDirection = normalize(uLightPosition);
        vec3 eyeNormal = normalize(uEyePosition);
        vec4 diffuseColor = vec4(1.0, 1.0, 1.0, 1.0);
```

```
                    float nDotVP = max(0.0, dot(normalDirection, lightDirection));
                                                                                //2
                    float nDotVPReflection = dot(reflect(-
              lightDirection,normalDirection),eyeNormal);
                    specular = pow(max(0.0,nDotVPReflection),shininess)*balance; //3
                    specularColorVarying=vec4(specular,specular,specular,0.0);   //4
                    colorVarying = diffuseColor * nDotVP*1.3;
                    gl_Position = uMVPMatrix * aPosition;
        }
```

▓ Line 1 declares a varying variable to hand the specular illumination off to the fragment shader.

▓ We now need to get the dot product of the reflection of the light and the normalized normal multiplied normally by the normalmatrix in a normal fashion. Line 2. Notice the use of the `reflect()` method, which is another one of the niceties in the shader language. `reflect()` generates a reflected vector based on the negative light direction and the local normal. That is then dotted with the `eyeNormal`.

▓ In line 3, the previous dot product is taken and used to generate the actual specular component. You will also see our old friend shininess, and just as in version 1 of OpenGS ES, the higher the value, the narrower and "hotter" the reflection.

▓ Since we can consider the sun's color just to be white, the specular color in line 4 can have all its components set to the same value.

Now the fragment shader can be used to refine things even further, as shown in Listing 10–16.

**Listing 10–16.** *The Fragment Shader That Handles the Specular Reflection*

```
        varying lowp vec4 colorVarying;
        varying lowp vec4 specularColorVarying;                                 //1
        precision mediump float;
        varying vec2 vTextureCoord;
        uniform sampler2D sTexture;
        uniform sampler2D sCloudTexture;

        void main()
        {
            vec4 finalSpecular=vec4(0,0,0,1);

            vec4 cloudColor;
            vec4 surfaceColor;
            float halfBlue;

            cloudColor=texture2D(sCloudTexture, vTextureCoord );
            surfaceColor=texture2D(sTexture, vTextureCoord );

            halfBlue=0.5*surfaceColor[2];                                       //2

            if(halfBlue>1.0)                                                    //3
            halfBlue=1.0;
```

```
            if((surfaceColor[0]<halfBlue) && (surfaceColor[1]<halfBlue))          //4
            finalSpecular=specularColorVarying;

            if(cloudColor[0]>0.2)
    {
                cloudColor[3]=1.0;
                gl_FragColor=(cloudColor*1.3+surfaceColor*.4)*colorVarying;
    }
            else
            gl_FragColor=(surfaceColor+finalSpecular)*colorVarying;               //5
    }
```

The main task here is to determine which fragments represent sea and which do not. It's pretty easy; the blue stuff is water (powerful wet stuff that water!) and everything that isn't isn't.

- In line 1, we pick up the `specularColorVarying` variable.

- In line 2, we pick up the blue component and divide it by half, clamping it in line 3, since no color can actually go above full intensity.

- Line 4 does the filtering. If the red and green components were both less than half that of the blue, it's a pretty safe bet that we can draw the specular glint on top of the water, instead of some place like Chad.

- The specular piece is now added to the fragment color in the last line, after first multiplying it with the `colorVarying`, because that will modulate it with everything else.

Figure 10–8 shows the results sans clouds, and Figure 10–9 shows the results with clouds.

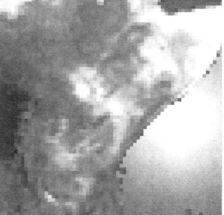

**Figure 10–8.** *A close-up on the right of the earth/water interface*

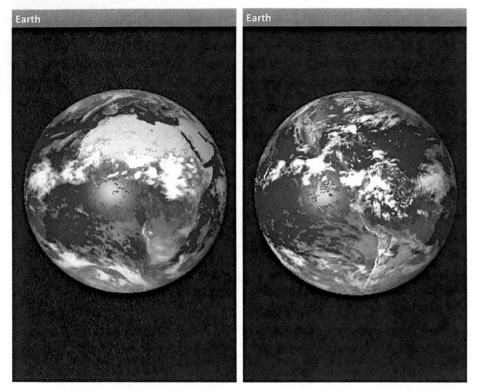

**Figure 10–9.** *The completed earth, for now at least*

This is just a single and very simple example of using shaders to enhance the realism of any scene you render. When it comes to space themes, for example, you might generate a hazy atmosphere around a planet or 3D volumetric textures to simulate galaxies or nebula. If only I had another ten chapters....

If you want to go ahead and reproduce the entire Chapter 8 project for extra credit with lens flare, widgets, and so on, feel free to do so.

## Summary

In this final chapter, you learned a little about OpenGL ES 2, the programmable pipeline version of ES, saw how and where shaders fit it in, and used them to add some extra detail to the earth. For extra credit, however, see about porting the rest of the simulator to version 2.

Throughout this book, you've learned basic 3D theory, both in the math involved and in the overall principles. I'd like to think that it's given you a basic feel or understanding of the topic, even knowing that the book could be many times larger, considering that we've barely touched 3D graphics.

The Khronos Group, the keepers of all things officially OpenGL, has published several extensive books on the subject. Affectionately known by the color of their cover, they have the Red Book (the official programming guide), the Blue Book, (tutorials and reference), the Orange Book (shading language), the Green Book, (Open GL on the Mac), and the Sort-of-Purplish Book (OpenGL ES 2). There are also numerous other third-party books that get much deeper then I've been able to go. Likewise, there are many sites on the Web dedicated to OpenGL tutorials; `http://nehe.gamedev.net` is by far one of the best with nearly 50 different tutorials as of this writing. And NVidia has a series of excellent guru-level books free for the downloading called GPU Gems. These cover things from rendering water caustics to waving fields of grass. They're certainly worth a look.

And as you're going over the work of other authors, be it from other books or on the Web, just remember that this book is the one that gave you the sun, the earth, and the stars. Not many others can claim that.

# Index

CPSIA information can be obtained at www.ICGtesting.com
Printed in the USA
LVOW051509120212

268318LV00006B/2/P